CHARLES DICKENS

Literary Lives
General Editor: Richard Dutton, Professor of English
Lancaster University

This series offers stimulating accounts of the literary careers of
the most admired and influential English-language authors.
Volumes follow the outline of writers' working lives, not in
the spirit of traditional biography, but aiming to trace
the professional, publishing and social contexts which
shaped their writing.

A list of the published titles in this series follows overleaf.

Published titles

Morris Beja
JAMES JOYCE

Michael O'Neill
PERCY BYSSHE SHELLEY

Cedric C. Brown
JOHN MILTON

Leonée Ormond
ALFRED TENNYSON

Peter Davison
GEORGE ORWELL

George Parfitt
JOHN DONNE

Jan Fergus
JANE AUSTEN

Gerald Roberts
GERARD MANLEY HOPKINS

James Gibson
THOMAS HARDY

Felicity Rosslyn
ALEXANDER POPE

Kenneth Graham
HENRY JAMES

Tony Sharpe
T. S. ELIOT

Paul Hammond
JOHN DRYDEN

Grahame Smith
CHARLES DICKENS

W. David Kay
BEN JONSON

Gary Waller
EDMUND SPENSER

Mary Lago
E. M. FORSTER

Cedric Watts
JOSEPH CONRAD

Alasdair D. F. Macrae
W. B. YEATS

Tom Winnifrith and Edward Chitham
CHARLOTTE AND EMILY BRONTË

Joseph McMinn
JONATHAN SWIFT

John Williams
WILLIAM WORDSWORTH

Kerry McSweeney
GEORGE ELIOT (MARIAN EVANS)

John Worthen
D. H. LAWRENCE

John Mepham
VIRGINIA WOOLF

Charles Dickens

A Literary Life

Grahame Smith
Professor of English Studies,
University of Stirling

First published 1996 by
MACMILLAN PRESS LTD
Houndmills, Basingstoke, Hampshire RG21 6XS
and London
Companies and representatives
throughout the world

ISBN 0–333–55718–2 hardcover
ISBN 0–333–55719–0 paperback

A catalogue record for this book is available from the British Library.

10   9   8   7   6   5   4   3   2   1
05   04   03   02   01   00   99   98   97   96

Printed and bound in Great Britain by
Antony Rowe Ltd
Chippenham, Wiltshire

Published in the United States of America 1996 by
ST. MARTIN'S PRESS, INC.,
Scholarly and Reference Division
175 Fifth Avenue, New York, N.Y. 10010

ISBN 0–312–12919–X

Contents

Acknowledgements

This book was written in its own context, the wealth of scholarship that began accumulating while Dickens was still alive. Specific borrowings are acknowledged in footnotes, but I would also like to record my indebtedness to all those scholars and enthusiasts who have assisted this work without being directly quoted in it.

I have benefited greatly from the advice of various friends and colleagues and I am grateful to them.

The research for this book was supported generously by grants from the British Academy and the Carnegie Trust for the Universities of Scotland which enabled me to use the library resources of the University of California at Los Angeles and the Huntingdon Library.

It is a lucky scholar who finds knowledgeable support in his own family. Helena Smith gave me the benefit of her own approach to Dickens, while Daniel Smith was particularly helpful in the areas of popular culture and film theory. As always, my work benefited immeasurably from the detailed attention of my wife and colleague, Angela Smith.

The faults are my own.

List of Abbreviations

Ackroyd   Peter Ackroyd, *Dickens* (London: Guild Publishing, 1990).

Forster   John Forster, *The Life of Charles Dickens*, 2 vols, ed. A. J. Hoppe (London: J. M. Dent & Sons Ltd, 1966).

Nonesuch   Walter Dexter (ed.), *The Letters of Charles Dickens*, 3 vols (London: The Nonesuch Press, 1938).

Pilgrim   M. House, G. Storey, K. Tillotson *et al.* (eds), *The Pilgrim Edition of the Letters of Charles Dickens* (Oxford: Clarendon Press, 1965 – in progress).

Speeches   K. J. Fielding (ed.), *The Speeches of Charles Dickens* (Oxford: Clarendon Press, 1960).

Chronology of Dickens's Life

Figures in parentheses indicate Dickens's age.

1812 Born in Portsea, Portsmouth, 7 February.
1815 (3) Family moves to London.
1817 (5) Family moves to Chatham.
1822 (10) Family returns to London, in increasing poverty.
1824 (12) Works at Warren's shoe-blacking factory. Father in Marshalsea Debtors' Prison for several months.
1825 (13) Attends school at Wellington House Academy.
1827 (15) Leaves school, becomes junior clerk in solicitor's office.
1829 (17) Freelance reporter at Doctors' Commons.
1831 (19) In love with Maria Beadnell. Becomes Parliamentary reporter.
1833 (21) Publishes first story, 'A Dinner at Poplar Walk'.
1835 (23) Engaged to Catherine Hogarth.
1836 (24) *Sketches by Boz*. Marries Catherine Hogarth. Begins *Pickwick Papers*.
1837 (25) *Pickwick Papers* completed. Sister-in-law Mary Hogarth dies. Editor of *Bentley's Miscellany*.
1838 (26) *Oliver Twist* (that is, completion of its serialization).
1839 (27) *Nicholas Nickleby*.
1841 (29) *The Old Curiosity Shop, Barnaby Rudge*.
1842 (30) Visits America from January to June. *American Notes*.
1843 (31) *A Christmas Carol*.
1844 (32) Stays with family in Genoa. *Martin Chuzzlewit*.
1845 (33) Returns from Italy.
1846 (34) *Pictures from Italy*. Briefly edits *Daily News*.
1848 (36) *Dombey and Son*.
1850 (38) Begins his weekly magazine, *Household Words*. *David Copperfield*.
1851 (39) Father dies.
1853 (41) *Bleak House*. Travels round Italy and Switzerland with Wilkie Collins.
1854 (42) *Hard Times*.
1855 (43) Lives in Paris for several months.

1856 (44) Fulfils boyhood dream by buying Gad's Hill Place.
1857 (44) *Little Dorrit*. Begins lifelong relationship with Ellen Ternan. Acting in Wilkie Collins's play *The Frozen Deep*.
1858 (46) Separation from his wife (whom he never sees again). Embarks on professional readings in public.
1859 (47) *A Tale of Two Cities*. *Household Words* merged with a new weekly periodical, *All the Year Round*.
1861 (49) *Great Expectations*.
1865 (53) *Our Mutual Friend*. Involved in serious railway accident.
1867 (55) Reading tour of America from November to May 1868.
1868 (56) Embarks on Farewell Reading Tour.
1870 (58) Gives last farewell reading in London in March. Starts *The Mystery of Edwin Drood*. Dies 9 June.

Chronology of Dickens's Times

Year	Literary Events	Historical Events
1812	Byron, *Childe Harold* I & II.	1811–20 Regency of Prince of Wales. 1812–14 War with America.
1813	Austen, *Pride and Prejudice.*	
1814	Austen, *Mansfield Park.* Scott, *Waverley.* Wordsworth, *The Excursion.*	
1815		Battle of Waterloo.
1816	Austen, *Emma.*	
1817	Keats, *Poems.* Austen dies.	
1818	Mary Shelley, *Frankenstein.*	
1819	Byron, *Don Juan* I & II. George Eliot born.	Peterloo Massacre.
1820	Keats, *Lamia . . . and other Poems.*	
1821	Keats dies.	Napoleon dies.
1822	Shelley dies.	
1823	Grimm Brothers, *German Popular Stories* (illus. by George Cruikshank).	Agricultural riots.
1824	Byron dies.	
1825		Opening of Stockton–Darlington railway.
1827	Blake dies.	University of London founded.
1828		Catholic Emancipation Act.
1830	Tennyson, *Poems, Chiefly Lyrical.*	Accession of William IV.
1831		First cholera epidemic
1832	Scott dies.	First Reform Bill.
1833	Carlyle, *Sartor Resartus.*	Abolition of slavery in British Empire. State funding of schools begins.

1834 Coleridge and Lamb die.   Tolpuddle martyrs. New Poor
                                              Law.
1837 Carlyle, *The French*   Accession of Victoria.
      Revolution.
1838   Anti-Corn Law League.
                                              Chartist petitions.
                                              London–Birmingham railway.
1839 Carlyle, *Chartism.*   First Factory Inspectors'
                                              Report.
1840 Hardy born.   Introduction of penny post.
1841 Carlyle, *Heroes and Hero-*
      Worship.
1842 Tennyson, *Poems.*   Chartist riots. Report on
                                              Sanitary Condition of
                                              Labouring Population.
1843 Carlyle, *Past and Present.*
1844   Rochdale Pioneers Co-
                                              operative Store.
1845 Disraeli, *Sybil.*   Railway 'mania' (speculation).
1847 E. Brontë, *Wuthering Heights.*
      C. Brontë, *Jane Eyre.*
1848 E. Brontë dies.   European revolutions.
      Thackeray, *Vanity Fair.*   Mass meeting of Chartists in
                                              London, movement collapses.
                                              Cholera epidemic.
1850 Tennyson, *In Memoriam.*   Pope appoints Catholic
      Wordsworth dies.   bishops to England.
      Wordsworth, *The Prelude.*
1851 Melville, *Moby Dick.*   Great Exhibition in London.
                                              J. M. W. Turner dies.
1852 Stowe, *Uncle Tom's Cabin.*   Duke of Wellington dies.
1853 C. Brontë, *Villette.*   Opening of Indian Civil
                                              Service to competition.
1854 Thoreau, *Walden.*   Crimean War.
      Wilde born.
1855 Gaskell, *North and South.*
      C. Brontë dies.
1856 Shaw born.   Crimean War ends.
1857 Flaubert, *Madame Bovary.*   Indian Mutiny.
1858 Eliot, *Scenes of Clerical Life.*
1859 Tennyson, *Idylls of the King.*

	Darwin, *On the Origin of Species.*	
	Mill, *On Liberty.*	
	Smiles, *Self-help.*	
1860	Collins, *The Woman in White.*	
	Eliot, *The Mill on the Floss.*	
1861		Death of Prince Albert (Victoria's husband). American Civil War begins.
1863	Mill, *Utilitarianism.* Thackeray dies.	Abolition of Slavery in USA.
1865	Carroll, *Alice's Adventures in Wonderland.*	Assassination of Lincoln. American Civil War ends.
1866	Dostoevsky, *Crime and Punishment.*	First Barnardo Home for orphans. Atlantic Cable laid.
1867	Marx, *Das Kapital.*	Second Reform Bill.
1868	Collins, *The Moonstone.*	
1869	Arnold, *Culture and Anarchy.* Blackmore, *Lorna Doone.*	Opening of Suez Canal. Mill advocates female emancipation.
1870	D. G. Rossetti, *Poems Lyrical.*	Education Act brings free public education in Board Schools. Franco-Prussian War.

Books concern printers, publishers, sales reps, booksellers, proof-readers, professors, illustrators, indexers, critics, text editors, literary editors, librarians, book-reviewers and bookbinders and bookkeepers, translators, typographers, Oxfam-fundraisers, whole university departments of soothsayers, manufacturers of thread and glue, auctioneers, lumberjacks, starving mice, wolves howling at the doors of authors of first novels, the Post Office book-bashing machine minder, religious bonfire fuel suppliers and libel-lawyers.

Foreword to J. L. Carr, *Harpole and Foxberrow General Publishers*

1

Authorship and Literary Production

Contemporary theories of authorship, especially those influenced by film studies, have taught us that the process of defining authors through naming them is more complicated than common sense would suggest. 'Dickens', a convenient and perhaps unavoidable label, masks a range of Dickenses which, taken together, constitute a highly complex whole. This very richness suggests the difficulty of holding the complete range of what can be meant by Dickens in one's head at any given moment. And, in fact, there is a tendency to privilege a single strand of this complex in relation to the discourse that currently preoccupies the reader and critic. There is, for example, a continuing debate in Dickens studies on the question of his relative conservatism or radicalism, especially in relation to supposed changes of view as he got older. If Dickens's journalism is privileged as a way of clarifying the issue a case can be made that he did, indeed, become socially and politically more conservative with advancing years. Concentration on the novels, however, might suggest very different answers to the problem.

The question of who or what is the 'real' person is, of course, a commonplace of ordinary human experience. Any individual may be a spouse, parent, friend, colleague, lover and so on, and possess what may seem like different qualities in these roles, although in most cases there is clearly a large degree of overlap. The question becomes more problematic, however, in the case of a 'great writer', particularly when that writer is Dickens. Dickens lived for much of his life at the centre of an extended family of parents, brothers and sisters, and children, many of whom looked to him for support, often financial, in ways that were frequently irksome to him. In addition, he initiated the trauma of separation from his wife after many years of marriage and he may have been the lover of Ellen Ternan, a woman young enough to be his daughter. After the other earlier trauma of his incarceration in a shoe polish factory at a crucial stage in his boyhood development, he became a lawyer's clerk, a legal and then parliamentary shorthand reporter, a newspaper reporter, the editor of (and regular contributor to) two best-selling weekly periodicals for a total of twenty years, and throughout his life engaged in a round of practical involvement with some of the worst social abuses of his day. He was a brilliant public speaker who was called on to support a full range of philanthropic causes and, through the immensely successful public readings of his own work, became what we would today call a media personality and one of the most famous people in Britain, America and Europe. Dickens's 'leisure' pursuits included walking, often twenty miles a day, and participation in amateur theatricals as actor, director and entrepreneur with an energy, and success, that are hardly distinguishable from professional activity. And he did also of course write fourteen completed novels.

It is, no doubt, that last contribution which gives interest to the rest of Dickens's numerous activities, but it seems clear that only a work of literary criticism in the narrow sense would be satisfied to privilege this segment of Dickens's life to the exclusion of all else. On the other hand, only the traditional narrative biography would seek to encompass a totalizing view of the whole of this experience, which probably explains the huge length of the recent extraordinary life of Dickens by Peter Ackroyd. The present study is, as its title states, a 'literary life'and this exerts its own pressure not to deal with the full range of Dickens's activity. Its concentration, then, will be on his professional career as a writer, partly through a description of the many aspects of this professional life, but also with the intention of offering some explanation for his specific achievements as a novelist through an emphasis on his life as a professional author. The bias of the book is, therefore, towards contextualization and so it will try to describe and analyse the literary contexts that surrounded Dickens when he was writing his novels. But although the emphasis will be on the literary it is hardly possible to seal this off from the social and political aspects of Dickens's life and period. Indeed, it will become clear that the economic aspects of his novel writing are a crucial aspect of his literary life. In short, this book will attempt to separate out at least some of the contextual forces that flowed through Dickens's pen along with the ink at the moment when he sat down to the ostensibly solitary and private process of making that series of black marks on white paper that we call novels.

It might be useful to begin by examining some of the ways in which this process is traditionally described. We often speak of novels as 'literature' or 'imaginative literature' and the process by which they come into being as 'creation' through the use of 'creative imagination'. If such language is analysed we can see that what lies behind it is a certain concept, historically determined, of what it means to be an artist, a concept that has the status of myth in our culture and that also operates at a popular level in governing the ways in which 'ordinary' people understand art and artists. These ideas, at both the serious and popular level, are inseparably bound up with notions of 'inspiration' and the creation of works of art through a process of 'creative agony'. In a way that is highly characteristic Dickens displays some contradictions in relation to this myth of the artist. Once his career was well under way, he revealed what might be called a business-like approach to the task of writing, disappearing for a set number of hours each morning and remaining in his study whether he was actually able to put pen to paper or not. On the other hand, he also displayed some of the classic signs of the artist in the grip of creative agony, above all in the earliest stages of writing a new novel. His letters are filled with vivid and comic descriptions of staring at blank sheets of paper, tearing at his hair, and restlessly pacing his study. But even in the later stages of a novel, moments of crisis such as the death of a beloved character like Little Nell or Paul Dombey would be marked by his famous all-night hauntings of the streets of London or Paris. One of his most striking evocations of this turmoil of creativity is contained in a letter of 1855 in which he was trying, as gently as possible, to evade a relationship with his former sweetheart, Maria Beadnell, who had reappeared in his life after a gap of some twenty-five years with disastrous consequences:

> A necessity is upon me now – as at most times – of wandering about in my own wild way, to think...I hold my inventive capacity on the stern condition that it must master my whole life, often have complete possession of me, make its own demands upon me, and sometimes for months together put everything else away from me...I can hardly expect you to understand...the restlessness or waywardness of an author's mind...Whoever is devoted to an Art must be content to deliver himself wholly up to it.[1]

These manifestations were unquestionably genuine and deeply felt, but they can be seen as the personal expression of a view of the artist and artistic creation which belongs essentially to the Romantic period, although some aspects of the whole process are even clearer in the Modernist art of the earlier twentieth century. What are some of the elements of this construct? Art itself is seen as obscure, difficult and unpopular, at least on its first appearance, while the artist himself (gendered conceptions of artistic creation are central to this mode of thought) is alienated from his society. Suffering is a crucial part of the artistic process and the artist is seen as quite different from the ordinary run of people through his possession of a creative power akin to that of God in His creation of the world. That such views are historically conditioned and so not universal is clear from some very different concepts of art and the artist held in the Middle Ages, the Renaissance and the eighteenth century. If we think of composers such as J. S. Bach and the painters of early Renaissance Italy we are presented with a quite different relationship between the artist and society. Whatever difficulties were involved in Church commissions and aristocratic patronage, the religious and social celebrators of cathedrals and great public spaces in music, painting and sculpture did not lack a social role. And the work produced under these conditions was frequently appreciated and admired on its first appearance. If artists have a social and economic function in the life of their times, they are liable not to be viewed as supermen, a different race of beings from their fellows. And the existence of studios for the training of apprentices emphasised the craftsman-like side of artistic production despite the recognition accorded to such obviously extraordinary figures as Leonardo da Vinci and Michelangelo. If, then, creative agony and an almost supernatural inspiration are not essential to the appearance of art, it may be possible to demystify this Romantic conception of the artist, just as it is possible to deconstruct the language which embodies this concept. One way to do this is to substitute the word 'production' for the word 'creation' and to see Dickens as a literary producer of texts rather than as a solitary, Romantically-agonized creator of works of the imagination. Such an approach is particularly fruitful if stress is laid on the material conditions of literary production, although this study will not restrict itself exclusively to that area.

The simplest example of the influence of material conditions on a literary text is, perhaps, the question of length. A traditional view of the artist as genius working under the pressure of inspiration would suggest that the length of a novel is the purest kind of artistic choice, governed by nothing but the internal demands of the work itself as the artist seeks to discover its organic form, the shape that the novel *must* take if it is to achieve its fullest degree of artistic expression. But a moment's consideration reveals that for most writers this is a luxury that they simply cannot be accorded, a situation that is rendered clearer by the public demands of, say, film and theatre. Although a fairly wide degree of toleration is acceptable here, it is obvious that a film which is less than roughly ninety minutes in length or a play that is less than an hour will not provide the 'evening out' or the 'night at the theatre' that the public expects in return for its money. Excessive length, on the other hand, may prevent the audience from getting home by public transport or, even, send it to sleep. These practical considerations may seem less applicable in the private, more individualized, world of novel reading, but investigation reveals that this is not the case. It is known for example that publishers frequently have practical problems in marketing the so-called novella, the prose narrative whose length hovers in the limbo between the long short story and the novel proper. Readers of modern paperback editions of Conrad's *Heart of Darkness* may have noticed how publishers and printers use devices such as unusually large typefaces, margins and line spacing in order to make the text look big enough to be worth purchasing as a single volume.

The point at issue here is obvious enough but important nevertheless. In the world of capitalism, the gap that exists between the production of a literary text and an audience's reception of it is filled by the contributions of agents, publishers, printers, booksellers and so on. In other words, the text cannot proceed directly to its audience, but is mediated by a complex series of factors, most of which are economic. And it is impossible for this screening process not to have some kind of influence on the work being screened. Certain writers in the history of the novel are traditionally singled out as heroic figures who have rebelled against these 'commercial' demands, whether because they had incomes independent of their activity as writers or because of an artistic purity which refused contamination by external pressures. Flaubert, Proust and Conrad come to mind here, but it can be shown that their supposed independence is less of a reality than a contribution to a myth of the heroic martyrdom of the artist who is, by definition, at odds with his society. In Conrad's case, for example, the influence of his publisher's reader, Edward Garnett, was crucial in permitting his work to make its fraught journey to a potential audience.

Nonetheless, it does seem sensible to make distinctions between kinds of writers on this issue. Although the personal isolation of Conrad and these others is seen traditionally as an aspect of their stance as literary heroes, authorship theory suggests that all acts of literary productivity are solitary only in the limited and not very interesting sense that *all* writers, all artists indeed, carry an immense amount of baggage into the study with them when they begin to write. Personal psychology, political views, economic pressures, not forgetting the passing events of mundane existence, are only some of the ingredients that enrich the supposedly private activity of putting pen to paper. That said, there do seem to be interesting differences between Dickens and these candidates for literary sanctification. However suspicious Dickens often was of such mediators in the communication process as publishers and printers, he seems not to have been hostile to the process itself, but to have collaborated eagerly in, and sometimes himself initiated, the means necessary to bring his work to the largest possible public. If there is an inescapably communal aspect to all forms of artistic production, there is a case for arguing that Dickens welcomed, rather than resisted, this feature of his working life. And a clue to the nature of his response may be found in the descriptive phrase attached to his weekly periodicals *Household Words* and *All the Year Round* as a way of defining Dickens's role as editor: 'Conducted by Charles Dickens'.

It is indeed possible to see Dickens as a conductor in many aspects of his life and career. His role in the amateur theatricals which dominated his life at different times can best be likened to that of the filmic auteur, the authorial director such as Orson Welles who dominates all aspects of the project in which he is involved. Dickens acted, produced, oversaw the production of sets, saw to the distribution of tickets, dominated the whole enterprise in fact but, again like Welles, with a charm that persuaded those contributing to give of their best. In short, his conducting of the large forces involved was dominated by *his* vision of the proceedings, but attuned to the recognition that this vision could only be realized through the contributions of others. The longevity of Dickens's need for this combination of power and mutual support is illustrated in a deeply revealing anecdote from the last few weeks of his life. Walking past Westminster Abbey in the summer of 1870 Dickens confided in a friend:

> 'What do you think would be the realisation of one of my most cherished day-dreams? To settle down now for the remainder of my life within easy distance of a great theatre, in the direction of which I would hold supreme authority. It should be a house, of course, having a skilled and noble company, and one in every way magnificently appointed. The pieces acted should be dealt with according to my own judgement; the players as well as the plays being absolutely under my command. There,' he said laughingly, and in a glow of merry fancy, *'that's* my day-dream.'[2]

His public readings, famous throughout the English-speaking world (he toyed with the idea of touring Australia towards the end of his life, but the readings were also a brilliant success in Paris), provide a particularly vivid example of his emotional sway over large audiences, drawing from them the responses he desired in the way that the orchestral conductor coaxes from, or imposes on, his forces the effects he wishes to evoke. Two incidents, which occurred in Ireland in 1858, evoke the sometimes hysterical atmosphere of these occasions and Dickens's own view of his power over an audience: 'I had a difficulty in getting in. They had broken all the glass in the payboxes. Our men were flattened against walls and squeezed against beams. Ladies stood all night with their chins against my platform. Other ladies sat all night upon my steps. You never saw such a sight. And the reading went tremendously.' This scene was repeated in Belfast, 'with the additional feature, that the people are much rougher...than in Dublin, and that there was a very great uproar at the opening of the doors...It ceased, however, the moment I showed myself.' (Nonesuch 3, 46–7)

Again, Dickens's longing (not too strong a word) to impose his will on a heterogeneous group can be seen in his burning desire to edit and indeed own a periodical, an odyssey that we can follow through his involvement with *Bentley's Miscellany*, his short-lived venture into newspaper editing with the *Daily News* in 1846, and which culminated in the success of *Household Words* and *All the Year Round*. A particularly interesting example of this interaction between the individual and the social can be seen in Dickens's orchestration, to change the metaphor, of the special Extra Christmas Numbers of *All the Year Round* as a series of stories by himself and others on a theme or subject determined by himself. We can catch a glimpse of his method in a letter to a friend and regular contributor to *Household Words*, the Rev James White:

> We are now getting our Christmas extra number together, and I think you are the boy to do, if you will, one of the stories. I propose to give the number some fireside name, and to make it consist entirely of short stories supposed to be told by a family sitting round the fire. *I don't care about their referring to Christmas at all;* nor do I design to connect them together, otherwise than by their names.
>
> (Pilgrim Vl, 780)

As the Pilgrim editors explain, Dickens chose four stories out of a total of ten, one by White and himself, and the others by Samuel

Sydney and Elizabeth Gaskell (n 5, 780). This somewhat casual approach contrasts with the method adopted for later efforts such as 'The Wreck of the "Golden Mary"' of 1856. For this Dickens wrote detailed instructions to his authors. He thus kept control of the framework of the enterprise and chose the stories for inclusion, but he was otherwise eager to collaborate with his contributors, although sometimes disappointed by what they submitted.

Serial publication will be dealt with in detail at a later stage, but it too can be seen as a species of conducting in relation to those who shared the enterprise with Dickens. The total visual impact of the novels in their own day, and to some extent later, cannot be separated from the contribution of the improbably named Hablot K. Brown, who adopted the signature Phiz to chime with Dickens's Boz and illustrated most of the novels from *Pickwick Papers* to *Little Dorrit*. Phiz may have been an orchestra of one, but Dickens's letters testify to the degree of control he exerted, although like any good conductor he was willing to give the soloist his head when he was playing well. Some idea of the intensity of Dickens's commitment to this area can be gained from a letter to Robert Seymour, his experienced, well-known and senior collaborator on *Pickwick*, who committed suicide before two monthly numbers had appeared, leaving the field clear for the 24-year old author:

> I have seen your design for an Etching to accompany it. ['The Stroller's Tale'] I think it extremely good, but still, it is not quite my idea; and as I feel so very solicitous to have it as complete as possible, I shall feel personally obliged, if you will make another drawing... The furniture of the room, you have depicted, *admirably*.'
>
> (Pilgrim VI, 146)

One can only guess at what the unfortunate Seymour would have thought of having his drawing of furniture complimented. It is, of course, crucial to this argument that the relationship I describe as conducting was a two-way process, that Dickens was influenced, as well as influencing, in this communal activity of professional writing. More will be said later of his involvement with his public, his publishers, and his friend, John Forster, all of whom can be seen as part of this metaphor of conducting.

The seductive charm of metaphors can, of course, give them a life of their own which reduces their value as part of a coherent argument aiming to analyse a phenomenon as complex as that of the literary career of a major writer. It might therefore be useful to clarify the senses in which it is being used here. What exactly does conducting mean in this context and what precisely is being conducted? If we think of Dickens as being in command, especially through serialization, of novels which can be described as multi-layered and contrapuntal, then he might more properly be called a composer. Novels such as *Bleak House* and *Little Dorrit* can reasonably be compared with works such as Beethoven's Ninth Symphony and Michelangelo's painting of the ceiling of the Sistine Chapel. In other words, they are achievements on a huge scale in which many elements are brought together in a unified whole and which draw attention to their own technical virtuosity as part of their aesthetic effect. But it is part of the essential purpose of this book to demonstrate that Dickens knew the score in more senses than one. If he was able to compose on a vast scale and paint an enormous canvas, as it were, he did so partly with an eye to the main chance of sales figures and their resulting income. It is this point that marks the transition from composer to conductor. However elaborate a musical score may be, it remains in some real sense inert until it is brought to orchestral life. Similarly, the literary text only comes fully alive when it is read, and it can only be read if it is brought before the public through all the processes of illustration, publication, advertisement and so on which will be described and analysed in this chapter and those that follow.

The truly complex feature of this process in Dickens's case is that he composed and conducted, if not simultaneously, then with remarkably little interval in between, since writing for serial publication on a monthly or weekly basis meant that the work was being read by a huge public almost as soon as it was written. This may allow the metaphor to be applied in a number of ways, perhaps, without its collapsing into incoherence. In addition to conducting the novels from silence into communication, Dickens can also be seen as conducting his vast public through the medium of his work and so eliciting from it the emotional and intellectual responses he sought. As we have seen, he himself saw his role in his periodicals as that of conductor of all the resources required to bring *Household Words* and *All the Year Round* before the public. And this clearly relates to the tasks he set himself in undertaking the amateur theatricals he so much enjoyed. Possibly the major usefulness of the metaphor is that it allows us to see ways in which Dickens combined, to a possibly unique degree in English literature, the solitariness of writing fiction with a commitment to communal activity. And it may also help us to perceive the inextricable nature of the connections between the private and the public in his life and work.

The fact that his novels invariably appeared in serial form, on five occasions as weekly serials and the remainder in the famous monthly numbers, created an especially intimate and fluctuating relationship between Dickens and his readers, one in which conducting could go hand in hand with the fine tuning of his work. He was, for example, in a position to estimate the public evaluation of his novels in terms of that most concrete of responses, weekly and monthly sales figures. And, on the comparatively rare occasions when sales dropped, he had at least the opportunity to try to remedy the situation. It is generally agreed, for example, that Dickens despatched the eponymous hero of *Martin Chuzzlewit* to America at least partly in an attempt to improve its rather poor sales figures, although this attempt to capitalize on his own American journey produced only a modest increase.

It was only in shorter works that Dickens achieved an ambition that surfaced from time to time, the desire to break free from serialization to write and publish a work as a complete whole. A striking example is the first, and best known, of the Christmas Books, *A Christmas Carol*, which Dickens wrote in a period of some six weeks for publication in December 1843. It was typical of Dickens the literary producer that he was writing the monthly parts of *Martin Chuzzlewit* at the same time, having to take a break from the *Carol* to finish his current number of the novel. But conducting is no less relevant a metaphor to describe how the *Carol* came into existence than it is with the serial works, since its success depended on the combined skills of the publisher, printer, illustrator and bookbinder, as well as those of the writer. Kathleen Tillotson has shown how complex was the work's genesis, reaching back as far as 1840 and Dickens's correspondence with the great philanthropist, Lord Ashley, on the horrific conditions endured by children working in coal-mines and factories.[3] The desire to strike with the force of 'a Sledge hammer' (Pilgrim III, 459) against these evils recurred over the years until it came to a focus in his idea for a new literary genre, a book for Christmas.

Peter Ackroyd suggests (407) that Dickens's social indignation on these issues came to a head after his well-documented visit to the Field Lane Ragged School on behalf of the philanthropist, Miss Burdett Coutts, for whom he acted as an unofficial agent. The Ragged Schools, a desperate attempt to educate the very poorest sections of society, provoked some of his most moving and interesting letters so it is surely no coincidence that he began work on the *Carol* only a few weeks later. But moral outrage and a desire to ease the sufferings of social outcasts went, as so often, hand in hand with the need for a sound financial return on the *Carol* as an investment. This was a period when Dickens felt himself to be particularly hard up, partly through the demands of his large extended family, and he clearly saw the book as the solution to a pressing need. And so we can follow in fascinating detail his conducting of the *Carol* into the public arena through his attempted control of a whole number of processes necessary for its successful appearance in the world.

The agreement with his publishers, Chapman and Hall, gave him an unusual degree of responsibility in that they were to publish the book on a commission basis so that Dickens would be in receipt of profits rather than royalties. But some matters had to be left in their hands and Dickens's intense practicality is revealed by the anguished tone of a letter complaining of their failure to advertise in the way he had expected: 'with the exception of Blackwood's, *the Carol is not advertised in One of the Magazines!*' (Pilgrim III, 604–5) From the very beginning, then, we can see that he was intensely concerned to reach the widest possible public, and also to produce the *Carol* as an attractive contribution to the Christmas scene at the lowest possible price. Anyone who has seen a first edition will confirm that it is a most beautiful little book. It contains four lovely etchings in full colour by John Leech as well as four black-and-white woodcuts. And the book's exterior is as attractive as its contents, the gilt design on its binding of red cloth echoed in the gilt edges of its pages. But despite Dickens's knowledgeable interest in the realities of book publishing, a crucial error was made in pricing the book too low, at five shillings, to recoup the costs involved in its expensive production. Although about six thousand copies were sold by Christmas Eve, and sales continued at a high level after Christmas, the profits from the first six thousand were about £130 rather than the £1000 Dickens had anticipated. Despite the universal acclaim lavished on the book by critics and public alike, the disappointment induced a reaction of near hysteria: 'Such a night as I have passed! I really believed that I should never get up again, until I had passed through all the horrors of a fever.' (Ackroyd 416.)

This pained response to a financial disappointment for a work whose central thrust is the rejection of a greedy materialism forms a fascinating commentary on the complexity of Dickens as a literary producer. There is no question that at one level the *Carol* arose from the deepest springs of Dickens's response to the aesthetic challenge of rendering social evils, as a letter describing, in the third person, the upheaval involved in its composition makes clear:

Over which Christmas Carol, Charles Dickens wept, and laughed, and wept again and excited himself in a most extraordinary manner, in the composition; and thinking whereof, he walked about the black streets of London, fifteen and twenty miles, many a night when all the sober folks had gone to bed.

(Pilgrim III, 2)

But for Dickens there was no contradiction between these transparently genuine feelings and his urge to conduct his work to maximum financial success through all the stages necessary to make contact with his public.

Equally complicated, although usually free from acrimony, was the special role occupied in Dickens's life by John Forster, a combination of friend, confidant, literary agent and corrector of manuscripts and proofs. In this last role Forster, like Phiz, was a solo performer and one who was allowed a great deal of leeway to cut and revise, especially when Dickens had overwritten the thirty-two pages that quickly became the standard format for the novels published in monthly parts and also during those not infrequent periods when Dickens was living abroad in Genoa, Lausanne or Paris, and posting manuscripts and proofs to London for printing and correction. The conducting in this case was of the most discreet kind, no doubt based on Forster's intimate knowledge of Dickens's tastes and intentions, and Dickens was frequently amenable to his friend's suggestions. But the dual nature of the literary relationships I am attempting to describe here holds in this case also; Forster made his own, sometimes independent, contribution to the enterprise, making it communal in some valid sense, although the ultimate decision-making remained with Dickens.

The key to the approach to be followed in this book is contained in Dickens's extraordinarily interesting explanation of why he so much enjoyed his practical stage activities:

As to the play itself...I derive a strange feeling out of it, like writing a book in company; a satisfaction of a most singular kind, which has no exact parallel in my life; a something that I suppose belongs to a labourer in art alone, and which has to me a conviction of its being actual truth without its pain that I could never adequately state if I were to try never so hard.'

(Nonesuch I, 825)

If, then, the theatricals were like writing a book in company, it might not be going too far to suggest that writing a book was like being in a play in private! There is no doubt an element of exaggeration in the claim, although anecdotes exist that show that for Dickens the writing process involved forms of behaviour that can be called dramatic, perhaps the most apt being his daughter Mamie's description of being privileged to observe her father's creative process when she was convalescing from an illness:

> One of these mornings, I was lying on the sofa endeavouring to keep perfectly quiet, while my father wrote busily and rapidly at his desk, when he suddenly jumped from his chair and rushed to a mirror which hung near, and in which I could see the reflection of some extraordinary facial contortions which he was making. He returned rapidly to his desk, wrote furiously for a few moments, and then went again to the mirror. The facial pantomime was resumed, and then turning toward, but evidently not seeing, me, he began talking rapidly in a low voice.
>
> (Ackroyd, 561)

This amazing incident, with its suggestive use of the word pantomime for Dickens's creative activity, reinforces the argument that in the act of writing his novels Dickens was conducting – with the pen as his baton – an amazingly varied range of materials which flowed into and helped to form the texts themselves. This theme will be pursued through a series of chapters concerned with such matters as publishers and serial publication, Dickens's reading, periodicals and journalism, Dickens and the theatre, Dickens's public, Dickens and social institutions, and language and the novel. Another note of clarification is perhaps worth striking. The subject of this study, for those who still accept the idea of a canon of great writers, is one of the major figures of world literature, second only to Shakespeare in English in his command of language, complexity of structure, creation of character and range of imagination. At the same time he was, and to some extent still is, a hugely popular figure whose name has become an adjective (Dickensian) in the English-speaking world to describe a range of experiences from the pleasures of Christmas to extremes of poverty. This combination of what the Romantic myth of genius would see as a contradiction in terms has sometimes seemed problematic to twentieth-century readers and critics. It would, however, have presented no difficulties for Dickens himself and should present none to us. Equally unproblematic for the writer and his contemporaries was the positive intervention of his work in the life of its own time which can appear unsophisticated to students of literature brought up on theories which seek to demonstrate a rigid separation between art and reality. Modern readers may shift uneasily at the descriptions of the crowds at the New York docks waiting for the latest instalment of *The Old Curiosity Shop* and shouting out to the approaching ship to ask if Little Nell were dead. And the frank acceptance of the influence of Dickens's work in the real world may seem embarrassing even when the source is the unsentimental Robert Louis Stevenson who wrote of the effect of reading the Christmas Books:

> I feel so good and would do anything, yes, and shall do anything, to make it a little better for people. I wish I could lose no time; I want to go out and confront someone; I shall never listen to the nonsense they tell me, about not giving money. I *shall* give money. Oh what a jolly thing it is for a man to have written books like these books and just *filled* people's hearts with pity.[4]

Stories of the practical effects of reading Dickens in his own day were not uncommon, an example being the 'factory owner [who] attended Dickens's Christmas Eve reading of the *Carol* in Boston in 1867 and was so moved by it that he ordered the works to be closed on Christmas Day. In following years the works were always closed, and every hand received a turkey.'[5] If these examples of the direct effect of literature on life seem implausible it might be as well to remember a twentieth-century example of the kinds of effect produced by Dickens, Arthur Miller's description of the first night of his play *Death of a Salesman* in Philadelphia in 1949 in his autobiography, *Timebends*:

> As sometimes happened later on during the run, there was no applause at the final curtain of the first performance. Strange things began to go on in the audience. With the curtain down, some people stood to put their coats on and then sat again, some, especially men, were bent forward covering their faces, and others were openly weeping. People crossed the theatre to stand quietly talking with one another. It seemed forever before someone remembered to applaud, and then there was no end to it. I was standing at the back and saw a distinguished-looking elderly man being led up the aisle; he was talking excitedly into the ear of what seemed to be his male secretary or assistant. This, I learned, was Bernard Gimbel, head of the department store chain, who that night gave an order that no one in his stores was to be fired for being overage.[6]

In this context, tales of the practical influence of Dickens's work may seem less unconvincing.

We are dealing then with a great popular genius, writing essentially comic novels which nonetheless aspire to intervene directly in the life of their own time. But Dickens is also a writer committed to a profound professionalism of attitude and practice, a professionalism that makes the attempt to describe and analyse his literary life particularly appropriate. This aspect of his career can be explored in a number of ways, in his deep respect for his own activity as a novelist as well as in an intense concern to extract his full pound of flesh financially from publishers and also, in a sense, from the public. An extended statement of Dickens's commitment to writing occurs in a letter to Thackeray, evidently in response to his praise of *Dombey and Son*:

> I *do* sometimes please myself with thinking that my success has opened the way for good writers. And of this, I am quite sure now, and hope I shall be when I die – that in all my social doings I am mindful of this honour and dignity and always try to do something towards the quiet assertion of their right place. I am always possessed with the hope of leaving the position of literary men in England, something better and more independent than I found it.
>
> (Pilgrim V, 227)

This letter reinforces the accuracy of Peter Ackroyd's statement: 'He was perhaps the first professional author to *act* as a professional, and to put what could have been notable skills as a Victorian businessman to good use.'(291). The last part of this judgement is also confirmed by his friend and fellow novelist, Bulwer Lytton, who claimed that Dickens understood 'the practical part of Authorship beyond any writer – Walter Scott not excepted.'[7] The two major figures in the nineteenth century before Dickens who could be regarded as professional writers were Scott and Byron, but both 'had their doubts about authorship as a profession'. Byron's dismissal is well known – 'No one should be a writer who could be anything better.' – while for Scott the lawyer it was 'the most fortunate thing...to have an established profession and professional character' outside of literature.[8] On the other hand, Dickens's belief in novel writing as a dignified career suffused his life at the personal as well as the social level. Despite his reputation as a great comic novelist, he disliked Thackeray's amusing series of fictional parodies, known as 'Punch's Prize Novelists', because 'I had a strong opinion of my own: and that it was, that they did no honour to literature or to literary men' (Pilgrim V, 82). Believing as deeply as he did in the novelist's right to 'rest his station and claims

quietly on Literature, and to make no feint of living by anything else'
(Pilgrim V, 289) Dickens could not resist introducing a note of criticism into his moving obituary of Thackeray after his death in 1863: 'I
thought that he too much feigned a want of earnestness, and that he
made a pretence of undervaluing his art, which was not good for the
art that he held in trust.'[9]

This public assertion of the value of his profession motivated Dickens
in a number of ways. He was a fervent supporter of the Guild of Literature
and Art, a somewhat ill-founded venture initiated by the novelist Bulwer
Lytton and himself which was designed, amongst other things, to provide support for unsuccessful writers. And he was a passionate advo-
cate of International Copyright to the extent of virtually ruining his first
trip to America by speaking out against its absence publicly despite the
storm of protest this generated in the popular press. The lack of copyright laws was sometimes defended by supporters of the purity of literature who claimed that it was sullied by being associated with
money-making and writers who lacked the 'well-balanced mind and
the delicate perceptions of a gentleman' (Pilgrim III, n. 5, 260) but Dickens
was outraged that his work could be pirated throughout the world by
publishers who rarely paid him a penny in return. This strength of feeling may have stemmed partly from his sense of the financial injustices
he thought were inflicted on him at the beginning of his career. Under
the pressure of early success, but before its full extent had become clear,
Dickens entered into a number of unwise commitments for fixed payments. This led to such exhausting entanglements as writing two novels at the same time, with a month divided between two weeks spent
on one serial part and the next two on a second. These overlaps occurred
from *Pickwick* to *Nicholas Nickleby* and induced bouts of exhaustion combined with fears of his talent drying up, worries not eased by the discovery that his rocket-like success was enriching publishers rather than
the writer himself. After this period of fame and uncertainty Dickens
insisted, as Ackroyd points out, 'that he would always participate in
the profits and thus increase his own income as his sales increased'
(291). Huge losses of temper on Dickens's part and the negotiating skills
of John Forster were required to extricate him from the worst of these
entanglements which he had, admittedly, freely entered into, but
Dickens remained throughout his life liable to outrage at what he saw
as the inordinate demands of publishers and susceptible to such slights,
whether real or imagined.

Dickens had an abiding hatred of patronage in all its forms, and literary patronage was a prime target, as a speech of 1840 makes clear:

'That huckstering, peddling, pandering to patronage for the sale of a book, the offspring of intellect and genius, would not now remain a stain upon their most brilliant productions.' (Speeches, 5.) One reason for the stain's disappearance was the increasing reliance on the public as the final arbiter of success through sales, a situation which for obvious reasons Dickens gloried in throughout his career: to be patronized by his money-paying audience was a central part of the dignity of literature as a profession, while financial support from an aristocrat would have been an insulting disgrace. But this appeal to the public was not simply a matter of their buying monthly parts or, even, a novel in its completed form. Throughout his career, Dickens's work was continually presented and re-presented to his audience in a complex range of ways through a system of what was called 'working the copyrights'. To take only a single example, *Oliver Twist* was published in the following formats in less than fifteen years. It appeared as a monthly serial in *Bentley's Miscellany*, a magazine edited by Dickens, from 1837 to 1839. It was then published by Richard Bentley in three volumes in 1838 (that is, before the serial publication was completed) with reprintings. Chapman and Hall, Dickens's next publishers, brought it out in three volumes in 1841. After another change of publisher, Bradbury and Evans issued it in ten monthly numbers in 1846 plus a one-volume edition in the same year. In addition to all this, which by no means exhausts the story, there were a mass of plagiarisms and pirated copies on the market. Once Dickens's career was fully under way a new work might be appearing in its monthly parts and being reviewed partly by way of long extracts as it came out, while at the same time earlier work would be circulating in a mass of authorized and unauthorized forms, as monthly and weekly parts and in single or three-volume editions. In the 1840s alone, Chapman and Hall were handling the Library Edition, the People's Edition, the Cheap Edition, and the Charles Dickens Edition of his works. In short, it might fairly be said that the market was saturated in Dickens's writings from as early as *Sketches by Boz* onwards. The full-blooded professionalism of this enterprise is indicated in a letter of 1847 in which Dickens is celebrating the Cheap Edition to a friend: 'I believe it is the greatest venture – indeed I have no doubt of it – ever made in books. If it should succeed (it must be an immense sale, to succeed sweepingly) I hope to get a great deal of money out of the idea' (Pilgrim V, 42.)

    It is interesting to put this intensity of activity in the general context of the volume of work Dickens seemed capable of throughout his career, a representative moment being well caught by Peter Ackroyd:

By early May [1836] he had also signed an agreement with John
Macrone to write a novel entitled *Gabriel Vardon, The Locksmith of
London*. This...only eventually emerged in completed form as *Barnaby
Rudge*...He received two hundred pounds for this, and then three
months later accepted a further one hundred pounds when he agreed
to write for Thomas Tegg a children's book to be called *Solomon Bell
the Raree Showman*. Then in the same month he made an agreement
with yet another publisher, Richard Bentley, for two novels, each
to be of the conventional three-volume length. He had also agreed
to write sketches for a new weekly paper, *The Carlton Chronicle* –and
all this at the time he was writing *The Pickwick Papers*, continuing
with his parliamentary duties for the *Morning Chronicle*, and prepar-
ing another volume of *Sketches* to be published by John Macrone.
(Ackroyd, 185)

We have seen that at other points in his earlier career Dickens found
himself committed to writing two novels at once and, although the
sheer pressure of novel-writing lessened later, any 'slack' was more
than taken up with his twenty years of magazine-editing from 1850
until his death, the amateur theatricals, his commitment to social work
as Angela Burdett Coutts's unofficial agent (as well as on his own
account), his public speaking and public readings, to say nothing of
a sometimes hectic social life punctuated by periods of foreign travel. But a note of caution needs to be struck here. A concentration on
writers as literary producers and committed professionals runs the
risk of turning them into puppets jerking convulsively under the pressures of money-grubbing literary output at all costs. And so it becomes
necessary to stress something of the full complexity of Dickens as man
and writer, something that can be apprehended through the comments of intelligent contemporaries. For Emerson he was 'too con-
summate an artist to have a thread of nature left. He daunts me! I have
not the key!', while for Henry James 'the offered inscrutable mask was
the great thing...a merciless *military* eye, I might have pronounced
it...a kind of economy of apprehension. 'An American Senator,
Cornelius Cole, remarked that 'Dickens in his numerous works has
created many original characters, but not one, I should say, more interesting than himself'.[10] These comments came towards the end of his
career when Dickens was world-famous, and so long practised in
guarding his inner life from prying eyes, but they do nonetheless gesture towards those depths that were most profoundly explored in the
great summing-up of Thomas Carlyle conveyed to Forster in com-
plimenting him on the completion of the third volume of his *Life:*

...you have given to every intelligent eye the power of looking down
to the very bottom of Dickens's mode of existing in this world...So
long as Dickens is interesting to his fellow-men, here will be seen,
face to face, what Dickens's manner of existing was; his steady practicality, withal; the singularly solid business talent he continually
had; and deeper than all, if one had the eye to see deep enough,
dark, fateful, silent elements, tragical to look upon, and hiding amid
dazzling radiances as of the sun, the elements of death itself.[11]

Nothing could suggest more brilliantly the various strands of
Dickens's personality: the reference to his business abilities is supported by many commentators as is the sternness indicated by James's
'merciless *military* eye'; but while Carlyle acknowledges the element
of joyful Pickwickian comedy in his 'dazzling radiances as of the sun',
his perception of the darkness of death is more than justified by aspects
of Dickens's work throughout his career. It is within this personal
context that I shall place my biographical emphasis on Dickens's professionalism as a writer.

2
Publishers and Serialization

That art does not simply arise unconstrained by external pressures is exemplified in the relationship between technology and music. Music is seen frequently as the 'purest' of art forms, the one most free from the inhibitions of content. But the history of music is at least partly the history of technological development and the possibilities this reveals for composers and performers. Until Mr Sax invented his instrument in 1840, the peculiar sound that we associate with the saxophone could not exist although there is an ancient tradition that conceives of musical forms as absolutes, of an ideal world in which all musical potentialities enjoy a Platonic form. But it is as absurd to imagine a composer longing to use a sound for the production of which no instrument existed, as it is to think of someone longing to take a photograph before cameras had been invented. The concept, as well as the reality, of photography could only be conceived of after the means to make it possible had come into being. This relationship between the material world and consciousness occurs also at a crucial moment in Dickens's career, the events which coalesced to make possible the appearance of *Pickwick Papers* in April 1836. The runaway success of *Pickwick* determined, with small variations, Dickens's method of publication for the rest of his writing life and provides perhaps the most dramatic example in the history of the novel of publishing practices affecting the form and content of works of literature. The combination of these practices and Dickens's active co-operation made possible the appearance of his work in a highly specific form and so gave Dickens's publishers, and publishing in the widest sense of the word, a key role in choices which can be regarded as artistic as well as practical.

Serialization lies at the heart of these choices and an accident of terminology has done something to obscure the special force of *Pickwick*'s achievement in this area. Just as a particular kind of cinematic success leads, in the commercial world of Hollywood, to the perpetuation of a genre until it has become financially exhausted, so the early success of serialization ensured that the form would remain dominant for a large part of the nineteenth century regardless of its unsuitability for some later writers. In discussions of this phenomenon, scholars and critics have a tendency to describe it as serial *publication* which collapses a distinction crucial to a proper understanding of Dickens's role in the process. The commercial domination of the serial led to a situation in which some works which had been written complete were cut up into segments and serialized after the event, as it were. The crucial point to make about Dickens in this regard is that he *wrote* serially for serial publication. In other words, as has already been pointed out, his novels were written discontinuously in separate segments, usually as a result of two weeks' writing a month, and then published in this form with a minimum of revision. After his initial successes, Dickens occasionally expressed the desire to come before the public with a complete novel in its traditionally serious and dignified guise of three volumes, but this ambition was superseded by his recognition of the power he exerted over a huge public through his skilful manipulation of this difficult form of writing and publication. These points indicate the themes that will be pursued in this chapter: first, the meaning for Dickens's career of the processes of publishing that flowed into the production of *Pickwick* and which, after its success, became dominant although always subject to modification; and second, the discontinuous process of writing separate units of a to-be-completed whole in monthly and, less frequently, weekly parts. What were the historical conditions that helped to bring *Pickwick* into existence? The need to order a complex mass of material into an explanatory form, whether for historical or biographical purposes, has a tendency to exaggerate the element of shaping which is a part of any good story. A dramatic opening and an exciting climax are desirable features of any narrative, but the desire to impose them on historical narratives may distort the flow that is an inherent aspect of historical process. Dickens's success at such a very early age with *Pickwick* is a marvellous yarn, but the desire to heighten it can lead to a number of such distortions. *Pickwick* is, of course, Dickens's first novel, which intensifies one's desire that it should also be his first book and, by the easy extensions of fantasy, that he should have been a completely unknown writer when he leapt so amazingly to prominence. However, the lure of the good story has to be resisted in favour of a rather more prosaic circumstantiality. The fact is that *Pickwick's* publishers, Chapman and Hall, approached Dickens solely to write the text for the illustrations that were seen originally to be the really important part of the enterprise. And they did so partly because he was already recognised as a rising young writer on the basis of the work that came to be known as *Sketches by Boz* on its first publication in book form in February 1836, a few days before Chapman and Hall proposed terms for *Pickwick*. Dickens's first published sketch, 'A Dinner at Poplar Walk', appeared anonymously in the *Monthly Magazine* in December 1833 and over the next few years he published some forty sketches that eventually formed the basis of the First Series of the *Sketches*. Contrary to the myth of Dickens's meteoric rise, and comforting fantasies about creativity, his career as a professional writer began not with his first novel, but with the sketches, at the moment when he secured extra payment for their appearance in the *Morning Chronicle* on which he was also a reporter.

Similar traps await the unwary on the question of the state of book publishing in 1836, as scholarly disagreements make clear. Again, it would be tempting to claim a number of firsts here: that Dickens's sales and remuneration were unparalleled in the history of literature, and that *Pickwick* single-handedly restored and revolutionized publishing from a period of decline. The picture is inevitably less clear than such a sharply defined sketch. In the early years of the nineteenth century two publishers, John Murray and Blackwood, paid large sums to writers who are still famous – Murray, for example, paid Byron £2000 (a huge sum in its day) for the third canto of his poem *Childe Harold*. Large payments were also made to writers who are now less well known such as Thomas Moore, who received £5000 for a life of Byron. And that publishing had already moved into what might be called its capitalist phase of development is shown by the bankruptcy of Constable for the then colossal amount of £250 000. All this is in the context of the sales achieved by Byron and Scott who were both best-sellers in their own time, Scott's *The Fortunes of Nigel* selling 7000 copies on its first day of publication.[1] The 40 000 copies of the monthly numbers of *Pickwick* which it settled into after the first appearance of Sam Weller is a much larger figure, but should be seen as quantitatively rather than qualitatively different from what had already occurred.

Similarly, caution is needed in accepting the view that publishing was at a nadir when Chapman and Hall, Dickens and *Pickwick* burst upon the scene. Admittedly, for one scholar 'The year 1832, when Richard Bentley [with whom Dickens was later closely involved] became an independent publisher, may be regarded as making a pause in British literary history. The flood of Romantic writing had waned, and little new talent had yet appeared'.[2] For other scholars, an interesting (if now little known) group of novelists working before the accession of Victoria perform an important role in the history of the form in clarifying that 'the years between Scott and Dickens are not a chasm but rather a bridge, a unique span that is valuable not only for what it joins but also for its own peculiar strengths'.[3] This disagreement is hardly resolvable in objective terms, dependent as it is on critical judgement. It is hard to disagree with the view that Dickens is the first major figure to appear in English literature after Scott's death, and that the excitements of publishing declined to some extent after the feverish successes of Byron and Scott. On the other hand, the writing, publishing and reading of novels was clearly being kept alive before Dickens by such figures as Captain Marryat, Bulwer-Lytton, Disraeli and others. We are on safer ground in seeing the 1830s as marking a momentous shift, in which Chapman and Hall played a significant role, from the market production of books by booksellers to the emergence of publishers in the modern sense. That all such shifts are transitional is emphasized by the fact that the terms 'bookseller' and 'publisher' were used interchangeably at the beginning of Dickens's career, sometimes by Dickens himself. In common with all other industrial activities, mass production in publishing necessitated the division of labour and Robert L. Patten clarifies what this process involved for a nineteenth century which was the 'age of the specialist publisher': 'Printing and binding, publishing newspapers, and selling stationery and books became separate businesses.'[4] In other words, a range of activities that had often been carried on by one employer under a single roof were hived off so that publishers sold direct to retailers only those books whose physical production they had themselves initiated from scratch.

Sober scholars are not afraid to use the world 'revolution'[5] about these changes in nineteenth-century publishing practices, although it is clear that they came about as a result of an amalgam of historical forces, personal initiative and pure chance. But regardless of origins, we can see our triumvirate of publisher, writer and text colliding with the dominant physical form taken by the novel from Scott's *Kenilworth* (1821) on, and which was to be 'the prevailing form for the next seventy-five years', the so-called three-decker.[6] A three-decker was a novel published in three volumes of roughly 300 pages each and selling for the considerable sum of 31s.6d. It is obvious that such an arbitrary form could be damaging to a number of writers as well as inhibiting to readers because of its expense. It offered a clear invitation to padding to reach the required length and, for the more scrupulous, the discomfort of trying to achieve a compromise between its demands and the forms they wished their writing to take. The three-decker arose from a complex of social as well as economic forces that clearly belonged to the pre-entrepreneurial stage of publishing. Novels at such a price were only available to the middle and upper classes and their class-bound ownership is mirrored in the 'weightiness' of their physical appearance, the reverse of the supposedly classless and ideally cheap modern paperback. Ironically, an entrepreneurial attempt to break this log-jam of restricted, permanent ownership had the effect of perpetuating the three-decker long beyond its useful life. Charles Edward Mudie founded the most famous of the Victorian lending libraries in 1852, constructing in the process an organizational and distribution network worthy of the Industrial Revolution at its most efficient. For a subscription of only one guinea a year, ladies and gentlemen all over the country were able to borrow books whose purchase would have been prohibitive even for the moderately well off. The Evangelical Mr Mudie's powers of censorship through the simple refusal of any book he did not care to stock may have been bad for the artistic health of the novel, but the economic equation was satisfying to the major parties concerned. Mudie flourished on his subscriptions while publishers had a perfectly safe outlet for a high proportion of their books as long as they were not likely to bring a blush to the cheek of the young person. The position is made clear by Richard Bentley's sales for a now-forgotten novel by an almost forgotten writer, Mrs Humphry Wood's *The Channings*. Mudie took 1000 copies, the booksellers Smith and Son 104, while all the other booksellers and London libraries accounted for only 479.[7]

Mudie's activities were still some way off when Dickens and Chapman and Hall were converging towards the production of *Pickwick*, but the respectability and economic conservatism generated by the three-decker and epitomized by Mudie's Select Library reveal some of the forces they pitted themselves against, even if only unwittingly. However, with characteristic flexibility Dickens was willing to co-operate with Mudie towards the end of his career. As Peter Ackroyd points out, *Great Expectations* was published shortly after its serialization in three volumes, for the only time in Dickens's career, to take account of the circulating library possibility, and Mudie did in fact purchase most of the first edition. (Ackroyd 902). What publisher and writer were bent on at this earlier stage, or what they came to be bent on as they began to understand *Pickwick*'s extraordinary success, was the commercialization of publishing in the interests of producing what has come to be called a commodity-text. In other words, they ignored the financial security guaranteed by Mudie of a marginal but secure profit on a relatively short run of expensive three-deckers for the dizzying prospect of enormous profits, which initially went mainly to the publishers, on a form of publication which could hardly have seemed more evanescent. The social disdain for such activities is one factor in that strand of criticism of Dickens in his own day for being ungentlemanly. A more interesting intellectual conservatism is represented in Emerson's objections to *American Notes*, Dickens's non-fictional record of his first visit to America which turned so bitterly from triumph to disappointment at a democracy that had failed to live up to his expectations: 'Truth is not his object for a single instant...As an account of America it is not [to] be considered for a moment...We can hear throughout the dialogue between the author and his publisher, "Mr Dickens the book must be entertaining – that is the essential point. Truth! damn truth!"' (Pilgrim III, n. 4, 271). We are so deeply familiar with this kind of criticism of the popular, of television say, in our own time that it is not too far-fetched to see Dickens, in the full range of his activities, as a precursor of the attempt to reach a mass audience which some find debased and others democratic in the best sense.

If the commercialization of publishing is to be seen as an aspect of the Industrial Revolution, then technology clearly has a role to play also since both are inseparably united as part of this historical process. For John Sutherland, 'By 1852 the English novel was as much a triumph of industrial progress as anything in the Great Exhibition'[8] and the roots of such a development can be seen in the attitudes and practices of Dickens and his publishers as their own historic enterprise got under way. The early 1830s was a period of far-reaching changes in book production brought about by the convergence of a number of technological developments, and Dickens's unprejudiced willingness to make use of these advances highlights his essential modernity of outlook. Dickens's nostalgia was for the lost Eden of childhood, but he had nothing but contempt for hankerings after the supposed good old days of merry England in the Middle Ages or in any other historical epoch earlier than his own. One positive aspect of what some have seen as a philistine rejection of the past is his celebration of the technical wonders of his own time. He talks, for example, of those 'blessed Railroads' which have virtually obliterated the distance between London and his beloved Paris, (Pilgrim V, 522) and an interesting link between technology and his mental processes is hinted at in 'Coming down in the railroad the other night (always a wonderfully suggestive place to me when I am alone)' (Pilgrim VI, 65). One of his numerous unrealized ideas for a book was 'bringing together two strongly contrasted places and two strongly contrasted sets of people, with which and with whom the story is to rest, through the agency of an electric message' (Nonesuch III, 302). Perhaps the most extended, and humane, example of this interest in the new, dates from 1849 with Dickens's insistence that his wife should have the benefit of the still controversial chloroform to ease her sufferings in childbirth. The letter to his friend Macready describing the incident is a striking example of Dickens's triumphalism in overcoming the forces of reaction, especially given that one current objection to its use in London – despite its acceptance in Edinburgh, France and America – was that it 'would excite improper sexual feelings and expressions in women' (Pilgrim V, n. 2, 487). But for Dickens, the advances of science and technology were not limited solely to the practical as he acknowledges in a review of 1848 which celebrates the 'ample compensation, in respects of poetry alone, that Science has given us in return for what she has taken away'(Pilgrim V, n. 1, 454).

This triumphalism at the victory of the new over tradition is echoed in the grimly satisfied tone of Dickens's comment on *Pickwick*'s success as a serial in the Preface to the Cheap Edition of 1847: 'My friends told me it was a low, cheap form of publication, by which I should ruin all my rising hopes, and how right my friends turned out to be, everybody now knows.' There is in all this a conjunction of the man with the moment, a moment at which a number of forces were combining to open the way to a much larger reading public than had ever existed before. One factor is the slow but sure spread of literacy, to which can be added increasing leisure for middle-class women, improved domestic and public lighting, and developments in transport facilitated by better roads and the introduction of the railways. These last advances eased the distribution of books and serial numbers throughout the country, while reading for travellers was made immeasurably easier by the train compared with the near impossibility of looking at a book on a horse-driven coach. And so it is not surprising that the railway bookstall soon came into existence although it did not have its major impact on novel buying until the advent of W. H. Smith and Son in the 1850s. One emphasis that can be selected from this welter of developments is the role of advertising which Dickens seems to have embraced willingly despite the reservations expressed to his trusted lieutenant W. H. Wills in 1851: 'You know that I have no faith in advertising beyond a certain reasonable extent.

I think it a popular delusion altogether.' (Pilgrim VI, 436.) However, this cautious approach appears to have been relinquished by 1859 in the interests of ensuring that the audience for *Household Words*, which Dickens was abandoning after a dispute with his publishers, would be transferred to his new weekly periodical, *All the Year Round*. In a letter to Forster, Dickens claimed that he was 'getting an immense system of advertising ready', a boast justified by the sending out and posting up of some 300 000 handbills to say nothing of asking W. H. Smith and Son 'to be good enough to distribute 240 000 small handbills relating to Mr Dickens's forthcoming publication'. Posters were 'displayed in railway carriages, at stations, in meeting halls and on omnibuses' while 'All over England, Scotland, Wales, and Ireland "good showy advertisements" on white or yellow show cards with black letters shaded in red announced the new publication.'[9]

All of this suggests that we are present at the birth of the modern world of publishing (a modernity now in its turn superseded by a range of new computer-based technologies) in the context of the Industrial Revolution with its constituent elements of technology, marketing, distribution, and so on. These forces can be seen as impinging on book production in two ways, on the book as physical object and as commodity-text. For example, an air of mystery surrounds Chapman and Hall's decision to issue *Pickwick* at the end of its serial run in 1837 in a single volume bound in cloth which would have been impossible 'before the technical innovations of 1830–32'. Some experts go so far 'as to link the general change to cloth binding directly to the success of *Pickwick*' and it may have been the extraordinary success of the novel which led Chapman and Hall themselves to issue it in this way. Their decision may also have been linked to another innovation, the move from paper labels for book titles to the mechanical stamping of gold lettering onto cloth which only became possible in 1832.[10] Whatever the motives, issuing *Pickwick* in this manner conferred on it something of the permanence associated with the status of literature, as distinct from the transience of miscellaneous periodical journalism which long continued to be associated with publishing fiction in monthly parts. The appearance of *Pickwick* as a book marks the beginning of a process of improvements in the quality of paper, printing and binding which, together with improved technical means of reproducing illustrations, led to a highly attractive level of book production, culminating in the care lavished on *A Christmas Carol*, a publishing event which establishes interesting links between the book as art object and as commodity-text. Writing in 1895, Percy

Fitzgerald, Dickens's younger friend and collaborator complained that nothing 'strikes us so much in modern publishing as the general lack of taste and elegance in the decoration and treatment of books' and contrasted this with an earlier period, 'Above all the five little Christmas Books of Dickens [which] are the most charming, entertaining little volumes that can be conceived...[especially *A Christmas Carol*] which is perfect in the writing, print, paper, binding, and illustrations'.[11] Contemporary readers are in a better position to appreciate the complex effects produced by the *Carol* as a physical object than earlier generations as the decoration of books has enjoyed a renaissance in recent years, one culminating example being Alasdair Gray's extraordinary novel *Lanark* which is illustrated and designed by the author himself in a riot of full-page and incidental illustrations, and a variety of typefaces.

Historians of any discipline must always be wary of references to ages of transition and periods of change: since history is process, perhaps any given moment of historical time is one of transition. But the facts and arguments of this chapter show that the point at which *Pickwick Papers* came into being was one of turbulence in publishing which carried with it, as periods of turbulence always do, possibilities of movement in a variety of directions. There could be nothing deterministic about the emergence of *Pickwick* in the form it actually took, but existing conditions clearly contained the seeds of that particular growth once the combination of intelligence, luck, initiative and chance involved had been brought into play. Despite an earlier warning about the seductive simplifications of exciting narratives, the story of the genesis of *Pickwick* is too good to be missed and is in any case central to the purposes of this chapter and, indeed, to the book as a whole. On 12 February 1836, five days after Dickens's twenty-fourth birthday, he was approached by the publishers Chapman and Hall with a proposal that he supply the text for a monthly publication whose major focus was to be the illustrations of Robert Seymour, a well-known and popular artist of the day. The subject was to be the comic misadventures of a group of middle-class gentlemen from London in their confrontation with rural sports such as hunting, shooting and fishing. The topic was hardly original and Seymour had, in fact, partly made his name with comic subjects of a similar kind. Dickens obviously appealed to the publishers as a rising and bright young man who had already proved himself in a series of brilliant sketches, although mainly of lower middle-class London life, but who would be amenable to the pre-ordained demands of the project and the role of his senior and more experienced partner. However, Dickens suggested modifications in the enterprise almost from the beginning, his opportunity for a more radical intervention occurring only weeks into the project when the unstable Seymour committed suicide having completed enough plates for only the first two numbers. Another artist, R. W. Buss, was hastily brought in but, his work for the third number proving unsatisfactory, H. K. Browne (Phiz) was engaged and remained Dickens's major illustrator up to and including *Little Dorrit*. From this point on Dickens became the major force, the amount of text was increased, the number of illustrations reduced, and the subject matter moved away from its emphasis on the rural to the urban scene with which Dickens was so intimately familiar. The venture was initially only modestly successful, selling some 400 copies a month, but it rose steadily until it achieved a monthly sale of 40 000, a triumph often associated with the appearance of Sam Weller in the fourth number, and regarded then and now as probably the most dramatic publishing success in the history of English literature.

As well as being pirated for the stage before its completion (a regular abuse of Dickens's novels given the lack of copyright protection), *Pickwick* was reviewed from a fairly early stage of its monthly life, a practice which continued for the rest of Dickens's career and was undoubtedly a factor in fostering his immense popularity. There seems little doubt that the high profile of Dickens's exposure to the public, to use what seem appropriate terms from the media and communications, was increased by the fact that his novels were accorded the bonus of widespread attention in the course of their appearance, often in the form of long quotations combined with critical comment, in addition to reviews of the completed works in their volume form. An early example of this kind of attention, in the *Morning Chronicle* of October 1836, serves to illustrate what appeared a problematic aspect of the text and one that highlights the freshness, if not the total originality, of the enterprise; for the *Chronicle* the monthly parts were 'entitled in every way to be placed among the periodicals; it is, in fact, a magazine consisting of only one article'.[12] This judgement clearly raises interesting questions of categorization. In fact, the extent to which *Pickwick* and, even, later works should be seen as a miscellany of individual sketches, as a magazine or periodical with only one article, as a novel and, if so, a novel that should be classified as literature or be seen more accurately as an entertainment of a more or less low and vulgar kind were questions that continued to vex Dickens's contemporaries throughout a large part of his career. Damning judgements were still possible as late as 1851, as a passage from a review of *David Copperfield* and Thackery's *Pendennis* in the *Prospective Review* makes clear:

> The serial tale...is probably the lowest artistic form yet invented; that, namely, which affords the greatest excuse for unlimited departures from dignity, propriety, consistency, completeness, and proportion. In it, wealth is too often wasted in reckless and riotous profusion, and poverty is concealed by mere superficial variety, caricature, violence, and confused bustle. Nine tenths of its readers will never look at it or think of it as a whole... No fault will be found with the introduction of any character or any incident however extraordinary or irrelevant, if it will amuse for an hour the lounger in the coffee-room or the traveller by the railway.[13]

Although this dismissal is couched in literary terms, its sub-text hints at social and perhaps political reservations, the vulgarity of the form itself being linked to a class of superficial readers lacking mature judgement. The serial violates the decorum appropriate to high art and the imagery of the passage embodies a distaste of profusion which could be likened to a class-based disdain for the crowded urban environment and dislike of such new-fangled phenomena as the railway. Such reactions were not uncommon and prompt questions as to their motives. One answer might be found in examining what precisely it was readers held in their hands when they took up a monthly serial number of a Dickens novel, once it had settled into what became its standard format. For the price of one shilling readers could purchase, on the last day of each month (although publication was nominally on the first day), 32 pages of print consisting of three or four chapters, plus two illustrations, bound in green paper covers, with several pages of advertisements before and after the text. As the climax to their reading experience, they could look forward to the final nineteenth instalment, a double number at two shillings with 48 pages of text, four illustrations, and a title-page, frontispiece, preface and the other preliminaries of a 'real' book. What can be learned from an analysis of this method of publication?

Although the price of a shilling put this publication out of the reach of the poorer strata of the urban working class and rural labourers, it clearly opened the way to something that might reasonably be called a mass reading public, at least in relation to the price of the three-decker, and so played a part in the democratisation of reading and novel buying made possible by the social and technological changes introduced by the Industrial Revolution. There is evidence, although it lacks volume and precision, that the monthly numbers reached the level of those who could not themselves afford a shilling and, even, to the illiterate. It is possible that little reading clubs were formed, organized on occasion by publicans, where for the contribution of a penny the illiterate poor could have a number read to them, the best-known example being that of an elderly charwoman who was told that Dickens was the sole author of *Dombey and Son*:

> Being further pressed as to what her notion was of this mystery of a Dombey (for it was known she could not read), it turned out that she lodged at a snuff shop kept by a person named Douglas, where there were several other lodgers; and that on the first Monday of every month there was a Tea, and the landlord read the month's number of 'Dombey'; those only of the lodgers who subscribed to the tea partaking of that luxury, but all having the benefit of the reading; and that the impression produced on the old charwoman revealed itself in the remark with which she closed her account of it. 'Lawk, ma'am! I thought that three or four men at least must have put together 'Dombey'!
>
> (Forster I, 453–4)

This method of publication necessitated a form of discontinuous, serial reading which could, of course, be contrasted with the more dignified reading experience of the three-decker (although a crucial part of the experience of all novels is that they are very rarely read at a single sitting). Again, the serial part was a mixed form, the literary text embedded in its surrounding illustrations and advertisements. A modern analogy might be the 'classic serial' on commercial television where the 'high art element' is surrounded by the 'vulgarity' of appeals to greed, vanity and materialism. In our case, however, the visual sophistication of the advertisements is often hardly separable from the skills employed in the adaptation itself, a process that threatens to flood art totally in commodification. In Dickens's day there was an overwhelming distinction between the quality of the literary text and Phiz's engravings, and the writing and illustration in the advertisements. Nevertheless, there is ample justification in this descriptive analysis to see why the serial might be dismissed, in Dickens's own words, as a 'low cheap form of publication' (in the Preface to *Pickwick Papers*). Its price enabled it to break through class barriers, it mixed commerce and literature (although, as we have seen, for some the text belonged more to the category of light entertainment), and it was both ephemeral and disposable in a way that even the dullest book was clearly not.

On the other hand, for many such features were aspects of Dickens's triumph. Kathleen Tillotson has disentangled the precise ways in which the form of *Pickwick* drew on and yet differed from previous serial publication, and her authoritative conclusion is that *Pickwick's* text, as opposed to its illustrations, 'so caught the public interest that it...initiated a virtually new method of publishing fiction, and established in the public the habit of buying novels as well as borrowing them'.[14] Many explanations of this widespread welcome for Dickens and his later success have been attempted, and the introduction of Sam Weller in the serial's fourth number can focus the critical-historical aspects of such accounts. There is general agreement that, whatever his literary antecedents, Sam embodied the appearance of a new type in English literature, an urban folk hero whose comic vulgarities of language were sufficiently refined by Dickens's artistry not to disgust a wide audience. Sam, and the later panoramas of London street life which were such a crucial part of Dickens's fictional development, also represented for his audience a recognition and an unmasking. Dickens was held to have created in fictional terms what many had seen and yet not really perceived, an urban comedy and drama which was coming into existence in the early years of the century along with its cause, the growth of London as the first metropolis of modern times. But for others who led blinder or more sheltered lives, Dickens was the unmasking explorer exposing the fun and the horror of the modern world to the amused, shocked, excited but above all entertained gaze of his fascinated audience.

Such explanations are interesting and valuable, but it might be possible to suggest some reasons for Dickens's popularity that relate more precisely to the fact of serial publication itself. The light-hearted ephemerality of the product may well have been a factor. Picking up a number of *Pickwick* was clearly a different experience from embarking on, say, Gibbon's *Decline and Fall of the Roman Empire*, the pleasure of Phiz's brilliant illustrations and the fun of the advertisements adding to the enjoyment of a text that was undemanding, at least as far as length was concerned. A deeper pleasure may have been gained, however, from what might be called the rhythm of seriality. In a letter of 1846 Dickens asked his publishers, 'I want to know...how soon after June you think we might safely, and with real effect, begin a story in Monthly Numbers – so that it should not commence at a dead time of the year'(Pilgrim IV, 2). Most of Dickens's serial novels started in March, April or May, and none in July, August or September; *Dombey* is the only one that started in October. At one level, this concern is an aspect of the practicalities of professional publishing, but the lightening of post-Christmas gloom (for some February is the cruellest month) for Dickens's huge audience by the anticipation of a regular serial addition to the joys of Spring is not to be discounted. This seasonal pleasure can be linked to the internal dating of the serial parts themselves. Although Dickens may have been vague about the years in which his novels are set, Paul Schlicke points out that 'the fictional seasons correspond closely to the time when the various episodes first appeared serially. Thus Nell leaves London in June, [in *The Old Curiosity Shop*] and Number 13, in which this action occurs, was published on 27 June 1840.'[15] The pleasurable expectations generated by this reading experience could be highly specific: a splendid example is Carlyle's story of the clergyman leaving the sick-room of a dying man after offering 'ghostly consolation' only to overhear the remark, 'Well, thank God, *Pickwick* will be out in ten days anyway!' (Forster I, 73) This rhythm of anticipation, gratification, and post-reading sadness moving on into a cycle lasting for nearly two years in the case of monthly serialization was no doubt often obliterated by the pressures of mundane existence. But the maintenance of a thread of pleasurable interest could have been reinforced by the combination of variety within continuity. Each serial part looked reassuringly familiar in its format and layout with its green covers, the front one bearing the title and the same decoration from month to month, and the two illustrations. Also, as John Butt and Kathleen Tillotson point out, it was 'Dickens's frequent, but not invariable practice, to design his first two chapters [of each monthly number] of equal length and importance, leaving the final chapter as a short appendix to them'.[16] It is not hard, surely, for us to identify with these pleasures although for us they are probably mainly generated by television. The anticipation of a regular weekly instalment of comedy or excitement and the seasonal hope that winter's darkness will be lightened by the unexpectedly new or the return of an old favourite are hardly foreign to our supposedly more sophisticated times, as viewers of material as diverse as 'Neighbours' and 'Middlemarch' would surely testify. And television even offers the occasional possibility of national unity at moments of crisis or celebration. There is reason to believe, therefore, that the hope contained in Dickens's advertisement for the launching of the Cheap Edition of his works in 1847 was not wholly empty:

It had been intended that this CHEAP EDITION, now announced, should not be undertaken until the books were much older, or the Author was dead...To become, in his new guise, a permanent inmate of many English homes, where, in his old shape he was only known as a guest, or hardly known at all; to be well thumbed and soiled in a plain suit that will be read a great deal by children, and grown people, at the fireside and on the journey; to be hoarded on the humble shelf where there are few books, and to lie about in libraries like any familiar piece of household stuff that is easy of replacement: to see and feel this – not to die first, or grow old and passionless, must obviously be among the hopes of a living author, venturing on such an enterprise.[17]

Through such ventures and, I would argue, serial publication Dickens achieved 'a kind of total and continual existence for the readers of his age'.[18]

Up to this point, serial publication has been taken to be monthly numbers published in their own self-contained pamphlet or booklet form, but Dickens also worked in two other, related, kinds of serialization. Both were weekly serials although appearing in different formats. *Old Curiosity Shop* and *Barnaby Rudge* came out in *Master Humphrey's Clock*, a format hard to explain to contemporary readers and, interestingly, one that did not appeal to Dickens's contemporaries. As we may have come to expect by now, the motives that brought it into being were mixed. Dickens hoped and expected that it would be a money-spinner, but he also gleefully saw it as a challenge to the pirates and plagiarists of monthly serialization, his 'object being to baffle the imitators and make it as novel as possible'.[19] *Master Humphrey* is best described as a miscellany based on such eighteenth-century models as the *Spectator* and Goldsmith's *Bee*, whose basic format centred on a 'club' consisting of Master Humphrey and his elderly friends. This unappetizing group were destined to meet once a week from 10 p.m. to 2 a.m. in order to be entertained by Humphrey's recounting of tales and other material found stuffed in the bottom of a grandfather clock. The initial response was very warm ('The Clock goes gloriously indeed. What will the wiseacres say to weekly issues *now*?' Pilgrim II, 50). But the wiseacres were right for the sales dropped disastrously when the public 'discovered that they were buying an old-fashioned periodical rather than a new novel in parts'.[20] Dickens's only recourse was to introduce a weekly fiction into the scheme and by the twelfth number *Master Humphrey's Clock* contained nothing but the *Old Curiosity Shop* followed immediately by *Barnaby Rudge*. The other weekly serials appeared in the brilliantly successful magazines that occupied a major portion of Dickens's time in the last twenty years of his life, *Hard Times* in *Household Words*, and *A Tale of Two Cities* and *Great Expectations* in *All the Year Round*. The use of fiction in the later periodical was, however, significantly different from that in *Household Words* and represents another major step in Dickens's continuing preoccupation with the practicalities of professional writing. In the words of John Sutherland, it put Dickens 'in the forefront of another major innovation, first-rate fiction in magazines and weeklies. In essence this was a new lease of life for serialization and did for it what monthly numbers had done in the forties and mid-forties.'[21]

We have seen that serial fiction was attacked, and defended, on the grounds of its commercialisation of literature and the breaking of class barriers in the interests of a mass reading public. But there was also intense debate concerning the purely artistic merits, or otherwise, of the form, a debate in which Dickens had many interesting things to say, although usually in his private capacity. He suggested to one correspondent that she read any two weekly numbers of *A Tale of Two Cities* or *Great Expectations* and 'notice how patiently and expressly the thing has to be planned for presentation in these fragments, and yet afterwards fusing together as an uninterrupted whole'(Nonesuch III, 461). But Dickens was also aware of the disadvantages of what he called this 'detached and desultory form of publication' (Pilgrim ll, 336). One major problem was that readers might jump to false conclusions as to where the story was tending before its underlying plan became clear. In the early stages of his career, Dickens obviously sometimes embarked on a novel not having taken fairly major decisions in advance, as Kathleen Tillotson suggests in an interesting discussion of the development of Nancy's character in *Oliver Twist*:

> Dickens's view of this crucial character seems to have developed in the process of writing, and can even be localized, in chapter XVI; nothing in the three previous chapters in which she appears anticipates her emergence as Oliver's defender, and this 'soul of goodness in things evil' can not have been meant solely as a surprise to the reader.[22]

Much later, with *David Copperfield*, we can see Dickens agonizing over an even more important problem, the death of a major character whose eclipse, or otherwise, would affect the whole future shape of the book: 'Still undecided about Dora, but MUST decide today' (Pilgrim VI, 94). For the reader who takes a romantic view of the creative process this can seem a fine way to go about writing a novel, but a little reflection suggests that there is no real difference between deciding on such issues well in advance of writing and within the writing process itself. In matters of this kind the proof of the pudding is in the quality of the finished product, regardless of how this was arrived at. Musical history informs us that the manuscript scores of Beethoven are an almost indecipherable mass of correction and revision while those of Mozart are miracles of clarity. This suggests that one composed on the page while the other composed in his head but this difference, interesting as it is, has no bearing on the quality of the music produced or on our criteria for judging it. In Dickens's case it might even be argued that last-minute decision-making in the midst of composition acted as a stimulus to the creative process.

A sometimes rather suspect delight in his own control of serial writing reinforces this view. A well-known example of the ills that serialization was heir to is the case of Miss Mowcher, the dwarfish hairdresser in *David Copperfield*, whose real-life original, Mrs Jane Seymour Hill protested at her portrayal and threatened legal action. Dickens's reaction, in a letter to Forster, reveals the ambiguity of his response to the situation: 'I have had the queerest adventure this morning, the receipt of the enclosed from Miss Mowcher. It is serio-comic, but there is no doubt that one is wrong in being tempted to such a use of power' (Pilgrim V, 676). It is interesting that Dickens makes no bones about admitting this use of a prototype, although poor Mrs Hill's identity is swallowed up, for him, in his fictional recreation of her. Obviously, there was nothing serio-comic about the matter for the victim and Dickens's recognition of his power did nothing to lessen his use of it, as the case of Harold Skimpole (based on Leigh Hunt) in *Bleak House* makes clear. Dickens had intended to make Miss Mowcher a kind of pimp, assisting Steerforth in his seduction of girls, and he regretted having involved a real person in such a fictional portrait. However, his reply to her solicitor's request that immediate changes be made in the character shows that for Dickens the novel very much came first:

I must beg you to understand that it [the changes] can only be made, in the natural progress and current of the story. Even if the next number were not already in the Press, it would be impossible to be made there, because the character is not introduced, and the course of the tale is not at all in that direction.

(Pilgrim V, 677)

There was nothing in the least 'natural' about the 'progress and current of the story', of course; its control lay entirely in Dickens's hands and he was simply not prepared to make the changes until he felt the novel was ready for the reintroduction of Miss Mowcher.

Another example of Dickens's pleasure in his power over the problems of serialization is to be found in his ill-concealed delight at the failure of others to master it, even when this involved the fortunes of his own publications. He intensely admired the work of Elizabeth Gaskell and was delighted to attract her into his stable of writers for *Household Words*. However, despite showering her with what he intended to be helpful advice about the intricacies of serial writing, he could not prevent a gleeful note entering into his comments to others on her deficiencies, a note similar to that struck in a letter on another female writer he admired greatly, George Eliot, whose novel *Adam Bede* forms the basis of the joke in what follows: 'Adam (or Eve) Bede is terrified by the novel difficulties of serial writing; cannot turn in the space; evidently will not be up to the scratch when Collins's sponge is thrown in.'[23] That Dickens associates the savageries of bare-knuckle fighting (coming up to the scratch or mark, etc) with a form of literary composition of which he had become such a powerfully successful master is revealing of some of his deepest feelings about it. But the concomitant of violence, triumphalism, and the exercise of power, is fear and we do have one example of the anxiety that could be induced by the nightmarish pressures of serialization in Charles Kent's report of a conversation with Dickens:

'Once, and but once only in my life, I was – frightened!'...somewhere about the middle of the serial publication of David Copperfield, happening to be out of writing paper, he sallied forth one morning to get a fresh supply at the stationer's...As he was about to enter the stationer's shop...for the purpose of returning home...and at once setting to work upon his next number, not one word of which was yet written, he stood aside for a moment on the threshold to allow a lady to pass in before him...[He then related with] 'mingled enjoyment and dismay' [hearing her ask for] 'the new green number.' When it was handed to her, 'Oh, this,' said she, 'I have read. I want the next one.' The next one she was thereupon told would be out by the end of the month. 'Listening to this, unrecognised...knowing the purpose for which I was there, and remembering that not one word of the number she was asking for was yet written, for the first and only time in my life, I felt – frightened!'[24]

This makes a wonderful yarn and the peculiar circumstances which generated it may have caused Dickens an especially intensified terror, but it is hard to believe that he was frightened by the enormity of his undertakings only once in his career. All writers dread drying up; the terror of drying up in mid-serial with a novel eagerly expected by a huge public must surely have visited him more than once. But again there is every reason to believe that this was not a destructive experience for Dickens. On the contrary, the combination of the responsibility to his readers, the artistic demands of the work in hand, his concern for sales and need for money, all worked to heighten and intensify his commitment to the writing process and can be seen as yet another of those collaborative elements in his career that this book is seeking to explore.

In an interesting letter to Forster, Dickens gave a general account of what he planned to do in *Dombey and Son*, then summarized the process: 'So I mean to carry the story on, through all the branches and off-shoots and meanderings that come up...This is what cooks call "the stock of the soup". All kinds of things will be added to it, of course' (Pilgrim IV, 590). It is well established that *Dombey* was the novel which saw the beginning of a new kind of attention to detail in the planning and preparation of his works' overall structure and thematic coherence which Dickens was to follow for the rest of his career. What this letter reveals is that he had worked out an aesthetic for the unification of fictions that were to be written serially. In other words, he was not interested in trying to write the kind of novel that has come to be called Jamesian (after the novelist Henry James) in which every detail is related to a thematic core with a rigour that is aesthetically beautiful, but which may sometimes seem lacking in spontaneity. Dickens continued to bemoan the problems of serialization, as we can see in comments on what is perhaps his most formally ordered work after *Hard Times*, *Great Expectations*:

> It is a pity that the third portion cannot be read all at once, because its purpose would be much more apparent; and the pity is the greater, because the general turn and tone of the working out and winding up, will be away from all such things as they conventionally go....As to the planning out from week to week, nobody can imagine what the difficulty is, without trying. But, as in all such cases, when it is overcome the pleasure is proportionate. Two months more will see me through it, I trust. All the iron is in the fire, and I have 'only' to beat it out.   (Nonesuch III, 216–17)

Dickens's mind is so saturated by his story of a blacksmith's apprentice that the final metaphor must have seemed to arise naturally, but what this letter also shows, I believe, is Dickens's total commitment to serial writing and serial publication. For him its faults and limitations were only the unavoidable difficulties attendant on *any* formal or aesthetic choice. Henry James may have laboured with exquisite care to render his fictions as formally perfect as he could, but there must always be a question as to how far such refinements can be perceived in detail by a readership doomed largely to desultory reading. Dickens may have longed occasionally to write a complete three-decker and so avoid some of the supposed weaknesses of the serial, but his comments on *Great Expectations* reveal the depth of the joy he experienced in circumventing its special difficulties in order to allow it to make its own special impact.

What this impact might mean for its audience is recorded suggestively in a review of *Dombey and Son* from 1848:

> An old friend has left us – the voice of a dear favourite is silent – *Dombey and Son* is completed...Those, and there are thousands of them, who have, like ourselves, discovered the work bit by bit – familiarizing themselves by long association with the every characteristic of the ideal personages depicted in the narrative – and coming at last to regard with a sort of tenderness even the green covers of the monthly instalment, as being connected in some fashion with the joys and sorrows of the story...will comprehend our regret at the dispersion of this imaginary multitude.[25]

3

Dickens's Reading

At one stage in Dickens scholarship and criticism the idea of writing at length on his reading would have seemed laughable or, at least, likely to produce only the slimmest of chapters. The notion that Dickens was an untutored genius, or an ignorant opportunist for those who failed to admire him, began early and was frequently overlaid with class responses. His flowing locks, bright clothes and jaunty manner signalled for some that he was not a gentleman, crucially lacking in the experience of public school and university that were seen as indispensable for those engaged in serious literature, as opposed to mere entertainment. Public school meant the classics and, in England, university spelled Oxford or Cambridge, 'advantages' which Dickens conspicuously lacked. George Henry Lewes, an intellectual author and scientist and the companion of George Eliot, was horrified when he visited the young Dickens at what he considered the inadequacy of his personal library. With increasing stability, a fine library was eventually acquired, but a lack of sustained critical discussion of his reading in Dickens's letters or essays contributed to the suspicion that he was a writer for whom books were not supremely important. But that Dickens saw himself as a habitual reader is shown by a letter of 1844 in which he remarks to Forster that he has 'been deep in Voyages and Travels, and in De Foe. Tennyson I have also been reading, again and again....I am all eagerness to write a story about the length of that most delightful of all stories, the *Vicar of Wakefield*' (Pilgrim IV, 198–9). Indeed, the evidence is that he read widely, from the research needed for his historical novels – 'All the time I was at work on the Two Cities, I read no books but such as had the air of the time in them' (Nonesuch III, 159) – to the byways of European literature:

> Sitting reading tonight, it comes into my head to say that if you look into Montaigne's *Journey into Italy* (not much known now, I think, except to readers), you will find some passages that would be curious for extract. They are very well translated into a sounding kind of old English in Hazlitt's translation of Montaigne.[1]

But this far from exhausts the extent of what might be called Dickens's serious reading, although he would have resented the implication that novel reading was a non-serious activity. Dickens was perfectly able to engage intelligent correspondents in discussions of some of the burning intellectual issues of the day including, for example, the controversy centring on the collection *Essays and Reviews* on which he took the 'progressive' side (Nonesuch III, 352). The volume appeared in 1860 and represented the views of liberal theologians in their attempts to think their way out of the dominant conception of the Bible as literally true. But we also find him encouraging one of his most important women friends, the Hon. Mrs Richard Watson, to follow a well-known contemporary dispute, a 'controversy between Whewell and Brewster, on the question of the shining orbs about us being inhabited or no. Whewell's book is called On the Plurality of Worlds; Brewster's More Worlds than One' (Nonesuch II, 603). Again, he took an intelligent interest in the geological debates which so fascinated Victorians:

> ...in these rocks she [science] has found, and read aloud, the great stone book which is the history of the earth, even when darkness sat upon the face of the deep. Along their craggy sides she has traced the footprints of birds and beasts, whose shapes were never seen by man. From within them she has brought the bones, and pieced together the skeletons, of monsters that would have crushed the noted dragons of the fables at a blow.[2]

Finally, his suggested reading list for a 'romantic' young aspiring author, Constance Cross, is hardly that which would come to mind for a frivolous or ignorant reader: 'Buckle's *Civilisation*, Mr Froude's writings, Macauley's *History* and *Essays* – especially the *Essays* – books of travel, biographies, no fiction'.[3]

The topic is, in fact, vast and this chapter will have to be highly selective in its treatment of it. The Bible and Shakespeare, for a start, were formative at the level of language, structure, character and theme. The texture of Dickens's prose, non-fictional as well as fiction, is imbued with imagery from both. The Bible, in its Authorized or King James version, and the Book of Common Prayer echo throughout Dickens. A minute number of examples can only hint at the range of this influence. Phrases abound, such as 'The one thing needful' (Luke 10.42), the title of the first chapter of *Hard Times*. The imagery of the Day of Judgement and of the sea giving up its dead can be found early, in *Oliver Twist*, and late, in *Little Dorrit*. The shadow of the devil follows such worthless gentlemen and pseudo-gentlemen as James Harthouse in *Hard Times* and Blandois/Rigaud in *Little Dorrit*, reminding us of *King Lear*'s 'The Prince of Darkness is a gentleman'. And the Bible, with Christianity as a whole, are shaping influences in Dickens's world view, helping to form his vision of the universe as a battleground between the forces of absolute good and absolute evil – in, for example, the competing worlds of Fagin and Mr Brownlow in *Oliver Twist*.

As with Dickens's reading in general, doubts have been cast on the depth of his involvement with Shakespeare, some scholars arguing that it is restricted to a relatively few number of fairly hackneyed references from a small range of plays. Again, however, the evidence suggests otherwise. Even at the level of mere counting, the forty-five references to Shakespeare in *David Copperfield* and the sixty-six in *Martin Chuzzlewit* indicate a more than superficial involvement.[4] For an intelligent friend, Annie Fields, Dickens was obviously 'a great student of Shakespeare, which is continually discovered in his conversation',[5] a judgement amply confirmed by the sometimes rarefied nature of his quotations. An invitation to a meal beginning 'Twice a year...I hold, not a solemn supper, but a solemn dinner...' (Pilgrim ll, 256), a reference to Macbeth's 'Tonight we hold a solemn supper, Sir', surely points to an in-depth grasp of some of Shakespeare's less noted passages. At a possibly more serious level, the painful early death of his beloved sister-in-law, Mary Hogarth, fused with Dickens's evident fascination with Cordelia, Miranda and other youthful heroines to produce one of his defining character types, an idealized version of young female innocence. That the results were not always artistically successful, as in Rose Maylie (*Oliver Twist*) and Nell (*Old Curiosity Shop*), does nothing to lessen the importance of this influence, especially as it was eventually to produce the more complexly interesting Esther Summerson of *Bleak House* and the eponymous Little Dorrit.

It would be possible to follow through these major shaping forces on Dickens's work in a number of ways. The structure of novels such as *Little Dorrit* and *Great Expectations* is founded on the image of life as pilgrimage, a journey through suffering and guilt to purgation and forgiveness, fictional reworkings of the Christian story which draw at least part of their power from complex patterns of language which echo and sometimes parody Biblical language. Again, *Bleak House* is saturated in Shakespearian imagery, an especially strong source being *Macbeth*, in a manner that gives the novel a tragic dimension as well as helping to create its atmosphere of blood and darkness. But this is all fairly familiar, if important, territory in Dickens studies and so it would be useful to explore slightly less well-known terrain. Two paths can be followed in attempting this, one into the formations that influenced Dickens at the deep level of a child's fascination with horror, the other leading from his more rationally conscious imaginative response to the pleasures of reading. One of Dickens's earliest memories was of being told the story of Captain Murderer who baked his wives in a pie a month after the wedding; eventually, having been poisoned, he turns blue, grows enormous, develops spots all over, and then explodes. This improving tale was imparted by his nurse which leads Dickens to his suspicion that, on investigation, 'we should find our nurses responsible for most of the dark corners we are forced to go back to, against our wills', a memory which he then extends:

> The young woman who brought me acquainted with Captain Murderer had a fiendish enjoyment of my terrors, and used to begin, I remember – as a sort of introductory overture – by clawing the air with both hands, and uttering a low hollow groan...This female bard['s]...name was Mercy, though she had none on me.[6]

There is no need to believe that these bloodcurdling recitals constituted a determining influence on Dickens's development, but there is every reason to think that they were connected with, even if they did not create, one of the most important threads in his personality. His childish response to such horror stories is remarkably similar to that 'attraction of repulsion' which led him so frequently to a heightened treatment of unpleasant subject-matter in his fiction. At the most general level, this can be seen in the ambivalence of response evoked in him by the fascinating horrors of the city; more specifically, it can be felt in the evocation of the oily disintegration of Krook through spontaneous combustion in *Bleak House*, the 'filth and fat and blood' of Smithfield Cattle Market in *Great Expectations*, and the disgustingly comic picture of Silas Wegg's wooden leg disappearing into the dustheaps of Boffin's Bower in his search for treasure in *Our Mutual Friend*. This complex of feeling relates also to Dickens's lifelong enjoyment, which is never entirely uncritical, of popular entertainment in all its forms: in the circus, boxing matches, performing dogs, Punch and Judy, and the broadest effects of the theatre of melodrama. The ways in which this material feeds into, and strengthens, his writing at its most serious is a key aspect of that confluence of forces we call Dickens and some attempt to analyse it will be made in this study's final chapter.

What I am calling the pre-rational roots of this engagement with the popular was something more than a fascination with the horrible. Delight in the macabre also linked to the celebration of fantasy through Dickens's pleasure in two forms of story-telling that were perhaps the most important touchstones of the reading experience throughout his entire life, fairy-tales and the *Arabian Nights*. One critic has referred to Dickens's Christmas Books as 'a new kind of fairy tale, the most pervasive of literary forms, and his own favourite'.[7] The meaning of fairy-tales for Dickens, and their role in his career, is too big a topic to be other than glanced at here. But their widespread importance in his writing can be understood from their effortless translation into personal experience and journalism, to say nothing of fiction. Dickens's letters to the beloved Mrs Watson were often tinged with the sadness evoked by the early death of her husband whom he regarded as one of his dearest friends. In 1860 he tells her that her letter to him

> ...quite stirred my heart. But we must not think of old times as sad times...We must all climb steadily up the mountain after the talking bird, the singing tree, and the yellow water, and must all bear in mind that the previous climbers who were scared into looking back got turned into black stone.

> (Nonesuch III, 178)

It is hard to imagine a lovelier use of the childhood realm for adult experience, a more public manifestation of which can be seen in the *Household Words* article 'Post-Office Money-Orders' which obeys one of the magazine's firmest rules, to invest the mundane world with the magic of fancy:

> A prosaic place enough at first sight, the Money-order Office is; but, when we went there to look about us, the walls seemed presently to turn to burnished gold, the clock to go upon a thousand jewels: the clerks to be the ministers of Fortune, dispensing, wisdom, riches, beauty, to the human race.[8]

It is no exaggeration to say that Dickens had a theory of the meaning of fairy-tales for human life in the nineteenth century, believing as he did that they helped to keep the imagination alive in an iron age of utilitarianism. The force of this commitment to what many dismissed as a world of unreal childishness emerged in Dickens's controversy with his friend and early collaborator, George Cruikshank. Compared with Phiz, Cruikshank's engravings have a savagery which testify to his links, as an older man than Dickens, with the Regency and its inheritance from the eighteenth century of the frequently obscene satire of Gilray and Rowlandson. Cruikshank was a hard-drinking companion of Dickens's early days who in later life became a fanatical supporter of teetotalism, a cause he advocated through the illustrated retelling of fairy-tales for propaganda purposes. Dickens's hostility to what he regarded as this didactic misuse of traditional stories was expressed in a *Household Words* article, 'Frauds Upon the Fairies' in 1853 in which he ridiculed Cruikshank's 'attempts to introduce temperance propaganda into the fairy-stories of childhood' (Ackroyd, 689).

Dickens was fearless in the face of the ridicule that was sometimes poured on a grown man's defence of the realm of childhood, and this principled affection was evoked even more strongly by what was the literary love of his life, the *Arabian Nights*, a work which played a formative role in the texture of Dickens's imagination. He loved the *Nights* from his first reading of them and returned to them throughout his life with never-diminished joy. They embodied a world of delicate fancy and the magical transformation of the mundane which fed his creative and personal life at every level, from the apparently supernatural goodness of his youthful female characters to the pantomime satire of his attacks on governmental red-tape. It is worth noting, in relation to this, that the version Dickens would have read was 'adapted...to European tastes, emphasizing the fantastic and the miraculous and carefully avoiding...candid references to sex'.⁹ But their darker side, the swift decapitations and abrupt changes of fortune, may also have nourished the violent aspect of Dickens's own imagination. Panks's utterly unexpected shearing of the Patriarch's hair in *Little Dorrit* and the justifiably cruel application of pepper to the horrible Fledgeby's wounds by Jenny Wren in *Our Mutual Friend* testify to their influence in even Dickens's later and, for some, more mature work. It goes without saying, of course, that the roots of such moments, and the happier examples of such influence, are complex. Christianity and Shakespeare, fairy-tales and the Arabian Nights, Smollett and Goldsmith, all and much else play a part in their formation. And there are levels which may be said to be personal to Dickens. The Patriarch's haircut may reveal him as a false Samson, deprived of a purely economic strength, but there are hints also of castration which may hark back to the most violent elements of folk literature but which also reveal Dickens's pre-Freudian insight into psychic complexities. The unravelling of individual strands in his make-up as literary producer must always be false to the total richness of the Dickens phenomenon, but it remains fair to isolate the *Arabian Nights* as a key aspect of this complex, if only because of the pervasive influence of its formal devices on his work. One striking example is the bewildering complexity of its use of the technique of framing. The whole work is framed by its beginning and ending with Scheherazade herself, but as her tales unfold they turn into a series of Chinese boxes as one leads into another with such convolutions that we are surprised to be returned to some original starting point. For example, the prologue itself is an immensely complex story of sexual betrayal involving two brothers and it is only when the elder, a king, has settled into his routine of marrying a virgin each day and having her killed after the wedding night that Scheherazade is introduced. Even then, her loving father (the king's vizier) attempts to persuade her against her apparently sacrificial marriage to the king by recounting a story of his own. This introduces the 'framework system of the *Nights*: the interlacing of several stories, narrated by different characters, into an organic whole; a system which owes its origin to Indian folk-tales and which was later on to be adopted by Boccaccio in the *Decameron* and Chaucer in *The Canterbury Tales*.'[10] We know that Dickens adopted precisely this method for the special Christmas numbers of *All the Year Round*, combining a group of stories by himself and others through a framework of his own devising. But the influence is evident in even one of his most artistically mature novels, *Little Dorrit*, where the main action is framed by an opening in Marseilles whose connections with the body of the text we are left to work out for ourselves. It is, alas, almost impossible to convey to the reader who is unfamiliar with them the peculiar delights of the magical world one is drawn into in the *Nights*. Their charm, humour, delicacy and formal brilliance remained a touchstone for Dickens of all that was best in literature, one that he sought constantly to emulate throughout his career. Indeed, they must be seen as a key factor in shaping him towards that poetic heightening of experience which is his true strength, rather than the straightforward realism he is sometimes supposed to exemplify.

We have seen that Dickens listened with fascinated horror to his Nurse's bloodthirsty tales and he no doubt picked up a whole range of such material through ears that were every bit as sharp as his 'clutching eye'. The evidence here can come straight from the fiction, in this case *David Copperfield*, since we know that its famous passage on David's absorption in books was directly autobiographical. Even the context (David's sustaining a private, imaginative life in the face of the Murdstones' cruelty) is significant, throwing as it does an emphasis on the life-giving role of reading in a hostile environment:

My father had left a small collection of books in a little room up-
stairs, to which I had access (for it adjoined my own) and which
nobody else in our house ever troubled. From that blessed little room,
Roderick Random, Peregrine Pickle, Humphrey Clinker, Tom Jones,
the Vicar of Wakefield, Don Quixote, Gil Blas, and Robinson Crusoe,
came out, a glorious host, to keep me company. They kept alive my
fancy and my hope of something beyond that place and time, – they,
and the Arabian Nights, and the Tales of the Genii, – and did me no
harm; for whatever harm was in some of them was not there for me;
I knew nothing of it...I have been Tom Jones (a child's Tom Jones, a
harmless creature) for a week together. I have sustained my own
idea of Roderick Random for a month at a stretch, I verily believe.
I had a greedy relish for a few volumes of Voyages and Travels – I
forget what, now – that were on those shelves...This was my only
and my constant comfort. When I think of it, the picture always rises
in my mind, of a summer evening, the boys at play in the church-
yard, and I sitting on my bed, reading as if for life.

(Chapter 4)

There is, again, an element of courage in Dickens's loving defence
of this reading material which would have been considered totally
unsuitable for a Victorian child. Indeed, the violence and frank sexuality of eighteenth-century fiction made it forbidden territory to well
brought up young women, at least until they were married. (In George
Eliot's *Middlemarch*, Dorothea Brooke's uncle tells her that he supposes she can read anything now that she is married.) The influence
of this reading on Dickens's early writing is clear. We have seen that
the beginnings of the *Pickwick Papers* were fortuitous; indeed, it is evident that when Dickens took control after Seymour's suicide he was
not altogether sure what he was up to. This unease is revealed in the
text's initially clumsy facetiousness and some changes of direction,
especially in the characterisation of Mr Pickwick. The somewhat desperate young man must have cast around for literary assistance and
it is obvious that he found it in his early reading, adapting what has
been called the picaresque aspect of earlier fiction for his own purposes. Mr Pickwick and Sam Weller are a kind of Don Quixote and
Sancho Panza, and their wandering adventures follow the essential
form of novels by Fielding, Smollett and others. The formula of a
young gentleman, down on his luck, accompanied by a faithful companion cum servant was followed in *Nicholas Nickleby* and *Martin
Chuzzlewit*, and less distinct traces of it can be found in *Oliver Twist*

and *Barnaby Rudge*. It is also arguable that Dickens, in fact, never abandoned the basic fictional premise of life as a journey although its simple use as a vehicle for adventure was enriched by layers of Christian symbolism. In this way, Pip's physical journey to London and riches in *Great Expectations* becomes a spiritual pilgrimage through guilt and suffering to forgiveness.

The outlines of this reading will be familiar to many readers, constituting as it does the classic beginnings of the English novel, but another key part of Dickens's early involvement with books is probably less well known and harder to explain. From an early age Dickens adored the periodical literature of the eighteenth century, what we would call magazines, such as the *Tatler*, the *Spectator*, the *Idler* and the *Bee*, to which should be added the essayists of the Romantic period, Hazlitt, De Quincey, Lamb and Leigh Hunt (who lived long enough to be an older contemporary of Dickens's and to be pilloried as Harold Skimpole in *Bleak House*). Dickens's lifelong involvement with periodical literature, including his ambition to have his own periodicals, will be the subject of the next chapter, but it requires some amplification at this point as part of the narrative of Dickens's reading. The link between these eighteenth-century and Romantic writers was a special form of the essay in which a strongly marked personality expressed his views on a wide variety of topics often with a gently satirical flavour. Favourite eighteenth-century topics were the absurdities of the newly imported Italian opera, the social foibles of ladies and gentlemen, attacks on duelling, indignation at the trials of poverty, and a celebratory form of literary criticism examining the beauties of writers such as Shakespeare and Milton. The most influential of these journals, the *Spectator*, was credited with having a civilizing effect on upper middle-class and aristocratic morals and social behaviour while, taken together, they paint a fresh and amusing picture of upper-class life in the period. As well as delighting in individual essays, Dickens clearly loved the serial miscellany as a form, with its regular appearance of material varying from sad to funny without touching the extremes of tragedy and farce. This format of a mixed bag of writing was continued by his favourite amongst the Romantic essayists, Charles Lamb, who adopted a pseudonym like Dickens and whose 'Essays of Elia' were a constant source of pleasure to him. Modern readers of this material tend to favour the intellectually robust William Hazlitt and find a feyness in Lamb which savours of escapist sentimentality. Through the heroic self-sacrifice of tending his sister Mary who had periodic fits of madness, in one of which she murdered their mother, Lamb was

...ied the marriage and children he evidently longed for. One of his
ost characteristic pieces, and a favourite of Dickens, 'Dream Children:
Reverie', stems from this deprivation in evoking an image of par-
nthood in a style of delicate, if possibly sentimental, fantasy which
early appealed to that side of Dickens which revelled in fairy-tales
nd the *Arabian Nights*. Elia, the protagonist of the essays, had been 'a
lame-footed boy' and the essay evokes an image of children who are
characteristically curious about their family's past: 'Children love to
listen to stories about their elders....It was in this spirit that my little
ones crept about me the other evening to hear about their great-grand-
mother Field, who lived in a great house in Norfolk'; this is followed
by their asking for 'stories about their pretty dead mother'. Eventually,
Elia wakes up and finds himself 'quietly seated in my bachelor arm-
chair', a conclusion which reveals that the children are indeed figments
of his imagination.[11] Some of the ingredients of what many would
regard as the weaker side of Dickens's own fantasy world can be traced
here. The lonely child, the pretty and so presumably young mother
who is dead, the nostalgia for an Edenic domestic past, the solitary
and probably eccentric bachelor with his dreams of a happiness he has
been denied – traces of all of these can be discovered in Dickens's work
from start to finish. But these influences also shed light on a key aspect
of Dickens the novelist, his capacity for an unremitting self-criticism
which is experienced directly in the work itself although it is not discussed explicitly in the letters or essays. Oliver Twist may be a rather
precious lonely child, but the stereotype is invested with real suffering in the Jo of *Bleak House*. Again, the pretty young mother whose
early death finally destroys the domestic Eden is rendered in *David
Copperfield* with an intensity of feeling and charm of manner that are
incomparable. Finally, the eccentric bachelor, insubstantial in the
Mr Brownlow of *Oliver Twist* or grotesquely implausible in the
Cheeryble Brothers of *Nicholas Nickleby*, is transformed in the later
fiction into the complex portraiture of Mr Jarndyce in *Bleak House* and
Arthur Clennam in *Little Dorrit*.

It has been argued that Dickens's major experience of reading was
the boyhood immersion we have seen recorded in *David Copperfield*
and that he read less as he grew older partly because he was simply
too busy and also because his emotional need for reading had lessened. There is ample evidence however that this is simply not so.
While he was away from home, for example, we find him sending 'a
carpet-bag-full' of books to his artist friend George Cattermole, who
was on his honeymoon, and describing his own holiday reading:

the Italian and German novelists (convenient as being easily ta?
up and laid down again...) Leigh Hunt's Indicator and Compani?
(which have the same merit) Hood's Own complete, A Legend ?
Montrose, and Kenilworth which I have just been reading wit?
greater delight than ever...I have Goldsmith, Fielding, Smollett, an?
the British Essayist handy.

(Pilgrim I, 576)

It is of course evident from this that Dickens had a tendency to reread old favourites, but later in the same year, 1839, we find him writing to Forster, 'I have just turned lazy and have passed into Christabel and thence to Wallenstein'. (Coleridge's chilling fantasy poem and his translation of Schiller's trilogy.) Again, we have the record of a close friend, James T. Fields:

There were certain books Dickens liked to talk about during his walks. Among his especial favourites were the writings of Cobbett, de Quincey, the *Lectures on Moral Philosophy* by Sydney Smith, and Carlyle's *French Revolution*. Of this latter Dickens said it was the book of all others he read perpetually and of which he never tired...He gloried in many of Hood's poems, especially in that biting 'Ode to Wilson'...One of his favourite books was Pepys's *Diary*...He preferred Smollett to Fielding, putting *Peregrine Pickle* above *Tom Jones*.[12]

One reason for the earlier twentieth century devaluation of Dickens as a reader is that, unlike George Eliot, he did not work up his opinions on literature into critical or theoretical essays. But he left in passing enough trenchant views on books and writers to demonstrate that his reading was not a mere time-consuming activity but an experience about which he felt and thought deeply, a judgement endorsed by at least one contemporary:

He was strongest in fiction and travels, and, not having gleaned his opinions of books through books, his judgements of them had a charming directness and independence. Many of the remarks which he let fall in conversation upon Shakespeare and others were original and true, and, had he cared to cultivate the faculty, he would have excelled in terse, distinctive criticism.[13]

A striking example of this 'terse, distinctive criticism' is contained in a letter to Forster discussing one of his favourite books, *Robinson Crusoe*:

You remember my saying to you some time ago how curious I thought it that Robinson Crusoe should be the only instance of a universally popular book that could make no one laugh and could make no one cry. I have been reading it again just now, in the course of my numerous refreshings at those English wells, [of literature, of course] and I will venture to say that there is not in literature a more surprising instance of an utter want of tenderness than the death of Friday. It is as heartless as Gil Blas [another favourite]...the second part [after Robinson's rescue] will not bear enquiry...[it] is perfectly contemptible, in the glaring defect that it exhibits the man who was 30 years on that desert island with no visible effect made on his character by that experience. Defoe's women too – Robinson Crusoe's wife, for instance – are terrible dull commonplace fellows without breeches; and I have no doubt he was a precious dry and disagreeable article himself – I mean Defoe: not Robinson. Poor dear Goldsmith (I remember as I write) derived the same impression.

(Nonesuch I, 767–8)

This mini-essay is clearly almost as revealing of Dickens's aims as a writer as it is of the achievements of Defoe's novel; his belief in tenderness, his desire to evoke tears and laughter, his interest in the finer discriminations of characterization are all evident here. But his observations also constitute an incisive critique of *Crusoe* as do his comments on *Uncle Tom's Cabin*, a bestseller in its day in both Britain and America: 'Of course you have been reading Uncle Tom's Cabin? I don't know whether Uncle Tom is a little too celestial, or whether I am a little in the opposite direction; but 'bating such things, it is an uncommonly fine book, and full of the highest power' (Pilgrim Vl, 826). The precise nature of Dickens's judgement is clarified if this letter is set beside a contemporary report: 'Speaking of *Uncle Tom's Cabin*, then just out, he said he thought it decidedly a story of much power, dramatic and moral, but scarcely a work of art....Uncle Tom evidently struck him as an impossible piece of ebony perfection, as a monster of excellence,' (Nonesuch II, 236). Of course, it has seemed to many readers, Dickens's contemporaries as well as those in the twentieth century, that *his* good characters are sometimes monsters of excellence. Dickens must have thought differently which suggests that he did see the presentation of goodness as an artistic problem, one that he laboured to make acceptable in a way that Uncle Tom was not for him. Again, his recognition of the book's power must relate to its didactic purpose, but the use of fiction for propaganda destroyed its effectiveness as art, however much he agreed with its aim of seeking the abolition of slavery.

A final example of the depth of Dickens's reading, and his ability to express his responses in critical terms, is indicated by his command of parody since successful parody can only stem from a real grasp of another writer's style and intentions. One of his most brilliant incursions into this area is his perfectly judged fragment on a writer he venerated, Thomas Carlyle, which occurs in a letter to Wilkie Collins in which he is evoking his actor friend, Regnier:

> As Carlyle would put it: A deft and shifty little man, brisk and sudden, of a most ingenious carpentering faculty, and not without constructive qualities of a higher than the Beaver sort. Withal an actor, though of a somewhat hard tone. Think pleasantly of him, ye children of men!
>
> (Nonesuch III, 515)

My contention is that with one part of himself Dickens lived in and through books, although it is central to this argument that he lived in and through a whole range of experiences: as journalist and public speaker, through the amateur theatricals and public readings, in his indignation at the sufferings of the urban poor, to say nothing of his more directly personal life. But if we make a crude division between the private and the public, there seems little doubt that reading was a central part of his inner life. And so when Dickens sat down to write his mind was full of the Bible and Shakespeare, popular horror stories and urban mythology, the periodical essayists and the eighteenth-century novel. But we can add even to this list in interesting and important ways. Whatever the responses of contemporary readers, Sir Walter Scott is a towering figure in the history of the novel and casts a long shadow over its development in the nineteenth and even the twentieth century. Scott invented the historical and the regional novel and, more important perhaps, revealed how fiction could deal successfully with the conflicts and partial resolution of social forces through the lives of individuals.[14] Writing the first of his two historical novels, *Barnaby Rudge*, in 1841 (although the book had been meditated on for several years before that), Dickens believed that its central set-piece, the Gordon Riots, were 'new material for fiction':

> This means that in 1836 [when he was still only twenty-four] he set out to write a serious historical novel, and by his choice of subject challenged comparison with Scott. The storming of the Tolbooth in the opening chapters of *The Heart of Midlothian* is the literary inspi-

ration of his central scene, as Madge Wildfire is of his central figure.[15]

Scott was a major part of what we can call Dickens's Romantic inheritance to which can be added his involvement with Wordsworth. A
highly intelligent review of one of the Christmas Books, *The Cricket
on the Hearth*, pointed out that Dickens was 'in one sense, ambitious
of becoming the Wordsworth of prose fiction', a judgement validated by the words of one of Dickens's closest friends, the actor Macready.
In his speech at the so-called Nickleby Dinner to celebrate the completion of his third novel Macready drew attention to Dickens's mastery of 'all the little details and minute feelings, of the every-day
intercourse of life, so finely...characterised in the lines of Wordsworth
as "Those nameless and unremembered acts,/That make the best part
of a good man's life."' The incident was reported by the painter, Sir
David Wilkie, who recorded that Macready's praise led Dickens to
talk about his admiration for Wordsworth.[16] One of Wordsworth's
greatest achievements was to imbue the lives of the rural poor with
a dignity and seriousness they had hardly been accorded in earlier
literature; Dickens's original contribution to the tradition is to trans-
fer this humane insight to the urban poor and lower middle class.

A last ingredient that can be added to this rich mixture is Dickens's
enthusiasm for his contemporaries which is, on the whole, warmly
generous. His commitment to his own status as a professional writer
seems to have extended to his fellow writers, and as the editor of two
popular journals for twenty years he had a practical reason for encouraging literary talent and feeling gratitude when it appeared. Thus
we find that he 'looked on *Vanity Fair* as an absolute masterpiece'
(Pilgrim II, 293) and felt, in the case of Tennyson, 'what a blessed thing
it is to read a man who can write!': 'I have just been reading Tennyson's
Idylls of the King. Most gallant and noble...they are all wonderfully
fine, chivalric, imaginative, passionate, admirable' (Nonesuch III, 118,
116). A commitment to the art of the novel and the ability to use language in interesting ways were of supreme importance to Dickens
and he was dismissive of those who failed to reach these standards
through carelessness or inattention to detail; on the other hand, he
frequently took immense pains to try to improve the work of unknown
and unimportant writers if he felt that they were serious in their
endeavours. He extended the warmest of welcomes to the early work
of Elizabeth Gaskell and George Eliot. (He was early convinced that
the latter's *Scenes of Clerical Life* was by a woman.) He encouraged
both to contribute to his periodicals and wrote movingly to Eliot of

his experience of reading her *Adam Bede*. Amongst living writers, however, he reserved his deepest respect for Thomas Carlyle, an influence signalled by the dedication to him of *Hard Times*:

> I have constructed it patiently with a view to its publication altogether in a compact cheap form...I know it contains nothing in which you do not think with me, for no man knows your books better than I.
>
> P.S. I wouldn't flourish to you if it were not in the nature of me.
>
> (Nonesuch II, 567)

Dickens may well have suspected what was the truth, that Carlyle, despite his love and admiration for him, despised novels and novel writing as fundamentally frivolous activities, an unease that can be sensed in his insistence on having composed *Hard Times* carefully with a view to its reaching the widest possible audience. And the P.S. is a touching little joke: Dickens's signature became increasingly baroque in its decorativeness, a display he felt was unbecoming in the face of the deeply, even dourly, serious Carlyle. The story of Carlyle's influence on Dickens is a fascinating one, but it is enough to note here that he was 'always reading you faithfully and trying to go your way' (Nonesuch III, 348).

Given that the discussion of Dickens's reading so far has been somewhat general, it might be useful at this point to look more closely at his involvement with a single writer as an example of how reading entered into Dickens's inner landscape. We have seen that he loved and admired many writers, but he clearly felt a special affection for Oliver Goldsmith, currently viewed as a rather minor figure, but one who loomed large in Dickens's view of the literary world. That Goldsmith loomed equally large in his interior life is demonstrated by the fact that of all the many quotations which stud the letters, speeches, journalism, and fiction the most frequently used is 'in a concatenation accordingly' from Goldsmith's comedy, *She Stoops to Conquer* (Pilgrim II, n. 1, 62). Goldsmith touched Dickens's life at a number of key points, from childhood to maturity. His novel, *The Vicar of Wakefield*, formed part of the early, intense experience of reading we have already looked at and Dickens's love for it can be felt in a letter of 1849 where it is 'a book of which I think it is not too much to say that it has perhaps done more good in the world, and instructed more kinds of people in virtue, than any other fiction ever written' (Pilgrim V, 517). Goldsmith was also an exponent of that periodical literature of which Dickens was so fond, editing his collection *The Bee* in the 1750s. In addition to his childhood reading, *The Bee* also figured in another key moment in Dickens's early life, his departure from the fairly uncomplicated happiness of Chatham, at the age of ten, for the uncertainties and increasing poverty of the period leading up to his incarceration in the blacking factory, probably at the age of twelve, in 1824. His Chatham schoolmaster, William Giles, kindly and well-educated, gave him a copy of *The Bee* as a going-away present; Dickens remembered that on the night before he left Chatham 'my good master came flitting in among the packing-cases to give me Goldsmith's *Bee* as a keep-sake. Which I kept for his sake, and its own, a long time afterwards.' (Ackroyd, 55). (It was Giles who later sent Dickens a silver snuffbox inscribed 'to the Inimitable Boz', a signature he had been using in *Bentley's Miscellany*, and a present which perhaps reinforced his only half-joking application of the phrase to himself in letters and conversation.) This involvement was increased in adult life by the pride and admiration Dickens felt for his intimate friend Forster's biography of Goldsmith, published in 1848. Significantly, it was Forster's moving account of Goldsmith's trials as a professional writer which particularly attracted Dickens's interest.

Goldsmith was a writer Dickens loved, admired, laughed and cried over, and reread constantly throughout his life. But this appreciation also touches on one of the deepest paradoxes of Dickens's creative and personal life. The suffering and humiliation of his early years are recorded in fictional form in *David Copperfield* and in the autobiographical fragment reproduced in Forster's *Life*, experiences which seem to have instilled in Dickens an iron resolve never to go the way of his improvident father. This determination to succeed is evident even quite early on in his dedication to learning the nightmarishly difficult form of shorthand then in vogue, 'that savage stenographic mystery' (*David Copperfield*, Chapter 43) in order to become a parliamentary reporter. Having become one, it is equally evident that he had to strive to become one of the best, just as he desired to be an outstanding reporter on the *Morning Chronicle*, in his own words leaving 'the reputation behind me of being the best and most rapid reporter ever known'.[17] His initial encounters with publishers left Dickens feeling, however unjustly, that he had been abused and exploited, and so one facet of his professionalism as a writer was his determination to secure the best possible financial terms for his work on all occasions. As we have seen, he became an important player in that increasing capitalization of writing and publishing which proceeded throughout the nineteenth century. In his work, on the other hand, the abuses stemming from wilful imposition on others, and the corruptions of money, are subjected to the most profound scrutiny. *Great Expectations* makes clear that this is at least partly a process of self-scrutiny. If Dickens is examining his own entanglements in materialism through transposing personal experiences into the fictional narrative of Pip, he is also examining in fictional form how these corruptions can become part of the structure of a whole society.

How does all this relate to Oliver Goldsmith? Goldsmith may have been a beloved fellow professional writer, but there all comparison with Dickens come to an abrupt end since Goldsmith's forty-six years consisted of a series of hilarious, if sometimes painful, misadventures. Stories about Goldsmith must always be treated with caution because of his economy or, perhaps, extravagance with the truth, but one is reluctant not to believe some of the best of them. Despite straitened circumstances, his family contrived to provide him with an education, but his attempts to launch himself in the world were signally unsuccessful. His love of finery led him to present himself as a candidate for ordination wearing scarlet clothes for which indiscretion he was ejected from the episcopal presence. On two occasions his relatives scraped together money, once to send him to America and the second time to enable him to train for the law in Dublin; twice he returned home penniless having blown the cash on good living and gambling. He was, however, musical and his flute 'proved a useful friend. He rambled on foot through Flanders, France and Switzerland, playing tunes which everywhere set the peasantry dancing, and which often procured for him a supper and a bed.'[18] His life as a literary hack in eighteenth-century London was hardly less eventful, although his talents secured him the friendship of some of the leading figures of the day including Dr Johnson, the actor Garrick, Edmund Burke and the painter Sir Joshua Reynolds. Indeed, with them and others he was one of the nine original members of the group which began as the Literary Club, although it has always been known simply as the Club. But Goldsmith's extraordinary appearance, clumsiness, and the disparity between the grace of his writing and the awkwardness of his conversation ('he wrote like an angel, and talked like poor Poll' according to Garrick) led him to feel an outsider even here. Despite eventually securing large earnings from his writings, he was finally overwhelmed by debt, dying from an illness which he insisted on trying to treat himself, despite the inadequacy of his early medical training. This led one friend to beg him to 'alter your rule; and prescribe only for your enemies' in response to Goldsmith's claim that he did not practise and made 'it a rule to prescribe only for my friends'.[19] What was there for Dickens to admire in this life, apart from the accident of Goldsmith's being a professional writer? He did, of course, add three fine works to British literature: a novel, *The Vicar of Wakefield*; a play, *She Stoops to Conquer*; and a poem, the *Deserted Village*; and we should not forget the importance to Dickens of his periodical, *The Bee*. Just as important, however paradoxically, is the fact that Goldsmith did not conform to the pattern of the Victorian self-made man which is a crucial element in Dickens's success story. If we ask who in Dickens's life he resembles most closely we have to say his father and his father's fictionalized transformation, Mr Micawber. John Dickens was generous, fun-loving and lovable, and in some essential ways hard-working and conscientious. Yet an ineradicable streak of improvidence meant that he was almost always that crucial sixpence over the expenditure of twenty pounds which, for Mr Micawber, spelt misery. Although this caused Dickens shame and vexation in the earlier part of his career, there is every reason to believe that love gradually triumphed over irritation. If, as almost all critics and scholars believe, the roots of Mr Micawber lie in Dickens's perception of his father, then we are forced to accept that he was capable of challenging at a deep level the very qualities that ensured his own success in the fiercely competitive world of Victorian publishing. 'Poor dear Goldsmith' belongs to the softer aspect of Dickens's personality as opposed to the harsh triumphalism of his exertions of will and power over all opposition in his professional life. This is the Dickens whose charm and gentleness with children were legendary, who found the sufferings of the urban poor sometimes unbearable, who sympathized so profoundly with the failures and disappointments of others. It is as though he saw, loved and admired in Goldsmith everything he himself was not in the arena of public success as a writer, where he was determined to dominate over the interests of publishers and the other money men who lived off literature.

But love for the man came after the love of the work and this affection can be traced from direct verbal borrowing to the more pervasive effect of Goldsmith's general tone and atmosphere on his own writing. In *She Stoops to Conquer*, the wonderful Tony Lumpkin, in one of the earliest recorded uses of 'morrice' in the sense of clearing off rapidly ('...Zounds! here they are! Morrice! prance!') must surely have been at least partly in Dickens's mind in Chapter 8 of *Oliver Twist* with the Dodger's invitation to Oliver on their first meeting: 'Up with

you on your pins. There! Now then! Morrice!' And Jeremy's protes-
tation from the same play, 'Though I'm but a servant' does of course
become the constant cry of the ineffable Miggs in *Barnaby Rudge*. Those
familiar with the Christmas scenes at Dingley Dell in *Pickwick*, with
A Christmas Carol, and with those moments of innocent jollification
so common in Dickens will recognise instantly their atmospheric pre-
figuring in *The Vicar of Wakefield*, with farmers who 'kept up the
Christmas carol, sent true love-knots on Valentine morning, ate pan-
cakes on Shrove-tide, showed their wit on the first of April, and reli-
giously cracked nuts on Michaelmas eve' to which can be added the
singing of old songs and the telling of old stories (Chapter 4). And
even scant attention to the 'structure' of the *Vicar* will reveal how
closely it adheres to the form of the miscellany which I shall argue
later was one of the deepest sources of Dickens's affection for eighteenth-century periodical literature and which he sought to emulate
in his own journalism and in the early novels. Goldsmith's book contains a ballad which lasts some six pages, the Vicar's son reading the
'fable' of 'a Giant and a Dwarf', the 'Elegy on the Death of a Mad Dog'
(which had already been used in *The Bee*), a virtual political essay in
Chapter 19, an interpolated tale, and the lovely and much antholo-
gized poem which finds an echo in T. S. Eliot's *The Waste Land*, 'When
Lovely Woman Stoops to Folly'. (Chapter 24). Rather than being a
novel in the conventional sense of a linear narrative it is, in fact, a
thoroughly mixed form of literature of a kind whose importance to
Dickens will be explored in the next chapter.

In the light of the evidence presented in this chapter one wonders
why Dickens has been displayed so persistently as someone for whom
reading was not a fully serious undertaking. One explanation may be
found in the quite extraordinary range of activities Dickens pursued
throughout his life. Those whose energies are less volcanic might well
wonder whether there could be room in such a life for reading, with
its demands for quiet and continuity. The fact is, however, that Dickens
did make space for it in his hectic schedule, just as he had to make
space for the process of writing itself. Indeed, one interesting thread
in the complex of Dickens's life is his repeated demand for periods of
withdrawal from social life and a kind of living unto himself which
he saw as crucial to his creative activity. Another major explanation
for the failure to take his reading seriously relates to a major theme
of this book, its attempt to present Dickens as a great popular genius
who lived much of his life in the glare of publicity and the hubbub of
practical affairs. In other words, he was at the furthest possible remove

from being either the artist locked away in an ivory tower or the writer as intellectual. Creative meditation was clearly an ongoing process for Dickens, one not dependent on prolonged separation from the world, and he had no aptitude for the extended exploration of ideas in, say, the essay-writing favoured by some major twentieth-century novelists and, in his own time, by George Eliot. To leap from these facts to the assumption that Dickens, like the protagonist of Samuel Beckett's *Murphy*, was 'a strict non-reader' is to fall into the abyss of false logic. This chapter has demonstrated that Dickens read, passionately and with commitment, throughout his life and the results of this reading are everywhere apparent in his work.

4

Periodicals, Journalism and the Literary Essay

The further one goes in exploring Dickens's professional career, the clearer it becomes that he was a very unusual kind of creative artist. Many major figures in English literature have had occupations and interests outside of literature, either from necessity or choice. T. S. Eliot's work as a banker and, later, his long involvement with the publishing house of Faber & Faber are well known, and biographies of Anthony Trollope chronicle in exhaustive detail his full-time commitment to a civil service career in the Post Office as well as his consuming passion for fox-hunting. A man capable of persuading the postal authorities of his day to introduce the pillar box for posting letters is clearly a force to be reckoned with. However, the range and depth of Dickens's extra-literary activities place him in a unique category. It is hard to say that any of these interests went deeper than another, apart from novel writing, but none exceeded his attachment to periodical journalism, for which his fascination never waned. The major purpose of this chapter will be to explore, and to explain, Dickens's engagement with this area.

The story begins on 12 April 1709 with the appearance of *The Tatler*, edited by Richard Steele, which 'was at once recognised as a new and brilliant departure', a new kind of publication which was both 'entertaining and educative'.[1] Steele was assisted by Addison (as Addison and Steele they form one of several eggs and bacon pairings in the history of English literature) and together they launched in 1711 a successor to *The Tatler*, the *Spectator*, which eclipsed its predecessor in popularity and fame, and so will receive most of the attention here. The *Spectator* was published daily on single sheets, printed on both sides in double columns, and although it had a relatively short life it was republished in a manner similar to Dickens's working of his copyrights, in monthly parts and various volume formats, culminating in the seven volumes of the First Collected editions with an eighth added in 1715. Since the *The Tatler* was 'a kind of prelude to the *Spectator*'

and 'the direct model for the literary plan and details of the later journal',[2] description of its format will serve as an indication of the *Specator*
and its contents: 'The paper was divided into five heads – gallantry
[personal behaviour, especially with regard to the relations between
the sexes], poetry, learning, politics, and "editorial".'[3] Its sales began
at three to four thousand, rising to twenty or, even, thirty thousand
on occasion while '10 000 copies probably represented the average
issue during the closing months' of its appearance in daily form.[4]

What was there in the *Spectator* that interested a child and continued to fascinate the man throughout his life? Dickens clearly adored
its miscellaneous character, the variety embodied in its range of material from grave to gay, from delight in popular amusements to social
satire. He may also, at some level, have responded to its attitude to
women, a kind of bantering seriousness towards female foibles, so
called, which was one cause of its immediate success, and expressed
in a tone not dissimilar to that frequently adopted by Dickens in letters to his women friends. Again, we know that Dickens was always
responsive to the idea of a literary club, whether in life or in art, and
have noted his beloved Goldsmith's membership of the first and most
famous of such groupings. Dickens himself was an inveterate joiner
at both the personal and formal levels. For some years he attended
meetings of a Shakespeare Club whose purpose was to discuss literary topics in convivial surroundings. Also, his relations with friends
and colleagues often took on a club-like quality in their adherence to
little rituals and in the organisation of activities such as holidays.
Those hostile to Dickens saw this habit of mind as leading to the establishment of cliques, a series of mutual admiration societies whose
major purpose was to advance his career through pushing his work
in a variety of ways. Particular hostility was generated by the group
of young men he gathered around him for the production of *All the
Year Round* who were seen as slavish imitators and disciples of the
great man's stylistic tricks. But for Dickens himself this 'networking'
was an essential part of his life as a professional writer and, at a personal level, an emotional bonding he found it difficult to live without. One of his most private rituals was the annual celebration with
his wife and John Forster of the day which was both his wedding
anniversary and Forster's birthday. Some of the happiest and most
hilarious times of Dickens's life, to judge by his letters, were spent in
the holidays he enjoyed throughout his life with a select circle of
friends. On his gruelling reading tours he clearly found support in
the creation of a clubbable atmosphere with his professional helpers,

a trait movingly evoked by the manager of his last tour, George Dolby, in his reminiscences of his life with Dickens.[5]

The club format Dickens used so often in his writing probably came most memorably to his attention for the first time in the character of the *Spectator*'s Sir Roger de Coverley:

> The character of Sir Roger had originated with Steele, but was never developed, and we owe to Addison almost the whole of the thirty papers which deal with the various aspects of Sir Roger's character, and more particularly with his life in the country. We are told how he manages his family, and chooses his chaplain; his fox hunting; his Tory politics; his adventures with gypsies round his country seat; his dispute with Sir Andrew Freeport; his return to London and his conversation in Gray's Inn walks; his reflections on the tombs in Westminster Abbey, and his remarks at the playhouse, are all related to us with perfection of style and humour, and finally an account is given of his death and legacies.[6]

The links from Sir Roger to such jolly figures of a bygone age as Mr Pickwick, his host at Dingley Dell, Mr Wardle, and Mr Fezziwig of *A Christmas Carol* are obvious enough. Sir Roger was introduced as early as the second number as a member of the club, although the format was not consistently maintained; however, the sense of him at the heart of a group of intimates can be seen as a forerunner of that use of Master Humphrey and his cronies as the story-telling mechanism of *Master Humphrey's Clock* which has already been discussed. Dickens delighted in the *Spectator* as a miscellany with hints of a club framework, but its most enduring fascination lay in the material itself which, for a lonely and imaginative boy, was conveyed with a delicate charm that stemmed from the graceful lucidity of its writing and the fanciful oddity of so much of its tone. If Sir Roger joined the ranks of the imaginary companionship of Tom Jones, Peregrine Pickle and the rest, we can also see that this material chimed with some of Dickens's deepest concerns as a mature adult.

When we read 'I was reflecting this Morning upon the Spirit and Humour of the publick Diversions Five and twenty Years ago, and those of the present Time', we know instantly that we are in territory Dickens would have delighted in, especially as this is followed by a lively paragraph on comic disasters in the theatre[7] and preceded by a description of what sounds like a quintessentially Dickensian form of entertainment, 'Signior *Nicolini's* Combat with a Lion in the Hay-Market'.[8] Equally appealing to Dickens, at the opposite end of the scale, is Mr Spectator's claim to deal in moral criticism and not just, say, attacks on fashion:

> I must therefore, once for all, inform my Readers, that it is not my Intention to sink the Dignity of this my Paper with Reflections upon Red-heels or Top-knots, but rather to enter into the Passions of Mankind, and to correct those depraved Sentiments that gave Birth to all these little Extravagances which appear in the outward Dress and Behaviour. Foppish and fantastical Ornaments are Indications of Vice, not criminal in themselves. Extinguish Vanity in the Mind, and you naturally retrench the little superfluities of Garniture and Equipage. The Blossoms will fall of themselves, when the Root that nourishes them is destroyed.'[9]

Such passages may well be the seeds of that hatred of gentlemanly dandyism which is attacked specifically in the person of Mr Turveydrop in *Bleak House* and becomes a more general focus of criticism in *Little Dorrit* and *Our Mutual Friend*. Abstemious himself, Dickens's life-long loathing of temperance movements and his joyful evocation of tipsiness in Mr Pickwick and his like seems to be foreshadowed by 'I am one of those who live in Taverns to a great Age, by a sort of regular Intemperance; I never go to Bed drunk, but always fluster'd; I wear away very gently; am apt to be peevish, but never angry.'[10] Readers unfamiliar with this material may perhaps begin to succumb to its charm and fun in this attack on doctors, part of a general campaign against divinity, law and medicine with which Dickens would have been fundamentally in sympathy:

> This Body of Men, in our own Country, may be described like the British Army in Caesar's time: Some of them slay in Chariots, and some on Foot. If the Infantry do less Execution than the Charioteers, it is because they cannot be carried so soon into all Quarters of the Town, and dispatch so much Business in so short a Time.[11]

This is followed in the next number by the truly delightful report of 'an eminent Italian Chirurgeon [surgeon], arrived from the Carnival at Venice...[who] has cured since his coming hither, in less than a fortnight, Four Scaramouches, a Mountebank Doctor, Two Turkish Bassos, Three Nuns, and a Morris Dancer'.[12] The *Spectator* is, then, filled with fun, wit, a lively observation of the social scene, a gently teasing attitude towards women, and a tender mockery of the relations between the sexes. All of this is pervaded by a charm of manner which can also accommodate consideration of the factors which indicate 'Society is upon a wrong Basis',[13] a mixture which not merely appealed to Dickens but which he attempted to reproduce, suitably modified, in his own periodicals.

It hardly needs saying, perhaps, that the *Spectator* was not the sole factor in forming Dickens's attitudes as a man and an editor of magazines; the whole point of this study is to attempt an unravelling of the complex of strands that went to the making of Dickens as literary producer. This complexity will be reinforced if we move to Goldsmith who, as we have seen, held an important place in Dickens's affections and whose periodical, *The Bee*, played a special role in his life. A glance at some of its characteristic moments will reveal how pervasively they seem to foreshadow Dickens's imagination. The dandyism touched on earlier which, in its moral form, is as important to the creation of the Harold Skimpole of *Bleak House* as it is to the social dandyism of Mr Turveydrop, is anticipated in Goldsmith's essay, 'Beau Tibbs, A Character' while the theatrical activities of Mr Vincent Crummles, the actor-manager of *Nicholas Nickleby*, is perhaps hinted at in the 'Adventures of a Strolling Player' whose father brought him up in 'his own employment, which was that of drummer to a puppet show':

> Thus the whole employment of my younger years was that of interpreter to Punch and King Solomon in all his glory...at the age of fifteen, I went and listed for a soldier...whom should I light upon but a company of strolling players...a paradise to me; they sung, danced, drank, and travelled, all at the same time...we resolved to exhibit *Romeo and Juliet*, with the funeral procession, the grave, and the garden scene.[14]

There is no doubt that the 'Adventures', Essay XXI, is one of *The Bee*'s most brilliant pieces of writing with its narrative drive, sense of character, and rich evocation of low life. So good is it, in fact, that one experiences real disappointment at its abrupt conclusion, necessitated presumably by the brevity of the form Goldsmith is working in, leaving the reader with the feeling that the material's full potential has not been developed. A similar experience results from the 'Distresses of a Common Soldier' with its gripping account of its protagonist being sent from parish to parish when he is orphaned at the age of five and then transported 'to the plantations' for poaching a hare. Apparently random detail brings the soldier vividly alive –'I hate the French because they are all slaves, and wear wooden shoes' – in a way that evokes one of the greatest passages in the whole of Dickens, Magwitch's life story in Chapter 3 of the third volume of

Great Expectations. The somewhat whimsical aspect of the essay tradition (taken up by Lamb in 'Dream Children') is present in 'A Reverie at the Boar's Head Tavern in Eastcheap' in a combination of dream and fancy that always appealed to Dickens, although this is combined with a vein of eighteenth-century bawdiness foreign to Lamb and to Dickens himself. The fat landlord of the Tavern turns into Shakespeare's Mrs Quickly as the narrator dozes before the fire at midnight:

> The prior of a neighbouring convent...gave me a license for keeping a disorderly house, upon condition, that I should never make hard bargains with the clergy, and that he should have a bottle of sack every morning, and the liberty of confessing which of my girls he thought proper in private every night.[15]

However, when 'she' starts to moralize this provokes a response from the narrator which was likely to have appealed to Dickens's conviction that art should imply morality, not state it: 'None of your reflections, Mrs Quickly...I love stories, but hate reasoning.'[16] 'On the Education of Youth' advocates a role for the state in children's education which must have elicited a positive response from Dickens, coinciding as it did with one of his own most deeply held beliefs: 'The care of our children, is it below the state....For the state to be the charge of all its children...might at present be inconvenient; but surely, with great ease, it might cast an eye to their instructors.'[17] Finally, 'A City Night-Piece' cannot fail to remind us of one of the most brilliant of the *Sketches by Boz*, 'The Streets – Night', although it moves quickly into abstractions and lacks Dickens's energy of detail and description: 'The clock has struck two...and nothing now wakes but guilt, revelry and despair. The drunkard once more fills the destroying bowl, the robber walks his midnight round, and the suicide lifts his guilty arm against his own sacred person...Why, why was I born a man, and yet see the suffering of wretches I cannot relieve! Poor houseless creatures!'[18]

Before leaving the eighteenth century this seems an appropriate moment to include William Hogarth as a visual equivalent of periodical literature and journalism, especially since he is such a seminal part of the total context within which Dickens came into being. In the words of the witty Rev. Sydney Smith, one of his early admirers, 'the Soul of Hogarth has migrated into the body of Mr Dickens', (Pilgrim I, n. 5 431) a judgement validated by Dickens's ceaseless praise of the artist and his evident role in the genesis of Dickens's work. Dickens and Hogarth had several things in common: both were self-made men and, in Hogarth's words, 'Shows of all sorts gave me uncommon pleasure when an infant...and mimicry, common to all children, was remarkable in me';[19] in addition, Hogarth embarked as a young man on a rigorous programme of training to correct his weak draughtsmanship similar in its intensity to the pains taken by the youthful Dickens to master shorthand and so enter on his desired career as a legal and parliamentary reporter. Hogarth was also a dedicated professional artist whose hostility to dealers led him to use engraving as a way of escaping the tyranny of the art market: 'By mechanical multiplication, advertisement, and display, Hogarth had found a medium and a method relieving him of the necessity of aristocratic patronage, and had created an audience for his images that any theater would be happy to share.'[20] Just as Dickens and Hogarth were proud of their professional independence, they also shared a consciousness of their own originality. In Hogarth's case this is clear from a fragment of autobiography:

> I then married, and commenced painter of small conversation pieces, from twelve to fifteen inches high. This having novelty, succeeded for a few years...I therefore turned my thoughts to a still more novel mode, viz. painting and engraving modern moral subjects, a field not broken up in any country or any age...I therefore wished to compose pictures on canvas, similar to representations on the stage; and farther hope, that they will be tried by the same test, and criticised by the same criterion...I have endeavoured to treat my subjects as a dramatic writer; my picture is my stage, and men and women my players, who by means of certain actions and gestures, are to exhibit a *dumb show*.[21]

These 'modern moral subjects' are, of course, his famous picture series such as the *Rake's Progress* and *Marriage à la Mode* and at this point we encounter a fascinating convergence of some of the crucial figures in Dickens's background. Hogarth influenced his friend and early collaborator, Cruikshank, above all in the 'serial images'[22] he created for his own series, *The Bottle* and *The Drunkard's Children*. Another major figure, Charles Lamb, reinterpreted Hogarth's own view of his work as theatre in favour of a literary analogy that is interesting in relation to Dickens's achievement: 'His graphic representations are indeed books: they have the teeming, fruitful suggestive meaning of *words*. Other pictures we look at, – his prints we read.'[23]

Leaving behind the feyness which can mar his more fanciful pieces, Lamb's essay on Hogarth is both brilliant and profound, deserving quotation at some length for the light it throws on Dickens through analysing so convincingly the strengths he was able to draw from his great predecessor. For the historical painters of the eighteenth century Hogarth could be seen 'as an artist of an inferior and vulgar class' for the very reason that his moral subjects are modern. Taking the example of the terrifying *Gin Lane*, Lamb points out that 'Disease and Death and bewildering Terror, in *Athenian Garments* are endurable, and come, as the delicate creatures express it, within the "limits of pleasurable sensation".' Everything in Hogarth's print, on the other hand, 'tells': 'the fascinating colours...and...the coarse execution...of the print, intended as it was to be a cheap plate, accessible to the poorer sort of people, for whose instruction it was done'. Again, it possesses 'that power which draws all things to one, – which makes things animate and inanimate, beings with their attributes, subjects and their accessories, take one colour, and serve to one effect...the very houses...tumbling all about in various directions, seem drunk, – seem absolutely reeling from the effect of that diabolical spirit of phrenzy which goes forth over the whole composition.' The disintegrating houses of Jacob's Island in *Oliver Twist* come easily to mind here. In another remarkable similarity with Dickens he claims that it is part of Hogarth's genius 'to trust so much to spectators or readers. Lesser artists show everything distinct and full, as they require an object to be made out to themselves before they can comprehend it.' Hogarth (and Dickens) have enough faith in their audience, and in their own powers, not to over-draw their picture. Lamb also praises Hogarth's work for what he calls its 'gratuitous doles which rich genius flings into the heap when it has already done enough, the over-measure which it delights in giving, as if it felt its stores were exhaustless'.[24] Finally, he comments with suggestive force on the total moral impression left by Hogarth's pictures: 'Is it an impression of the vileness and worthlessness of his species? or is it not the general feeling which remains...*a kindly one in favour of his species*? was not the general air of the scene wholesome? did it do the heart hurt to be among it?'[25] Lamb believes that Hogarth's prints are 'analogous to the best novels of Smollett or Fielding'[26] and so opens the way to a point-by-point comparison between Hogarth and Dickens via two of his favourite writers. One last example may demonstrate the similarity of tone, as well of artistic technique, between Dickens's writing and Hogarth, as interpreted by Lamb:

> that aged woman in *Industry and Idleness* who is clinging with the fondness of hope not quite extinguished to her brutal vice-hardened child, whom she is accompanying to the ship which is to bear him away from his native soil...in whose shocking face every trace

of the human countenance seems obliterated, and a brute beast's
to be left instead, shocking and repulsive to all but her who watched
over it in his cradle before it was so sadly altered, and feels it must
belong to her while a pulse by the vindictive laws of his country
shall be suffered to continue to beat in it.[27]

There is something almost prophetic in this analysis which combines a perceptive insight into Hogarth with a foreshadowing of a
major aspect of what we mean by Dickensian. It seems appropriate to
return to the discussion of the periodical essay at this point with Lamb
himself, this time in his role as Romantic essayist. Leigh Hunt, another
favourite of Dickens and a personal friend, defined Lamb's work in
this form as 'among the daintiest productions of English *wit-
melancholy*',[28] a description which is liable to raise modern hackles with
its hints of a rather fey delicacy. However, although Lamb's writing
in this mode lacks the intellectual power of his analytic celebration of
Hogarth, the charm to which Dickens was so responsive can be felt in
'A Complaint of the Decay of Beggars in the Metropolis':

> The all-sweeping besom [broom] of societarian reformation...is uplift
> with many-handed sway to extirpate the last fluttering tatters of
> the bugbear Mendicity from the metropolis. Scrips, wallets, bags –
> staves, dogs, and witches – the whole mendicant fraternity, with
> all their baggage, are fast posting out of the purlieus....I do not
> approve of this wholesale going to work, this impertinent crusa-
> do...proclaimed against a species. Much good might be sucked from
> these beggars....There was a dignity springing from the very depth
> of their desolation; as to be naked is to be much nearer to the being
> a man, than to go in livery.[29]

The charm here lies in comic outrage, a fantastic fling at the
respectable world of work in favour of idleness conceived as a spectacle whose loss is part of a 'progressive' regimentation towards dull-
ness. Once more we can disentangle the complex interlocking of some
of the key forces in Dickens's context in ways that relate directly to
the work. In a passage that could have suggested the fate of Simon
Tapperpit in *Barnaby Rudge*, whose legs are crushed as a result of his
role in the Gordon Riots in 1780, Lamb writes of one particular beggar in the vein of Harold Skimpole (in *Bleak House*) whose prototype,
we remember, was Leigh Hunt:

> These dim eyes have in vain explored for some months past a well
> known figure, or part of the figure of a man, who used to glide his

comely upper half over the pavements of London, wheeling along with most ingenious celerity upon a machine of wood; a spectacle to natives, to foreigners, and to children...Few but must have noticed him; for the accident which brought him low took place during the riots of 1780, and he has been a groundling for so long...He was a grand fragment; as good as an Elgin marble.[30]

We have a suspicion in such passages that our legs may be being pulled, a possibility denied to Lamb's beggar, which can induce a longing for the certainties of satire, the hope that Lamb's outrage is directed at the evils of a society that can permit such heartless abuses. But the outrage is, in fact, outrageousness and the heartlessness lies in a comic celebration of the moral lessons to be learned from a hideously maimed individual whose deformity renders him 'a grand fragment; as good as an Elgin marble'.

It is a difficult business to sort out the precise nature of Dickens's enjoyment of such passages, his responses to Leigh Hunt in life, and his rendering of this material into fiction. What is clear, however, is the similarity of tone between Lamb's piece and Harold Skimpole 'moralizing' on the sufferings of others to his own benefit in Chapter 15 of *Bleak House*:

> Well, it was really very pleasant to see how things lazily adapted themselves to purposes. Here was this Mr Gridley, a man of robust will, and surprising energy – intellectually speaking, a sort of inharmonious blacksmith – and he could easily imagine that there Gridley was, years ago, wandering about in life for something to expend his superfluous combativeness upon – a sort of Young Love among the thorns – when the Court of Chancery came in his way, and accommodated him with the exact thing he wanted! There they were, matched, ever afterwards! Otherwise he might have been a great general, blowing up all sorts of towns, or he might have been a great politician, dealing in all sorts of parliamentary rhetoric; but, as it was, he and the Court of Chancery had fallen upon each other in the pleasantest way, and nobody was much the worse, and Gridley was, so to speak, from that hour provided for.

To see Chancery as a benefit to Gridley is as great an outrage as comic admiration of the physique of a cripple, although the ends to which these effects are being employed are different. We seem once more to be in the shifting territory that involves Dickens's father, Mr Micawber and the writer's recognition of the need for an irresponsible light-heartedness in the face of the routines of self-made respectability.

We are on surer ground with 'On Some of the Old Actors' which has affinities with the evocation of the singers of the past in Joyce's wonderful story, 'The Dead', and a celebration of bygone theatricality that Dickens would surely have enjoyed, especially emanating from a writer who had been 'indulged with a classical conference with Macready', the actor who was one of Dickens's dearest and oldest friends. In fact, it is in the area of enjoyment of the theatre that we can find one of the closest similarities between Dickens and Lamb, one close enough to suggest either direct borrowing or the tenaciousness of Dickens's memory. A glance at Lamb's 'My First Play' and Dickens's 'First Fruits' is enough to make the point. Lamb first:

> The afternoon had been wet, and the condition of our going (the elder folks and myself) was, that the rain should cease. With what a beating heart did I watch from the window the puddles, from the stillness of which I was taught to prognosticate the desired cessation! I seem to remember the last spurt, and the glee with which I ran to announce it....It was all enchantment and a dream. No such pleasure has since visited me but in dreams.[31]

Dickens's evocation of this great event is even more vivid, an example of the charm of manner which was one of his great personal attractions, but which has been insufficiently appreciated as a feature of his work (the first two hundred pages or so of *David Copperfield* are a key example):

> We went to the play and were happy. The sweet, dingy, shabby little country theatre, we declared, and believed to be much larger than either Drury Lane or Covent Garden....Dear, narrow, uncomfortable, faded-cushioned, flea-haunted single tier of boxes...the warnings not to 'talk loud,' in defiance of which (seeing condonatory smiles on the faces of those we loved) we screamed outright with laughter...then...we for the first time 'sat up late,' and for the first time ever tasted sandwiches after midnight, or imbibed a sip, a very small sip, of hot something and water.[32]

The ecstatic nostalgia in these pieces for his pre-Warren's Blacking childhood, and there are many of them in Dickens's later journalistic essays, forms a key aspect of *Copperfield* in a manner which suggests that a Dream Childhood is being explored in the style of Lamb's 'Dream Children'.

Again, 'Poor Relations' has a strong flavour of that shabby genteel quality which recurs so constantly in Dickens's work from *Sketches* onwards, the poor relation being known 'by his knock....A rap, between familiarity and respect; that demands, and at the same time seems to despair of, entertainment.'[33] But there are darker intimations in Lamb also, as in the schizophrenic existences of the clerks and tradesmen who, reminiscent of Wemmick in *Great Expectations,* must suppress their inner lives at the behest of the pressures of business, like the shopkeeper who calmed himself by beating his family and 'when the heat was over, would sit down, and cry faster than the children he had abused; and after the fit, he would go down into the shop again, and be as humble, courteous, and as calm as any man in the shop, meek like a lamb'.[34] 'The Superannuated Man', based on Lamb's own sudden and traumatic retirement from the East India House, is suffused with elements that Dickens seems to have taken over for his own purposes. When, for example, the Superannuated Man tell us that 'it is now six and thirty years since I took my seat at the desk in Mincing Lane' we must be reminded of one of Dickens's most penetrating studies of a favourite type, the London clerk, in the Mr Wilfer of his last completed novel, *Our Mutual Friend.* In response to his daughter's 'And how have they used you at school to-day, you dear?', which forms part of the novel's pattern of reversal in parent–child relationships, he answers 'I attend two schools. There's the Mincing Lane establishment, and there's your mother's Academy. [A reference to his unhappy domestic life.] Which might you mean, my dear?' (Book 4, Chapter 5). Lamb's essay continues in a way which seems to foreshadow Dr Manette (*A Tale of Two Cities*), Arthur Clennam (*Little Dorrit,*) and Mr Boffin (*Our Mutual Friend*), as well as a host of faceless clerks and the London which forms their home: 'It is true I had my Sundays to myself; but Sundays, admirable as the institution of them is for purposes of worship, are for that very reason the very worst adapted for days of unbending and recreation...I miss the cheerful cries of London, the music, and the ballad-singers – the buzz and stirring murmur of the streets. Those eternal bells depress me.' Under the pressure of his enforced leisure, the Superannuated Man was 'in the condition of a prisoner in the Old Bastile (*sic*), suddenly let loose after a forty year's confinement'.[35]

The contextualization provided by this chapter thus far surely makes Dickens's enthusiasm for journalism, and the control and editing of a periodical, seem less obsessive. This commitment can be understood as a facet of his burning ambition to be a financially independent, professional writer through assuming the mantle of a well-established tradition in English literature. Initially, of course, journalism seemed an obvious route for a bright young man who wished to rise in the world but whose education suited him only to the lower reaches of the law, and for whom university and the gentlemanly professions that might have flowed from it were shut off for reasons of inclination as well as family circumstances. Dickens started his second working life, at the age of fifteen, as solicitor's clerk and began his laborious process of self-advancement by forcing himself to acquire proficiency in the fiendishly difficult Gurney system of shorthand. This skill enabled him to become a freelance reporter at Doctors' Commons, a bizarrely antiquated branch of the English legal system, which did nothing to increase his respect for the law, and in 1832, aged twenty, he joined *The Mirror of Parliament*, a rival to *Hansard* in taking down the proceedings of the House of Commons. He soon became a parliamentary reporter on an evening paper, *The True Sun*, and reported the debates which preceded the abolition of slavery and the passing of the first Reform Bill. Dickens served the *Morning Chronicle* as a reporter from 1834 until 1836, a period evoked in one of his most famous speeches, to The Newspaper Press Fund in 1865, some thirty years after the events it so memorably evoked:

> I have pursued the calling of a reporter under circumstances of which many of my brethren at home in England here, many of my modern successors, can form no adequate conception. I have often transcribed for the printer from my shorthand notes, important public speeches in which the strictest accuracy was required, and a mistake in which would have been to a young man severely compromising, writing on the palm of my hand, by the light of a dark lantern, in a post chaise and four, galloping through a wild country, all through the dead of night, at the then surprising rate of fifteen miles an hour. The very last time I was at Exeter, I strolled into the Castle Yard there to identify, for the amusement of a friend, the spot on which I once 'took', as we used to call it, an election speech of my noble friend Lord Russell, in the midst of a lively fight maintained by all the vagabonds in that division of the county, and under such a pelting rain, that I remember two good-natured colleagues, who chanced to be at leisure, held a pocket handkerchief over my notebook after the manner of a state canopy in an ecclesiastical procession.... I have been, in my time, belated on miry by-roads, towards the small hours, in a wheelless carriage, with exhausted horses and drunken postboys, and have got back in time for publication, to be received with never-forgotten compliments by the late Mr Black,

[his editor] coming in the broadest of Scotch from the broadest of hearts I ever knew.

(Speeches, 347)

The range of experience provided by this period to a brilliantly observant young man is obvious; he was clearly able to follow politics in all its manifestations in distinctively different parts of the country in a way that added greatly to the store of impressions that would eventually flood out in his fiction. However, as Peter Ackroyd points out, this activity cut deeper than merely acquiring subject matter for his sketches, novels and journalism:

> he learnt how to produce 'copy' to a deadline with a punctiliousness that would prove invaluable for his novels in later life but, more importantly, it is significant that the greatest novelist of the English language should have been trained first as a journalist and reporter. He was at once made aware of an audience which he had to address, and whose tastes he would need to satisfy, if he were to be taken seriously at all.

(Ackroyd, 187)

And we can also trace here the roots of one of Dickens's most defining characteristics, a fusion of qualities that are usually seen as mutually exclusive in a writer: a commitment to the most minute, if vivid, recording of the social life of his time combined with the ability to translate the mundane into realms of fantastic and surreal comedy and tragedy. As early as *Pickwick Papers*, for example, he transformed the events of the trial involving Lord Melbourne, the Prime Minister, and his supposed adultery with Caroline Norton – admittedly grotesquely absurd and obscene in itself – into the sublime comedy of the trial of Bardell v. Pickwick which, rooted in reality, nevertheless takes flight into a realm of sublime laughter at the ridiculousness of human institutions.

Having established that Dickens was both a star parliamentary and newspaper reporter, it seems obvious enough that his ambitions might extend to being a star editor and owner of a weekly periodical and such indeed seems to have been the case from an early stage in his career. The first step on this journey occurred when Dickens agreed with the publisher Richard Bentley in November 1836, just before *Pickwick* began to take off on its meteoric rise to success, to edit his monthly *Bentley's Miscellany* at a salary of £20 a month, a large sum which promised a degree of financial stability to a newly-married freelance writer aged twenty-four. Dickens edited the *Miscellany* until February 1841 and his second novel, *Oliver Twist*, appeared in it in the monthly parts that may have already begun to look like his trademark given *Pickwick*'s fame. *Bentley's Miscellany* was followed by the curious publication in weekly parts *Master Humphrey's Clock* which, after the early failure of its 'club' and miscellany aspects with their attempt to reintroduce old favourites such as Mr Pickwick and Sam Weller, turned into the vehicle for the publication of two novels, *Barnaby Rudge* and *The Old Curiosity Shop*. Abortive attempts then followed, a periodical called *The Cricket* which came to nothing and Dickens's misguided decision to edit a new national newspaper, the *Daily News*, which was first published in January 1846 and which he abandoned as editor some three months later. Solid and long-lasting success arrived with *Household Words* in 1850 which Dickens virtually transformed into *All the Year Round* in 1859 and edited until his death in 1870.

Although *The Cricket* project was pushed aside in the excitement of the *Daily News* attempt, something of what Dickens was after in all his periodicals is summed up by the recipe for *The Cricket*: 'Carol philosophy, cheerful views, sharp anatomization of humbug.' (Pilgrim IV, 328). The 'philosophy' referred to is, of course, that of *A Christmas Carol* with its message of hope, love and genial good fellowship, a kind of Christmas all the year round. But for Dickens there is no incompatibility between this and satirical attacks on the abuses and corruptions of Victorian society. His tenure at *Bentley's* provides a model both of what Dickens hoped to achieve in the world of periodical publishing and what was necessary for him to attain total success. Clearly, he saw himself as the conductor of this early enterprise in the sense that has been discussed in Chapter 1, although the governing metaphor of his role as editor in his Editor's Address on the Completion of the First Volume of *Bentley's* is theatrical: 'At the end of a theatrical season it is customary for the manager to step forward...' and the metaphor is continued throughout the Address with Dickens sometimes presenting himself as the stage manager.[36] A glance at the contents of this first volume reveals his desire to emulate the miscellaneous quality of his beloved eighteenth-century periodicals: biographical sketches, poems, comic Irish sketches, popular history and literary criticism. Dickens's own contributions included the 'Public Life of Mr Tulrumble, Once Mayor of Mudfog' which also formed, in the first sentence of the novel as it appeared in *Bentley's*, the birthplace of Oliver Twist.

But who, and what, was Dickens conducting in this venture? Not, for a start, contributors of his own generation and choosing, for although he became friendly with some of them his contributors were essentially friends of Bentley whose names, plus that of Cruikshank, would have suggested to potential buyers 'a compendium of Cockney fun and satire' mixed with a 'kind of linguistic rowdiness'[37] which was at odds with Dickens's softening of Regency horse-play. Also, Dickens's Address admitted to a certain lack of political engagement with its claim that 'we have nothing to do with politics. We are so far Conservative....We are so far Reformers...'[38] Although Dickens's later periodicals never announced themselves in narrow party political terms, he would have choked on the admission of conservatism as an abandonment of his commitment to 'sharp anatomization of humbug'. Finally, with Bentley as owner, Dickens lacked the total control he thought essential to such an enterprise: 'I must beg you not to allow anybody but myself to interfere with the Miscellany. I have received a note from Lever, complaining with some justice...of the whole disposition of his Dialogue having been altered after he saw a proof. If we do this, we may go look for contributors in Grub Street.' [The mythical haunt of hack writers.] (Pilgrim I, 224).

When the moment for *Household Words* was ripe Dickens had the clearest possible conception of how he would run the journal and what, essentially, it was for. His general approach to its material is clearly expressed in a letter to his right-hand man Wills of November 1853: 'KEEP "HOUSEHOLD WORDS" IMAGINATIVE! is the solemn and continual Conductorial Injunction.' (Pilgrim VII, 200) More specifically, the opening number contained 'A Preliminary Word' to its readers which stated quite explicitly the fully worked-out ideas which motivated the enterprise. The aim was to write about 'the stirring world around us, the...many social wonders, good and evil', but in 'no mere utilitarian spirit, no iron binding of the mind to grim realities'. The intention was, rather, to 'tenderly cherish that light of Fancy which is inherent in the human breast'.[39] That there was nothing sloppy in Dickens's championing of imagination over the mundane is clear from a warning to Wills: 'Nothing can be so damaging to Household Words as carelessness about facts. It is as hideous as dulness, (Pilgrim VII, 51). A vein of deep seriousness is mined by this remark, a responsible concern both for his public and his own project. As Dickens well knew, a sentimental disregard for facts as unimportant is the worst possible position from which to mount an attack on the materialism of a society dominated by the wrong kinds of facts. With his sense that the miscellaneous nature of the journal needed to be unified in some manner, Dickens turned to his eighteenth-century predecessors for a variation on the club format. He developed the idea of the Shadow, which could go everywhere and see everything, an idea which 'sets up a creature which isn't the Spectator, and isn't Isaac Bickerstaff' but which was intended to possess a 'charm for their [the readers'] imagination, while it will represent common-sense and humanity' (Pilgrim V, 623). However, Dickens soon saw that the idea would not work and it was dropped, perhaps because he grasped at an early stage that the unifying presence, and presiding genius, would be himself. From the beginning Dickens set his heart on the largest possible readership, accepting everything that was entailed in aiming for 'so large an audience as this of ours – in which the constant endeavour is, to adapt every paper to the reception of a number of classes and various orders of mind at once'(Pilgrim VI, 719). Crucially, as we have seen, this entailed no writing down to his public as far as Dickens was concerned and this general approach was certainly validated by the periodical's sales. Although the readership of *Household Words* was essentially middle class, it was cheap enough at two pence to be within the reach of the literate working class and cultivated enough to reach the upper, a breadth of readership which ensured sales in the region of 36 000 to 40 000 a week.[40]

What did Dickens's contemporaries discover as they so eagerly opened these pages? To plough our way through twenty-four pages of closely printed text in double columns with no relief from illustrations might seem a daunting experience for modern readers, but this was not the Victorian response. A 'typical issue might contain a sociological or political piece, a poem, a story, a historical or biographical piece, an article of "useful" knowledge, and an article of exotic or sensational or amusing information'.[41] The first number, for example, contained two poems, by William Allingham and Leigh Hunt, both good if minor poets; a piece on the French tragic actress Mdlle Clairon by George Hogarth, Dickens's father-in-law; the opening chapter of Elizabeth Gaskell's 'Lizzie Leigh'; 'A Preliminary Word' and 'The Amusements of the People' by Dickens; an information piece, 'Valentine's Day at the Post-Office by Dickens and his trusty secretary Wills; and 'A Bundle of Emigrants' Letters' by Dickens and Mrs Caroline Chisholm, a philanthropist active in the field of emigration whom Dickens satirized as Mrs Jellyby in *Bleak House*. The range and depth of Dickens's involvement in the venture can be sensed from this list alone. In fact, about half of the material was by Dickens and his staff (W. H. Wills, R. H. Horne, Henry Morley, and Wilkie Collins), the remainder by regular or occasional contributors. A glance at the detail of Dickens's workload on *Household Words*, a weekly demand which was only part of a huge volume of activity, is enough to justify the ironic dismissiveness of a letter to Leigh Hunt: 'I don't mention such trifles as that great humming-top Household Words which is always going round with the weeks, and murmuring "Attend to me"' (Nonesuch II, 621). In a letter to Wills of 1856, Dickens suggested the following topical subjects: 'The Police Enquiry'; the 'constitution of foreign armies, especially as to their efficiency'; the 'prices of fares on foreign railways'; safety laws on British and foreign railways; compensation for injured people; the tyranny of a Scottish landlord, the Duke of Argyle, over his tenants; the question of whether proposals for Life Assurance are ever refused; poisoning as a crime and the sale of poisons; and, less topically, a 'light' article on coaches, coaching and coaching inns (Nonesuch II, 725–6). Something of Dickens's attitude to his collaborators, and to the enterprise as a whole, is revealed in a discussion with Wills about Wilkie Collins being taken on as a salaried staff member: 'He is very suggestive, and exceedingly quick to take my notions' (Nonesuch II, 800). There is thus ample justification for his claim in a letter of 1853 that 'I diffuse myself with infinite pains through Household Words, and leave very few papers indeed, untouched' (Pilgrim VII, 220). Given that Dickens also spent hours each week in the minute correction of material ('I have had a story to hack and hew into some form for Household Words this morning, which has taken me four hours of close attention' (Nonesuch II, 782), it is hardly surprising that he should have encouraged an element of co-operation as well as control in the running of the magazine's affairs; concerning a controversy with Harriet Martineau on the dangers, or otherwise, of factory machinery he writes to Wills: 'If you think any little thing I have put in, too hard, consult Forster. If you both think so, take it out. Not otherwise' (Nonesuch II, 721). On the other hand, Dickens would never countenance the expression of opinions which ran counter to his own known views or to the general policy of the magazine: 'I should like Morley to do a Strike article...But I cannot represent myself as holding the opinion that all strikes among this unhappy class of society who find it so difficult to get a peaceful hearing, are always necessarily wrong; because I don't think so' (Nonesuch II, 722). One way of understanding Dickens's role as the Conductor of *Household Words* is through the analogy of the Renaissance artist's studio, an idea prompted by Peter Ackroyd's description of its activities: '...there were many occasions when with Wills, Morley or others he would collaborate in "composite" articles, Dickens characteristically providing the opening and ending to set the tone of the piece, while his collaborators filled in the rest....Some of his articles were also written in collaboration with their subjects...various members of the Detective Department at Scotland Yard', most notably Inspector Fields, a prototype for Inspector Bucket in *Bleak House* (Ackroyd, 599). The flavour of this kind of collaboration is indicated in some of his instructions to Wills: 'I want a name for Miss Martineau's paper...[he suggests three]. Take which one you like best' and 'If you have to take out more, [for reasons of length] take it from Dr Pablo after his marriage and the loss of his wife's fortune' (Nonesuch II, 553).

It is impossible to illustrate fully the range and variety of *Household Words*'s material, but a few of its more interesting directions can be indicated. Dickens's love of France and the French set him apart from the sometimes crude chauvinism of British patriotic feeling and he sought always to modify such absurdities as middle class suspicion of French immorality, which inevitably meant sexual misbehaviour rather than the corruptions of the gross materialism he so disliked in contemporary Britain. Nowhere is this more lightly achieved than in 'Our French Watering Place', a loving acknowledgement of holidays spent regularly in Boulogne, with its tribute to the figure based on Dickens's landlord: 'Good M. Loyal! Under blouse or waistcoat, he carries one of the gentlest hearts that beat in a nation teeming with gentle people.'[42] This represents the kinder side of Dickens's attempts to modify the limitations of his society. More hard-hitting are two articles written with W. H. Wills, 'The Doom of English Wills', which take to task the nepotism and inefficiency involved in the storage of wills in cathedral towns. In one case, based mainly on Lincoln and Lichfield Cathedrals, the

> Registrar is a person of almost inordinate power; beside his seven thousand-pound-per annum place, he is Chapter Clerk, Town Clerk to the Magistrates – a Proctor, moreover in boundless practice. He lives in great state; he keeps horses, carriages, dogs, and a yacht; he is – could he be anything else? – a staunch tory; he generally proposes the tory members for the county, and has been known to pay the entire electioneering expenses of a favourite tory candidate.[43]

Dickens never loses sight of the role of humour in these attacks: another registry 'produces to its fortunate patentees twenty thousand pounds per annum; about ten thousand a year for the Registrar who does nothing, and the like amount for his Deputy who helps him'.⁴⁴ But there is no incompatibility between this satirical comedy and the deadly seriousness with which Dickens viewed such abuses. *Household Words* was a campaigning vehicle for all the causes Dickens believed in, none more passionately than sanitary reform which with education formed the basis of his programme for a social transformation which he regarded literally as a matter of life and death. Normally such issues had to be treated in a manner which adhered to the journal's policy of presenting all topics in a bright, lively and interesting way to the widest possible audience. However, the issue for 7 October 1854 began with a 'leader', 'To Working Men', provoked by Dickens's horror at the unnecessary deaths from cholera and typhus produced by the avoidance of the most elementary precautions for public health, a rage which led him into a fierceness of attack which offended at least some readers:

> It behoves every journalist, at this time when the memory of an awful pestilence is fresh among us, and its traces are visible at every turn in various affecting aspects of poverty and desolation which any of us can see who are not purposely blind, to warn his readers whatsoever be their ranks and conditions, that unless they set themselves in earnest to improve the towns in which they live, and to amend the dwellings of the poor, they are guilty, before God, of wholesale murder.

One cause of Dickens's anger is revealed by the kind of occurrence which fuelled his never-ending contempt for Parliament and all its doings; in the course of a debate in the House of Commons on recent outbreaks of disease, 'Lord Seymour, the member for Totnes, exhibited his fitness for ever having been placed at the head of a great public department by cutting jokes, which were received with laughter, on the subject of the pestilence then raging.' His advice to working men is to join with the members of the responsible middle class to bring about changes which will ensure the creation of 'a government so acted upon and so forced to acquit itself of its first responsibility, that the intolerable ills arising from the present nature of the dwellings of the poor can be remedied'.

One reader who was offended was his close friend the wealthy philanthropist, Miss Burdett Coutts, for whose complex charitable activities Dickens acted as agent, perhaps most interestingly with the home for prostitutes, Urania House. Despite her humane work for the poor

Miss Coutts was politically conservative, a fact that Dickens usually ignored both out of deep friendship and in the interests of the good work he helped her to fulfil. On occasion, however, he was forced to protest, as over her blaming the individual worker for the existence of class warfare in Victorian society: 'I differ from you altogether, as to his setting class against class. He finds them already set in opposition...You assume that the popular class takes the initiative. Now as *I* read the story, the aristocratic class did that, years and years ago, and it is *they* who have put *their* class in opposition to the country – not the country which puts itself in opposition to *them*' (Nonesuch II, 661). This disagreement touches on a debate which has raged in Dickens studies intermittently over the years, the question of the balance of radicalism and conservatism in his general make-up and political outlook. It has been argued in relation to *Household Words* that the topical issues which it took up for satirical attack had already come to public notice elsewhere and that Dickens was risking nothing by ventilating subjects with which his readers would have been familiar. However, even if this point is accepted, and there are grounds for not doing so, it could be argued that the verve, humour and, sometimes, savagery of its exposure of public abuses deserve to be seen as something better than a stale rehash of the campaigns of others. Perhaps the last word on this matter can be left safely to the editors of the Pilgrim edition of Dickens's letters who argue that, for the years 1853 to 1855, '*Household Words* is often as much a crusading journal as a miscellany' (Pilgrim VII, x).

Household Words had been a glittering success, but Dickens achieved the summit of his journalistic career when it was superseded for a number of characteristic reasons, in May 1859, by *All the Year Round* which Dickens edited until his death in 1870. Dickens had parted from his wife in May 1858 and, against strenuous advice, published a vague statement in *Household Words* denying the truth, without specifying their nature, of 'all the lately whispered rumours' concerning his role in the separation.[45] Dickens attempted to have this statement appear in *Punch* which was published by Bradbury and Evans who were the printers of *Household Words*. When this was refused, he quarrelled with his printers and undertook the complex steps necessary to wind up his periodical and replace it with *All the Year Round*, to the title of which was added the words 'with which is incorporated *Household Words*' thereby denying the use of the title or its goodwill to anyone else. In controlling three-quarters of the magazine while Wills owned a quarter, Dickens was essentially its publisher and so he had 'at last, what he had always yearned for: absolute mastery of a great popular weekly, and with that mastery the unhampered power, day in and day out, to extend his personal influence into every corner of English life'.[46] In addition, Dickens had the grim satisfaction of seeing it become 'a phenomenal financial success'[47] with a circulation extending, on occasion, to as high as 300 000 a week.[48] But as always throughout his career, whether as novelist, reader or journalist, Dickens was never content to rest on the laurels of past triumphs and with *All the Year Round* he achieved yet another brilliant success. As we have seen, its innovation was to make original fiction its dominant offering to the public, to the extent of being the lead item in each issue; only once, in fact, did an issue fail to begin with a work of fiction.

The change of tone associated with these developments can be registered in the gravity of Dickens's statement of aims: 'We purpose always reserving the first place in these pages for a continuous original work of fiction....And it is our hope and aim, while we work hard at every other department of our journal, to produce, in this one, some sustained works of imagination that may become a part of English Literature.'[49] But this seriousness of purpose was also central to the journal's non-fiction aspect as in Dickens's definition of its aims several years after it started publication when he described it as 'a collection of miscellaneous articles interesting to the widest range of readers, consisting of Suggestive, Descriptive and Critical Dissertations of the most prominent topics, British and foreign, that form the social history of the past eight years'.[50] *Household Words* may have been bright, informative and satirical, but it could only be described as a social history of its time by default and not as part of Dickens's conscious intention. One sign of these changes is the explicit concern with economic theories evident in some instructions to Wills: 'In cutting the Cotton paper to such dimensions as you can find room for, take nothing out of the first slip. Because the Manchester School deserves all the schooling it can get, touching its reduction to the grossest absurdity of the supply-and-demand dogmatism, and its pig-headed reliance on men's not going to war against their interest. As if the vices and passions of men had not been running counter to their interests since the creation of the World!' (Nonesuch III, 321) *All the Year Round* was then less personal than *Household Words*, and more professional, partly because Dickens wrote less for it himself than he had done with the first journal: 'Unlike other journals, *All the Year Round* treated such difficult subjects as scientific advances, the postal system, and the London water supply in an attractive way, and in a way that, while not patronizing, was comprehensible to readers unaccustomed to making any intellectual effort.'[51]

It is, therefore, appropriate that the pages of *All the Year Round* should have seen the climax of Dickens's career as a writer of periodical essays, the form in which he made his first attempts at professional writing in the pieces which were collected as the *Sketches by Boz*. *The Uncommercial Traveller* is the title given to a collection of essays which appeared in *All the Year Round* from January 1860 onwards and which contains some of Dickens's greatest writing. Their basic format was a modernized version of the spokesperson of Addison and Steele's journal, Mr Spectator, the disinterested observer who took no 'practical part in life'.[52] Significantly, and as always, Dickens fastened on an emerging contemporary type here, the traveller – in his case, uncommercial rather than commercial, a distinction explained in the introduction:

> Figuratively speaking, I travel for the great house of Human Interest Brothers, and have rather a large connection in the fancy goods way. Literally speaking, I am always wandering here and there...seeing many little things, and some great things, which because they interest me, I think may interest others.[53]

This series of periodical essays, which ran for some three years, gave Dickens the opportunity to fuse social and personal observation in a style that combined journalistic vivacity with meditative introspection, one example of which is the contrast between the present and the past made possible by the return to his 'birthplace', Dulborough Town:

> ...the first discovery I made was, that the Station had swallowed up the playing-field...The coach that had carried me away was melodiously called Timpson's Blue-Eyed Maid, and belonged to Timpson, at the coach-office up street; the locomotive engine that had brought me back, was called severely No. 97, and belonged to S.E.R., and was spitting ashes and hot water over the blighted ground.[54]

However, these memories are by no means uniformly nostalgic. The Traveller is taken as a child to see four or, even, five dead babies born to the same woman lying 'side by side, on a clean cloth, on a chest of drawers; reminding me by a homely association, which I suspect their complexion to have assisted, of pig's feet as they are usually displayed at a neat tripe-shop'.[55] The Traveller's meeting, in another piece, with a 'very queer small boy' whose father had told him that he might some day come to own Gad's Hill Place reinforces the suspicion that *The Uncommercial Traveller* is the vehicle for a meditative exploration of Dickens's own life. And he did of course make a similar attempt, in a highly fictionalised way, in *Great Expectations* which appeared in the same year as the essays began to be published in *All the Year Round*. The novel was serialized in Dickens's periodical from December 1860 and earlier, in September, Dickens used a huge bonfire at Gad's Hill to destroy 'the accumulated letters and papers of twenty years'.[56] Dickens destroyed his correspondence partly because he had a horror of biographical intrusion into his own life and that of his friends. But it is hard not to feel that such a decisive action must have linked to some attempt to come to terms with himself in relation to the past and the present. At the very least, it must have prompted a host of those memories which seem inseparable from letters, especially at the moment when they are about to be destroyed for ever. All of these circumstances, including his separation from his wife after more than twenty years of marriage and the disturbance created by his relationship with Ellen Ternan (whatever its precise nature), conspired to produce an exploration of self and circumstance with which it is easy to identify:

> Ah! who was I that I should quarrel with the town for being so changed to me, when I myself had come back, so changed, to it! All my early readings and early imaginations dated from this place, and I took them away so full of innocent construction and guileless belief, and I brought them back so worn and torn, so much the wiser and so much the worse.[57]

One example of this 'innocent construction' is that he and his schoolfriend, Joe Specks, read of Roderick Random (the hero of Smollett's novel of the same name) together and 'had believed him to be no ruffian, but an ingenuous and engaging hero'.[58] Dickens had demanded of public and friends alike that only an innocent construction be placed on what was clearly a momentous event, leaving his wife and entering into a relationship with a woman young enough to be his daughter, especially when the man in question was the most famous Victorian celebrator of hearth and home. Dickens was so convinced that he was the ingenuous and engaging hero of his own drama that he took the extraordinary step of publicizing his separation in a statement in *Household Words* which he clearly regarded, against the advice of most of his friends, as a satisfactory justification of his behaviour.

That this period of upheaval was creative in its outcome is demonstrated not merely by the power of *Great Expectations*. It can also be experienced in such wonderful essays as 'Night Walks' which sees the sane and insane as equal in the world of dreams since, if sleep can be called the death of each day's life, dreams might be regarded as the insanity of each day's sanity. 'Some Recollections of Mortality' evokes a pitiless absence of fellow-feeling in a sketch of a corpse being taken out of the Thames. 'Tramps' provides a vividly comprehensive description of different categories of down-and-out while 'A Small Star in the East' evokes an unbearably painful picture of the lowest reaches of Victorian poverty:

> I could enter no other houses for that one while, for I could not bear the contemplation of the children. Such heart as I had summoned to sustain me against the miseries of the adults failed me when I looked at the children. I saw how young they were, how hungry and how serious and still. I thought of them, sick and dying in those lairs. I think of them dead without anguish; but to think of them so suffering and so dying quite unmanned me.[59]

The Small Star is, in fact, the East London Children's Hospital whose work is described with a beautiful absence of sentimentality, but whose efforts are seen, realistically, as a tiny gesture towards an ocean of suffering. Despite the hospital's wonderful work, the essay is a tragic vision of human pain rather than a propagandist appeal for social change.

The Uncommercial Traveller contains some of Dickens's most controversial writing, pieces such as 'The Ruffian' which are crucial to the debate on the reactionary versus radical direction in his later development. Although deplorable for its advocacy of 'perpetual imprisonment' and corporal punishment ('I would have his back scarified often and deep'), the essay is charged with an enormous comic energy as in the description of a group of ruffians: 'This fellow looks like an executed potboy of other days, cut down from the gallows too soon, and restored and preserved by express diabolical agency.'[60] Also, the essay is careful to distinguish the horseplay of navvies who fight mainly among themselves and who 'work early and late, and work hard' from the eye-gouging and ear-biting activities of ruffians who commit indecent assaults on women in broad daylight. And comfortable liberal outrage is immediately overturned by 'On An Amateur Beat' which is at the opposite extreme from ranting about ruffians:

> Walking faster...I overturned a wretched little creature who, clutching at the rags of a pair of trousers with one of its claws, and at its ragged hair with the other, pattered with bare feet over the muddy stones. I stopped to raise and succour this poor weeping wretch,

and fifty like it, but of both sexes, were about me in a moment, begging, tumbling, fighting, clamouring, yelling, shivering in their nakedness and hunger. The piece of money I had put into the claw of the child I had overturned was clawed out of that wolfish gripe, and again out of that, and soon I had no notion in what part of the obscene scuffle in the mud, of rags and legs and arms and dirt, the money might be.[61]

The hopelessness of charity in the face of such a mass of misery is rendered with bitter power and provides ample proof of the inexhaustible vitality of Dickens's writing throughout his career. This chapter has traced the emergence of Dickens as journalist and editor in relation to the eighteenth century which meant so much to him, and these culminating examples of his mastery of the periodical essay demonstrate how sustaining and yet liberating this context was. But the power of the *Uncommercial Traveller* pieces indicates that Dickens did in the end have to make the form his own. The contradictions and complexities of his own life and his response to the times in which he lived were not ultimately containable within the safe limits inhabited by the earlier users of the form which he loved so much. One of these contradictions can be seen in his role as editor. He clearly enjoyed being a genial father-figure to his contributors, especially to the young men he gathered round him in the *All the Year Round* period, many of whom testified to their enjoyment of such a relationship with him. On the other hand, his need for total control of everything that emerged from under his name was little short of fanatical. Similarly, the loving husband and father was ruthless in enforcing the arrangements he insisted on in leaving his wife of so many years. Catherine was well provided for materially, but Dickens never saw her again after their separation, even at the marriage of their daughter Katey, to which she was not invited. We have seen, too, that there were deep divisions in Dickens's social thinking between his conservative and radical impulses. The richness of all this ensures that even a literary life is unable to keep solely within the literary realm if it is to hope to explain a writer as complex as Dickens. The influence of the eighteenth century in forming him as journalist, editor and essay writer is undeniable. But the life outside of literature, in all its ramifications, has also to be called into play if we are to take the full measure of Dickens's culminating achievement as journalist and periodical essayist in *The Uncommercial Traveller*.

5

Theatre and Popular Entertainment

On 14 April 1860 Dickens issued an invitation, some might say a challenge, to one of his more distinguished friends, Austen Henry Layard, the famous archaeologist: 'Here is a queer question I am going to ask you. Have you any curiosity to see the Great Fight (at a cost of Three Guineas)?...it is to come off at Daybreak on Tuesday morning' (Nonesuch III, 155–6). As so often Dickens's insatiable curiosity prompted him towards an event of some general interest, in this case in the history of sport. The Great Fight was a 42-round, two hours and twenty minutes' encounter between the Englishman Tom Sayers and the American John Heenan which is generally regarded as the first international boxing match to achieve media status through being widely reported in the British and American press. (Sayers became a national hero when the fight ended in a draw because of spectators invading the ring.) The wonders of the Victorian postal service enabled Dickens to write to Layard again on the same day in a manner which indicates that his 'queer question' received a negative response. That Dickens was not put off by such rejections from his more sophisticated companions is evident from the fact that he attended a black-and-white minstrel show, Buckley's Serenaders, less than a year later in the company of his younger and raffish friend, Wilkie Collins, at the very moment when he was writing *Great Expectations*, often considered one of his most serious, mature and dignified novels. Dickens's epistolatory style in issuing these invitations to fun and frolic is well conveyed by a letter to Collins of January 1853:

> If you should be disposed to revel in the glories of the eccentric British Drayma on Saturday evening, I am the man to join in so great a movement. My money is to be heard of at the Bar of the Household Words, at five o'Clock on that afternoon.
>
> Gin Punch is also to be heard of at the Family Arms Tavistock, [his home, Tavistock House] on Sunday at five, when the National

Sparkler will be prepared to give Lithers [one of Collins's stage roles] a bellyful if he means anything but Bounce.

(Pilgrim VII, 12)

What do these glimpses of Dickens's social life tell us about the man and the writer? He was, quite evidently, 'game' for any possible variety of jaunt – what he often called an 'out' – in the field of popular entertainment. Apart from indecency, which was in plentiful supply in Victorian London, Dickens had a boundless appetite for this kind of pleasure: the circus, performing dogs, puppets, pantomime, melodrama, panoramas and magic lantern shows, all inspired him with enthusiasm and, on occasion, joy. There was hardly anything in the way of entertainment and spectacle he was not prepared to go and see, including the public hangings which provided both for a large segment of London's population. That the high and low-brow distinction meant nothing to him is evident from the fact that these pleasures coexisted easily with the deepest respect for, and interest in, the serious theatre, above all Shakespeare. And it was also characteristic that his delight in the popular prompted him to a response to its meaning for the life of his time, especially as part of the gradually developing urban culture which he observed and recorded at first hand, and thought about deeply. It is of course central that the novels cannot be understood apart from this context, whether we are laughing at the riotous fun of the Crummles company's appalling performance of *Romeo and Juliet* in *Nicholas Nickleby* or being moved by later work such as *Great Expectations* where another dreadful rendering of Shakespeare is perpetrated to more serious, although still comic, effect. This side of Dickens, sometimes dismissed in his own day as vulgar and in ours seen as conduct unbecoming to a serious writer, is one we ignore at our peril.[1] We can experience fully its importance for Dickens in one of the most joyous celebrations of popular art he ever wrote, a marvellous letter to Forster from Rome on a puppet-theatre, which fuses perfectly childlike delight with mature judgement, displaying in Dickens himself one of his most admired human traits, that 'genial disposition to be pleased which is one of the finest qualities to be found in the heart of Man' (Pilgrim VII, 251):

It was a wet night, and there was no audience but a party of French officers and ourselves. We all sat together. I never saw anything more amazing than the performance – altogether only an hour long, but managed by as many as ten people, for we saw them all go behind at the ringing of a bell. The saving of a young lady by a good

fairy from the machinations of an enchanter, coupled with the comic
business of her servant Pulcinella (the Roman Punch) formed the
plot of the first piece. A scolding old peasant woman, who always
leaned forward to scold and put her hands in the pockets of her
apron, was incredibly natural. Pulcinella, so airy, so merry, so life-
like, so graceful, he was irresistible. To see him carrying an umbrel-
la over his mistress's head in a storm, talking to a prodigious giant
whom he met in the forest, and going to bed with a pony, were
things never to be forgotten. And so delicate are the hands of the
people who move them, that every puppet was an Italian, and did
exactly what an Italian does. If he pointed at any object, if he salut-
ed anybody, if he laughed, if he cried, he did it as never Englishman
did it since Britain first at Heaven's command arose – arose – arose,
etc. [from Rule Britannia] There was a ballet afterwards, on the same
scale, and we really came away quite enchanted with the delicate
drollery of the thing. French officers more than ditto.

> (Pilgrim Vll, 202)

This chapter will, then, describe Dickens's lifelong involvement with
the theatre and popular entertainment as crucial influences in the formation of his personality and work.

It is entirely appropriate that when the eight-year-old Dickens was
lost in London – the subject of a *Household Words* piece of 1853, 'Gone
Astray' – he should have whiled away the time by seeing a play in
which the protagonists were a good sailor, who was very good, and
a bad sailor, who was very bad; it goes without saying that the first
was a success and lived happily ever after while the second came to
a bad end. If we think of contemporary children as culturally formed
by television, their mythology and inner life to some extent conditioned by cartoons, game-shows and the rest, we need to think of the
tiny Charles as the focus of a range of simple but more varied pleasures. We have noted already the importance of his childhood reading and of the horror stories told him by Mary Weller. To this can be
added the activities announced by his command to the servant, 'Now,
Mary, clear the kitchen we're going to have such a game',[2] an announce-
ment followed perhaps by a magic lantern show or an extravaganza
based on his toy theatre over which, anticipating later days, Charles
would preside as actor, designer, director and, on occasion, play-
wright. (One of his more notable efforts was *Misnar The Sultan of India*,
a tragedy based on the *Tales of the Genii*.) Popular songs were another source of fun, Charles singing such comic ditties as 'The Cat's Meat

Man', accompanied by his sister Fanny on the piano. To his amused mortification in adult life, Dickens remembered his father's pride in the comic singing taking the form of standing him on a table to sing to grown-up friends.

But Dickens's central experience of popular culture was and remained the theatre. This enthusiasm never flagged, from the unforgettable first visit ('We went to the play and were happy'[3]) to his mature theatre-going in, for example, 1860 only ten years before his death, during a period when he was living at the *All the Year Round* office: 'I pass my time here (I am staying here alone) in working, taking physic, and taking a stall at the theatre every night' (Nonesuch III, 196). Throughout his life Dickens saw every possible kind of play and theatrical spectacle, including of course the 'delights – the ten thousand million delights of a pantomime' even 'of the pantomime which came lumbering down in Richardson's waggons at fair-time to the dull little town in which we had the honour to be brought up'.[4] This exuberant praise comes from the introductory chapter to the memoirs of the famous clown, Joseph Grimaldi, which Dickens was induced to edit in 1837, a possible tribute to his childhood 'veneration for clowns, an intense anxiety to know what they did with themselves out of pantomime time, and off the stage'.[5] Pantomime was hard to miss, even for the conscientiously serious playgoer, as the opening night of the Drury Lane programme in December 1841 makes clear: '*The Merchant of Venice*, followed by the new Christmas pantomime *Harlequin and Duke Humphrey's Dinner; or Jack Cade, the Lord of London Stone*' (Pilgrim II, n. 2 453). That this took place under the management of one of Dickens's dearest friends, the actor W. C. Macready who was notable for his 'reversion to the genuine text, [of Shakespeare's plays] and careful regard for the poetical idea of each drama' (Pilgrim II, n. 2 453) makes clear that the popular was a key element in Victorian theatre as a whole. The bizarre richness of this pantomime experience is hinted at by a contemporary account: 'No words can express the animation, the gaiety, the boldness, the madness, the incoherence, the coarseness, the splendour, the whimsical poetry, the brutality of these Christmas pantomimes' (Ackroyd, 37).

If, as I have suggested, Dickens did not simply revel in such pleasures but thought about their meaning for social and personal life, what conclusions did he come to? An early effort in this direction is a piece in *Bentley's Miscellany*, 'The Pantomime of Life': 'We revel in pantomimes...because ...A pantomime is to us, a mirror of life; nay more, we maintain that it is so to audiences generally, although they are not aware of it; and that this very circumstance is the secret cause of their amusement and delight.'⁶ The essay does not really explain what it is that audiences are not aware of and leaves its subject abruptly, a sign that Dickens is not yet able to work out fully the nature of his own insights. With sanitary reform and education, popular entertainment was one of the topics closest to Dickens's heart, and mind, and as late as the year of his death, 1870, we find him ruminating on theatre's social importance in a letter to his son Henry, advising him on a speech he is to make at university:

> Your next Tuesday's subject is a very good one. I would not lose the point that narrow-minded fanatics, who decry the theatre and defame its artists, are absolutely the advocates of depraved and barbarous amusements. For wherever a good drama and a well-regulated theatre decline, some distorted form of theatrical entertainment will infallibly arise in their places. In one of the last chapters of Hard Times, Mr Sleary says something to the effect: 'People will be entertained thomehow, thquire. Make the betht of uth, and not the wortht.'
>
> (Nonesuch III, 769)

Twenty years earlier, in *Household Words*, 'Shakespeare and Newgate', written with R. H. Horne, tackles another aspect of the subject:

> There are not many things of which the English as a people stand in greater need than sound rational amusement. As a necessary element in any popular education worthy of the name; as a wholesome incentive to the fancy, depressed by the business of life; as a rest and relief from realities that are not and never can be all-sufficient for the mind, – sound rational public amusement is very much indeed to be desired.⁷

And it is significant that Dickens should have felt impelled to confront this subject in the essays collected as *The Uncommercial Traveller*, in 'Two Views of a Cheap Theatre'. In this essay Dickens makes a suggestive contrast, which cannot have been agreeable to all sections of his public, between the presentation of plays and a religious service, both in the same building. The building itself wins Dickens's approval for the ways in which it has been designed to be servicable to its working-class audience with 'convenient places of refreshment and retiring rooms...Magnificently lighted by a firmament of sparkling chandeliers', part in his view of 'an unquestionably humanising influence in all the social arrangements of the place'. He notes of the acting in the pantomime that 'the people who kept the shops...had no conventionality in them, but were unusually like the real thing – from which I infer that the audience are not to be done as to anything in the streets' and registers, with an unsentimental aside, the moral force of the melodrama about which they 'all agreed (for the time) that honesty was the best policy, and...were hard as iron upon Vice'. The contrast with the service is comprehensive, the Uncommercial Traveller thinking it a 'very difficult thing...to speak appropriately to so large an audience and speak with tact. Without it, better not to speak at all. Infinitely better, to read the New Testament well, and to let *that* speak.' In contrast to this, 'a suppositious working-man was introduced into the homily, to make suppositious objections to our Christian religion and be reasoned down...not only a very disagreeable person, but remarkably unlike life...[with] a suggestion of a dialect that I certainly never heard in my uncommercial travels...as far away as fact as a Chinese Tartar.'[8] Nothing could reveal more clearly that Dickens did more than simply enjoy popular entertainment than this fascinating discussion. He clearly respects the audience's unwillingness to be 'done' (fooled) about anything of an unrealistic nature presented to it, and the distinction between morality in art and in life is recognized. The role of popular theatre in instructing through pleasure is contrasted favourably with the unconvincing propaganda of the religious service.

Entertainment, in its widest sense, is therefore a central element in civilized life as far as Dickens is concerned. At its simplest, it provides a tired workforce with rest and recreation, the pleasure of being taken out of itself into the escapism of other worlds and exotic locations. But in its form as popular theatre, above all melodrama, it also has an ethical force, inculcating moral lessons through the triumph of good over evil. Dickens also sees popular drama as having its own kind of cathartic effect, akin to the catharsis traditionally ascribed to tragedy. In 'Lying Awake', one of the so-called *Reprinted Pieces* taken from *Household Words*, Dickens argues that in melodrama and pantomime audiences are entertained by the spectacle of events turning out well on the stage which would be disastrous in real life. The relevant passage is so interesting and such a definitive refutation of those who suggest that Dickens is incapable of real thought in his non-fictional writing that it is worth quoting at some length:

> This particular public have inherently a great pleasure in the contemplation of physical difficulties overcome; mainly, as I take it, because the lives of a large majority of them are exceedingly monot-

onous and real, and further, are a struggle against continual difficulties, and further still, because anything in the form of accidental injury, or any kind of illness or disability, is so very serious in
their own sphere. I will explain this seeming paradox of mine. Take
the case of a Christmas Pantomime. Surely nobody supposes that
the young mother in the pit who falls into fits of laughter when the
baby is boiled or sat upon, would be at all diverted by such an occurrence off the stage. Nor is the decent workman in the gallery, who
is transported beyond the ignorant present by the delight with which
he sees a stout gentleman pushed out of two pair of stairs window,
to be slandered by the suspicion that he would be in the least entertained by such a spectacle in any street in London, Paris, or New
York. It always appears to me that the secret of this enjoyment lies
in the temporary superiority to the common hazards and mischances
of life; in seeing casualties, attended when they really occur with
bodily and mental suffering, tears, and poverty, happen through a
very rough sort of poetry without the least harm being done to anyone – the pretence of distress in a pantomime being so broadly
humorous as to be no pretence at all. Much as in the comic fiction
I can understand the mother with a very vulnerable baby at home,
greatly relishing the invulnerable baby on the stage, so in the
Cremorne [a popular theatre] reality I can understand the mason
who is always liable to fall off a scaffold in his working jacket and
to be carried to the hospital, having an infinite admiration for the
radiant personage in spangles who goes into the clouds upon a bull,
or upside down, and who, he takes it for granted – not reflecting
upon the thing – has, by uncommon skill and dexterity, conquered
such mischances, as those to which he and his acquaintances are
continually exposed.[9]

Popular entertainment acts, then, as a kind of safety-valve against
the chances and accidents of a pre-welfare-state world. The foreclos-
ing of a mortgage in melodrama and the tumble from a beanstalk in
pantomime would, in reality, be terrifying intrusions of fate into a
social world which lacked welfare provision except at the most basic
level of the workhouse and personal charity. The laughter they gen-
erate in the theatre is thus a barrier erected against what would be
their inevitable consequences in real life.

This escapist role for popular entertainment is part of a deeply
thought-out response by Dickens to what he saw as some of the essential features of his society and their effects on human lives. We have
seen that Dickens was essentially a progressive with a profound belief

in the triumphs of chloroform, railway travel and telegraphic communication. But he also recognized that a price has to be paid for these advances in human terms. At its worst, he saw his own time as dominated by an iron-bound utilitarianism which reduced men and women to functional operatives in a vast industrial process. Dickens's ideas in this area are worked out with great complexity, although embodied in totally fictional terms, in *Hard Times*, where factory workers are seen solely as 'hands' and thus reduced to the level of tiny cogs in a vast machine. Such reductionism ignores everything which makes people fully human, their capacity for emotion and the ability to inhabit realms of imagination and dreaming having no place in a purely rational organization of society and labour. This explains the thematic role of fairy-tales in the novel since the presentation of its major villains in these terms undermines what they stand for in the most subversive manner possible. When Stephen takes himself off to 'the red-brick castle of the giant Bounderby' (Book the Second, Chapter V), the latter is ridiculed by the kind of literature he would dismiss most completely for its childish lack of relevance to the 'real world'. But Dickens takes the enemies of unimaginative industrialization, capitalist excess, and utilitarian dogmatism seriously and in that sense not liable to be easily defeated. And so we return to escapism and one of Dickens's most deeply held beliefs that 'Human kind', in T. S. Eliot's words in *Four Quartets*, 'cannot bear very much reality' ('Burnt Norton' I). *Little Dorrit* is a key example of this aspect of Dickens's thought in characters such as Mrs Plornish who comforts herself for a limited and cheese-paring life with the delusion that the urban squalor of her home is a rural 'Happy Cottage'. The final remarks of Mr Meagles on the sacrifice of his beloved daughter to a 'good' marriage bear directly on the point:

> 'she's very fond of him, and hides his faults, and thinks that no one sees them – and he certainly is well connected, and of a very good family!'
> It was the only comfort he had in the loss of his daughter, and if he made the most of it, who could blame him?
>
> (Book the Second, Chapter 34)

Humble people who 'live lives of quiet desperation'[10] need illusions and day-dreams to make existence tolerable and, for Dickens, a night at the pantomime, circus or melodrama is, like a night at the pictures for a later generation, an important release from everyday cares into a world in which everything can be made to come right in the end.

On the other hand, we should not be deluded into thinking that Dickens took an uncritical view of popular culture. Almost any kind of entertainment, within the bounds of decency, was better than none at all, but he sought constantly to raise the standards of what was on offer to the Victorian public at both the popular and the more serious level. Dickens's critical attitude to the theatre can be followed in two areas where his personal involvement was close, adaptations from his own work and the amateur theatricals so dear to his heart. Throughout his career Dickens did occasionally take a hand in the adaptations inflicted on him and one reason for doing so is relevant at this point:

> ...finding that I could not prevent the dramatising of my last story, I have devoted myself for a fortnight to the trying to infuse into the conventionalities of the Theatre, something not usual there in the way of Life and Truth.

> (Nonesuch III, 148)

An invitation to his production of *The Lighthouse* suggests a very similar motivation: 'The real Theatre is so bad, that I have always a delight in setting up a sham one – besides deriving a pleasure from feigning to be somebody else' (Nonesuch II, 668). In fact, as a historian of the theatre makes clear Dickens was explicitly part of a movement committed to a root and branch improvement of the English theatre:

> Of Dickens's contemporaries, Macready, Browning, Forster, and Lewes are of special importance. The five men were in agreement about the great objective of making the English playhouse fit for a modern drama that would be a worthy descendent of the work of Shakespeare...[they] saw in the young Browning a man who might create a modern English drama of great poetic and theatrical power.[11]

However, they were ultimately defeated by a number of factors, perhaps the major one being that 'physical conditions and conventional expectations made it impossible for the lyrical sensibility at the heart of contemporary English poetry to flourish in the huge theatrical spaces of the patent theatres'.[12] The leading figure in this enterprise was, of course, W. C. Macready. He is credited with restoring *King Lear* to the theatre in something like its original form after the bowdlerization of Nahum Tate which held the stage throughout the eighteenth century, a version in which Lear and Gloucester are spared and Cordelia marries Edgar to complete the happy ending. Macready presented his restored Shakespeare for several seasons in which the plays were intelligently directed, and brought to life imaginatively with appropriate scenery and decor. Dickens was unstinting in his praise of these efforts and sympathetic when they ended, as they usually did, in financial failure.

Dickens's involvement with the theatre was, then, as comprehensive as one could imagine. He was a delighted spectator of all kinds of entertainments throughout his life. He also wrote a number of plays without, admittedly, much success or distinction, although he and Wilkie Collins achieved a 'hit' with *No Thoroughfare* in 1867. His more important contribution to the English-speaking stage, however, lay in the adaptations of his novels and stories which were a staple of English and American drama from *Pickwick* on. Indeed, one Victorian theatre critic was led to ask, 'What will become of the English stage when the public has grown weary, if it ever does grow weary of dramatic versions of the stories of...Mr Dickens?'[13] And on his second visit to America Dickens himself remarked to Forster of the New York stage that 'comic operas, melodramas, and domestic dramas prevail all over the city, and my stories play no inconsiderable part in them' (Nonesuch III, 581–2). Eye-witnesses testify that he was an actor of great intensity who might well have pursued a successful professional career. In addition, his amateur productions were evidently outstanding in all aspects of their stagecraft with the exception that not all of his fellow actors performed on his high level. Finally, as a solo performer, he was a brilliant magician, and a reader of his own work of such distinction that the subject demands more detailed discussion elsewhere. We have already noted his confession to Charles Kent nearly at the end of his life, of his ambition to run an English National Theatre as a benevolent tyrant; he had already confessed to an identical desire nearly thirty years earlier: 'I begin to be once more of the opinion that nature intended me for the Lessee of a National Theatre – and that pen, ink and paper have spoiled a Manager' (Pilgrim III, 243–4). But if even Dickens was unable to achieve this aim on top of all his other activities, he clearly did enjoy a symbiotic relationship with the theatre, shaping it through the pervasive influence of his work as well as the adaptations from his fictions, while being influenced by it in his turn. Nicholas Nickleby, for example, is 'a genuine "Adelphi [a popular theatre] walking gentleman": his manner, heroic bursts, protection of his sister, bearding of Ralph, etc., were all elements in the Adelphi melodrama; and though the author appreciated the absurdities of the "Adelphi guests," etc., he was certainly influenced by the place.'[14] Nicholas is, of course, a character from an early novel, but it can be demonstrated convincingly that Dickens's work retained important theatrical elements throughout his entire career.

It might be useful at this point to look in more detail at some of those aspects of Dickens's involvement with the theatre that have already been touched on. That Dickens did seriously consider a career as an actor is not in doubt since we know that he prepared very carefully for an audition which had to be called off at the last moment on grounds of ill-health. He had written to the manager of the Covent Garden Theatre in 1832 telling him 'exactly what I thought I could do; and that I believed I had a strong perception of character and oddity; and a natural power of reproducing in my own person what I observed in others' (Pilgrim IV, 244–5). This dual ability, the fierce intensity of observation made possible by his 'clutching eye' *and* the ability to reproduce his observations through mimicry had been noted years before when the fifteen-year-old was employed in his first major job as a solicitor's clerk (that it is a central feature of the power of his writing goes without saying). A fellow clerk recorded for posterity his admiration of Dickens's ability to 'imitate, in a manner I never heard equalled, the low population of the streets of London in all their varieties, whether mere loafers or sellers of fruit, vegetables, or anything else' (Ackroyd, 117). Dickens refined and developed this talent over the years partly through his almost obsessive theatre-going but also, amazingly enough, at this stage through practising 'often four, five, six hours a day'. His request for a Covent Garden audition was granted, but on the day appointed he 'was laid up...with a terrible bad cold and an inflammation of the face' and so could not attend, although it is worth noting that he wrote to the manager explaining that he would try again for the next season. Whether his indisposition was psychosomatic, some internal warning against taking a wrong direction, can only be a matter of biographical speculation. It is, however, hardly possible to doubt that his audition would have been successful if it had occurred, with results incalculable for the development of English and, indeed, American and European literature. That this urge towards public performance remained strong throughout his life is evident not merely from the amateur theatricals; his skill as a magician in the family circle, his brilliant public speaking and, above all, the charismatic readings of his own work testify to an unquenchable thirst for self-expression and approbation in the public arena.

Equally unquenchable was the theatre's appetite for, and reliance on, adaptation of his writings throughout his entire career. Some of the statistics alone are staggering and justify the view that the mass production of plays from Dickens was a major part of what might legitimately be called the Victorian entertainment industry. For example, 'by 1850 Dickens had been dramatized in at least 240 productions', nearly twenty-five per cent of them plays from *Nicholas Nickleby*[15] and a total of well over 3000 productions have appeared up to the present. Dickens was, however, only one of the more striking instances of what had become a tradition of adaptation which included Defoe, Fielding, Richardson, Smollett, Sterne, Goldsmith and Scott, to name only the major figures involved. This, with a number of other factors such as the lack of copyright protection, gave novels the status of a kind of public property, open to use by other media as part of the general domain of popular entertainment, so that 'Dickens came of age as a novelist when dramatic adaptation was the fate of novels'.[16] The nature of this fate is clarified by the fact that *Nicholas Nickleby* opened as a play – adapted by one of the best known practitioners of the craft, Edward Stirling – after only eight of the novel's nineteen monthly parts had appeared.[17] In the circumstances Stirling was forced to invent a plot and ending for the later parts of the book but, in a delicious example of the fluid relationship between art and reality made possible by serial publication, Dickens had his revenge by 'introducing and denouncing him at Mr Crummle's farewell supper' at a later point in the novel (Forster, vol 1 101). The cavalier attitude taken by figures such as Stirling is amusingly indicated by his self-defence:

> Some apology is due to Mr Dickens, for the liberty taken with him in finishing his work before its time; but the great increase of popularity it must have received from my putting it on the stage, will, I think, more than excuse a step to which I was urged rather by circumstance than desire. Some injudicious friends of Mr Dickens...have chosen to display a soreness at the complete manner in which I have triumphed over all the difficulties I had to surmount in my undertaking.[18]

Impudence could hardly go further, especially in the case of a work which was currently achieving an enormous popular success. But Stirling was only a single player, if a major one, in a process that points again towards the 'industrialized' commodification of literature for purposes of mass entertainment: 'The early nineteenth-century entertainment industry generally followed certain empirically tested principles in manufacturing products for public consumption: among these was the distillation of a novel to its lowest common emotive denominator, its most elemental appeal.'[19] The division of labour inseparable from mass production is one way of understanding the theatrical careers that were built on Dickens's achievement, not merely by adaptors such as Stirling but by actors who specialized in playing specific characters, sometimes a single character for long stretches of their careers. One of the best-known teams involved in this process were the Keeleys, a husband and wife who 'were probably the first truly important theatrical folk to take several important roles in Dickens dramas.'[20] It is an extraordinary fact to the modern sensibility that Mrs Keeley played Oliver Twist in 1839 at the age of 33! For one contemporary critic she had little to do in the role but 'dress and undress', a remark which suggests at least one reason for the audience's interest in such breeches parts. Indeed, a contemporary illustration of Mrs Keeley as Smike in *Nicholas Nickleby* suggests a shapeliness in trousers quite at odds with the character's misshapen physique.[21] It is perhaps worth noting in this context that Dickens himself wrote Forster an enthusiastic letter urging him to see a brilliant impersonation of a boy by a Miss Wilton who, in the great tradition of the English theatre, eventually became Lady Bancroft (Nonesuch III, 81). It is amusing as well as interesting that by the time of *The Uncommercial Traveller* Dickens is prepared to admit that his 'first metropolitan pantomime' was marred because of 'dreadful doubts of Mr Barlow's considering the costumes of the Nymphs of the Nebula as being sufficiently opaque, obtruding themselves on my enjoyment'. (Mr Barlow is a spoilsport character from a novel Dickens hated for its sanctimonious do-goodism, *The History of Sandford and Merton*.) This interest in the female form is continued, in the same piece, in reminiscences of going to a burlesque:

> ...an uncompromising burlesque, where everybody concerned, but especially the ladies, carried on at a very considerable rate indeed. Most prominent and active among the corps of performers was what I took to be (and she really gave me a fair opportunity of coming to a right conclusion) a young lady of a pretty figure. She was dressed as a picturesque young gentleman, whose pantoloons had been cut off in their infancy; and she had very neat knees and very neat satin boots.[22]

What did this conveyor-belt of adaptation mean for Dickens? Not money, as we have seen, or at least very little of it since his work was initially simply pirated, although at a later stage he did devise means for securing some modest recompense. From an artistic standpoint Dickens had serious and well-reasoned reservations about the whole business:

My general objection to the adaptation of any unfinished work of mine simply is, that being badly done and worse acted it tends to vulgarize the characters, to destroy or weaken in the minds of those who see them the impressions I have endeavoured to create, and consequently to lessen the after-interest in their progress.

(Pilgrim I, 463)

Since, however, the process was unavoidable he did have the satisfaction of the kind of indirect material return suggested by another infamous adapter, W. T. Moncrieff: 'Let these "high intellectuals" speak to Mr Dickens's publishers, and they will learn it has rendered them, by increasing their sale, the most fortunate of chapmen and dealers.'[23] In other words, his 'audience was much larger than a mere reading public'[24] and so his fame was extended by those who poured into theatres to see versions of his novels whether they had actually read them or not. The well-known argument that reading is increased by the viewing of 'classic serials' on television may well have applied in Dickens's case also, although the shocks which can be involved in the former may have been just as disturbing in the Victorian period. It is one thing to see Richardson's *Clarissa* in a manageable number of instalments on television, quite another to read its more than a million words. A similar experience might well have been in store for those who hurried from their evening in the theatre to one of Dickens's massive novels, especially in its complete volume form.

It is, of course, almost impossibly difficult to re-experience the tone and texture of these adaptations from the written texts that have come down to us. One of the most unlikely examples, *Our Mutual Friend*, does in fact read surprisingly well, mainly because it is heavily reliant on the novel's amusing dialogue in the domestic exchanges between the martyred Mrs Wilfer and her high-spirited daughters, the pert Lavinia and the wilful Bella. On the other hand, the book's densely complex plot moves with startling rapidity, Rokesmith revealing himself as Harmon to Mr Boffin at the beginning of Act III after only twenty-one pages of text.[25] London, the river and the great panorama of society are nowhere to be seen. A version of *David Copperfield*, called *Little Em'ly*, is much less successful. It dispenses entirely with Dora, beginning with Agnes and David at Yarmouth, already in love, with Emily and Steerforth in the offing. Unlike the version of *Our Mutual Friend* much of the early dialogue is given over to plot exposition between Agnes and David while the absence of Dora disposes of David's internal conflicts and gradual maturing at one fell swoop. It does, however, seize the opportunities presented by the original for 'tableaux vivants' and extravagant scenic effects. The role of tableaux vivants, an unfamiliar experience to contemporary theatre-goers, in adaptations of Dickens's work is best described by an expert in the field, H. Philip Bolton:

> The stage technique of 'realizing' the 'pictures' from the novel that had begun with stagings of *Pickwick Papers* very much continued and developed with stagings of Oliver Twist. Barnett's version at the Pavilion in May 1838 had one such imitation of Cruikshank's plates, for example. Almar's version at the Surrey in 1838 and 1839 especially featured 'scenery either from the Designs made upon the spot by Mr Brunning, or from the Etchings which so richly illustrate the Work, by the talented GEORGE CRUIKSHANK'. This became very much an established convention in the staging of Dickens, so that we find a contemporary critic praising the Adelphi, 1839, version for supplying 'tableaux such as George Cruikshank himself would not have despised.' Nor was this a short-lived tradition. We find it again in 1855, at the Pavilion, which especially promoted 'the living pictures' in the piece. The method was at least nostalgically revived in 1909 at the Broadway Theatre's production of Dexter's and Harry's 'Oliver Twist', which concluded with a tableau of Fagin in 'The Condemned Cell.'[26]

As far as scenic effects are concerned we should remember that a key aspect of the theatre in the context of the Industrial Revolution is that the Victorian period is the great age of that stage machinery which made possible the realisation of a range of excitements such as storms, fires and earthquakes with a realism not exceeded until the advent of the cinema.[27]

It might be possible to illustrate both of these theatrical devices from the *Little Em'ly* already referred to. Emily runs off at the end of Act 1 and this is followed by the stage direction 'All form picture' which is indicated in the play script as follows:

                                     Peggotty
Mrs Gummidge
        Barkis   Copperfield
                             Ham

CURTAIN

One crucial feature of the tableau, which can be inferred from the above, is its static nature; as in the cinematic freeze-frame, motion is arrested and this is clearly an important factor in the generation of emotion which itself can hardly be separated from the pleasure of recognizing the source in the novel from which the living picture has been created. The play then moves to its conclusion after the death of Steerforth and Ham as, in the distance, the 'Wreck breaks up and mast falls'. Uriah Heep is unmasked in Act IV Scene I while Scene II is wordless. The directions for Scene III then follow:

> Ship at Wharf. Discover on ship, Peggotty, Mrs Gummidge, Barkis, Martha, Emily grouped picturesquely. In a row-boat...Captain, Agnes, and a Boatman...Music 'Rule Britannia', 'Girl I Left Behind Me', etc. Ship is worked to R[ight]. Picture. All clear and wave hats and handkerchiefs.
>
> Curtain (slow).[28]

Although this may seem like a farrago of nonsense to the modern reader, it is by no means foreign to aspects of even the later novels as a passage from *Bleak House* makes clear:

> Mr George strides through the streets with a massive kind of swagger and a grave-enough face. It is eight o'clock now, and the day is fast drawing in. He stops hard by Waterloo Bridge, and reads a playbill; decides to go to Astley's Theatre. Being there, is much delighted with the horses and the feats of strength; looks at the weapons with a critical eye; disapproves of the combats, as giving evidences of unskilful swordsman-ship; but is touched home by the sentiments. In the last scene, when the Emperor of Tartary gets up into a cart and condescends to bless the united lovers by hovering over them with the Union-Jack, his eye-lashes are moistened with emotion.
>
> (Chapter 21)

Mr George is not free from faults, he broke his mother's heart by running away to be a soldier as a young man, but his willingness to be moved by this simple entertainment is as much a testimony to his fundamental goodness as is that hearty enjoyment of food which figures prominently in *Bleak House*.

We will not be surprised to learn that *Bleak House* itself was adapted in a version known as *Lady Dedlock's Secret*, first performed in Aberdeen in 1874, on which we have an exasperated comment by Dickens's son, Charley: 'It is, perhaps, excusable that Krook should have murdered Mr Tulkinghorn and have been denounced by Jo, who was a witness to the transaction, also that Jo should...describe Lady

Dedlock as...a servant though not with manners to conform. But the conclusion of the play in which Lady Dedlock (out of her mind) is escorted back to Chesney Wold by Jo, and has a regular conventional knockabout death scene, while Jo...does not die' clearly goes too far for Charley's filial piety.[29] Perhaps more interesting, though, is another facet of adaptation which has a bearing on our time, the composition, while the novel was still appearing in serial form, of a number of songs by C. W. Glover called *'Bleak House* Lyrics'! Although not positively identified, they were probably 'The Story of Esther Summerson', 'Farewell to the Old House', and 'Ada Clare' (Pilgrim VI, 715).

One of the truly engrossing aspects of the study of Dickens is the fact that these waves of adaptation have never really ceased, although they have ebbed and flowed to some extent, right up to the present day so that his work has continued to live in the English-speaking and European world in a number of different forms of which television serials are only the most obvious example. Three of the most striking are the brilliant musical show *Oliver!*; the two-part, six-hour adaptation by David Edgar for the Royal Shakespeare Company, *The Life and Adventures of Nicholas Nickleby*; and another two-part, six-hour effort, Christine Edzards's film of *Little Dorrit*.[30] Edgar's stage version has been given permanent form on video, but no one who saw this amazing event in the theatre is ever likely to forget it. The sense of audience and actors involved in a vast communal experience suffused with laughter, tears and a quite unsentimental social indignation was like, to paraphrase Dickens's words, *reading* the book in company, and audiences appear to have left the theatre with an overwhelming sense that Dickens was still vividly alive for the contemporary world, a making-over from one medium to another of which he would surely have approved. Interestingly, when the play's director Trevor Nunn visited the Gorky Theatre in what was then Leningrad, he discovered that the company was working on an adaptation of *Pickwick* and was told by the Artistic Director 'it was common to adapt Dickens for the stage in the USSR'.[31]

Despite the difficulties in attempting a purely mental recreation of the dramatic effect of the scripts of adaptations, it would be useful at this point to continue the story of Dickens's involvement with the theatre by looking at an example of his amateur productions. *The Frozen Deep*, ostensibly by Wilkie Collins, is a particularly good choice, occurring as it does at a time of crisis in Dickens's life and also precipitating an even more radical upheaval in his circumstances. In addition, examination of its genesis reveals the richness of context within which such productions took place. Dickens suggested that Wilkie Collins write a melodrama on a subject currently agitating the public and of great personal interest to Dickens himself, the disastrous Arctic expedition of Sir John Franklin which ended in death for all of its members and provoked rumours of cannibalism within the party. The play's action centres on a polar expedition during which the character played by Dickens, Richard Wardour, dies in rescuing his successful rival for the love of Clara Burnham who has rejected him; the climax is Wardour's death in Clara's arms, her unrestrained tears covering his face. The first performance took place on 6 January 1857 in a specially constructed theatre in the schoolroom of the Dickens home, Tavistock House, and was closely followed by a number of repeat performances.

The sense in which the whole effort should be seen as amateur is the first of a number of questions raised by *The Frozen Deep*: the scenery for two of the three acts was painted by a dear friend and distinguished artist, Clarkson Stanfield, who had begun his career as a theatrical scene painter; and the incidental music and overture were composed by a young professional musician, Francesco Berger. It was also professional in another way, through the efforts made by Dickens to ensure that this apparently domestic entertainment in a private house received what we would today call media exposure. The 'select audiences' for the play included important legal figures and the President of the Royal Academy but, apart from the world of 'the great and the good', Dickens 'intended that the performances and the audience's reaction should be publicized, for he invited professional reviewers and encouraged them to comment freely on anything they saw that might be of public interest'.[32] His reward, in general excitement and approbation, was very great. Reviewers hailed the production 'as the outstanding dramatic event of 1857';[33] Queen Victoria was anxious to see the play and so a private performance was arranged; and *The Illustrated London News* of 17 January contained an illustration of its third act. At the same time, the death of an old friend, Douglas Jerrold, prompted a number of benefit performances in public, culminating in three at the Manchester Free Trade Hall for audiences of over 2000 each evening, the whole enterprise raising the enormous sum of £2000 for the Jerrold family.

What specifically did Dickens contribute to this public event of which the *Saturday Review*, a periodical often mildly hostile to Dickens, remarked 'there was nothing to be seen at present on the English stage which equals the Frozen Deep'?[34] As so often in his career, innovation was the hallmark of his transformation of this essentially commonplace material:

all the reviewers...found the spectacle and acting unusually fresh and natural, in contrast to...the professional stage...Some reviewers thought that Dickens's acting...'might open a new era for the stage'. All of them...regarded him as an innovator...Dickens has deliberately sought the support of realistic spectacle...the principal 'natural' effect depended upon the scenery and lighting.[35]

In other words, it is possible to see this production as part of his campaign for an improved and more serious drama, an example in practice of what he might have attempted had he fulfilled his ambition of becoming the benign dictator of an English National Theatre. It is fascinating, in this context, to learn that some considered his acting as 'quiet, strong, natural, and effective. It appeals to the imagination of the audience...is free from exaggeration'.[36] In view of a later part of this study, it is worth noting that the production's lighting effects supervised, like everything else, by Dickens were praised as subtle and understated. It was this aspect of stage technique that Dickens himself singled out for commendation in describing a Parisian production of the opera *Faust* to the obviously knowledgeable Macready: 'Stage management remarkable for some admirable and really poetical, effects of light. In the more striking situations, Mephistopheles surrounded by an infernal red atmosphere of his own. Marguerite by a pale blue mournful light. The two never blending.' (Nonesuch III, 342–3) Such expressive uses of lighting are now more often seen in the cinema and the filmic analogy is particularly relevant in considering the relationship between the bare bones of the play's script and what it became in Dickens's realization of it:

it is little more than the skeleton of an unconventional melodrama. It makes the intense excitement of Dickens and the enthusiastic praise of admirers, including professional reviewers, Macready, and Queen Victoria seem incomprehensible. But the script is skeletal because it is little more than a scenario. From the beginning, 'The Frozen Deep' was planned as a peculiar kind of stage performance with the script to be merely an essential means for implementing this performance. The performance, not the script, excited Dickens and his audiences. All the reviewers knew that it was Dickens's synthesis of the various elements of the stage performance which made it seem so strikingly harmonious, novel, and powerful.[37]

But if Dickens put a great deal into the whole enterprise, he did undeniably also get a great deal out of it, perhaps in some ways more than he bargained for. The enormous size of the Free Trade Hall necessitated the use of professional actors, including Ellen Ternan whom Dickens came to love for the rest of his life and with whom he may well have had an affair. Although his marriage was already over in spirit if not in the separation that was soon to occur, this link between the theatre and the trauma of the 45-year-old upholder of domestic happiness entering a liaison with a woman of eighteen is a fascinating field for psycho-biographical speculation. In addition, it has been argued that the shattering experience of impersonating, in Wardour, a man denied the only love he ever desired who yet triumphs in a final sacrifice of the self, exorcised Dickens's inhibitions about representing human complexity in fictional terms and 'permitted the creation first of Carton and later of Pip and Eugene Wrayburn'.[38] An appropriate conclusion to this self-reflexive fusion of life and art might be a word concerning a play reportedly presented in Melbourne in 1895 called *Dickens: A Comedy*:

> Mr Garraway's play, it appears, was in one act...and set in one scene, which is behind the scenes, at the amateur performance given in Manchester Town Hall of Wilkie Collins' 'Frozen Deep', August 1857. In this remarkable concoction are introduced Mrs Cowden Clarke and Miss Ternan, who played in several pieces with Dickens....John Forster, Douglas Jerrold, Mark Lemon also appear.[39]

There truly is, it seems, nothing new under the sun as this anticipation of both Stoppard and post-modernism so clearly suggests.

This chapter has surveyed an area which binds Dickens's life and work in a seamless web. The novels themselves are characterized by the very fun which Dickens so much enjoyed in the popular theatre and entertainment of his own day. But there is nothing simplistic in this relationship. Just as Dickens subjected popular amusements to a searching enquiry as to their social meaning and moral purpose, without ever losing a sense of the pleasure they created, so the novels combine charm and sometimes almost violent high spirits, sunny geniality and dark obsessions. The relationship provides, in fact, one of the clearest examples of how Dickens was of his time, without being totally submerged within it. He saw the necessity of simple and, even, crude pleasures for those whose lives were marked by toil and deprivation, but he never slackened in his pursuit of a refinement of popular taste, a passionate quest to which his own novels stand as the ultimate testimony.

6

Dickens's Public: Adulation and Constraint

The subject of this chapter takes its starting point from Kathleen Tillotson's remark that 'with *Pickwick*, Dickens embarked upon his lifelong love-affair with his reading public; which, when all is said, is by far the most interesting love-affair of his life'.[1] A topic as rich as this will have to be broken down into its constituents, many of which are controversial, if it is to receive anything like satisfactory treatment. The size and nature of Dickens's audience, his roles as a public personality, the readings of his own work, all are parts of a complex of forces which make up a fascinating segment of Dickens's career. Description and analysis will again be brought to bear on these processes with the final aim of evaluating the balance of liberation and constraint involved in the adulation to which Dickens was subjected from the appearance of Sam Weller in the fourth number of *Pickwick Papers*.

The size and range of Dickens's audience is a question that has stimulated colourful anecdotes and much speculation, some of it wild, although we are fortunate that scholars such as Richard D. Altick have brought some order into this chaos. We have already encountered (in Chapter 2) the story of the illiterate old woman being read to in a little group of subscribers; rather higher in the social and educational scale is the following:

> The idle apprentice read from 'Pickwick', and soon the laughter became epidemic, with such an improvement in the rapidity of the work that the master appointed idle Tom to be reader in general, with the best success. Mr Chadwick told this fact to Dickens, assigning to Tom, the reader, the function, economically, of a fifer or drummer to animate, regulate, and quicken the march of production.[2]

There is something faintly sinister, perhaps, in the utilitarian role assigned to literature in this episode, although Dickens would no doubt have taken the pragmatic view that since the work had to be done it was better to encourage it with something of real value. Colourful anecdotes aside, the hard-headed can grapple with the mass of statistics dealing with sales figures although even these require careful assessment. Altick points out, for example, that in a *Household Words* article 'The Unknown Public', Wilkie Collins distinguished four publics for books:

> the religious public...the public which reads for information...the public which reads for amusement, and patronizes the circulating libraries and the railway bookstalls...[and] the public which reads nothing but newspapers.

Altick himself comments that all 'of these, except the last, had existed for centuries. The great difference was that all except the first were growing prodigiously'.[3] This growth meant that the probable potential reading public for a publisher in 1852 was between five and six million which makes a possible sale of something like half a million for *Dombey and Son* remarkable. On the other hand, these impressive figures are put into perspective by 'the amazing vogue of *Uncle Tom's Cabin*, the biggest sensation the English book trade had ever known'. The book was probably read by 'a million immediate buyers', although this figure was only achieved by stretching the potential book-buying public to its greatest limits. One interesting discrepancy in all of this is that between sales figures and those for readership. In the case of Dickens, for example, we can pose the question of how many individuals read a single monthly number of, say, *Dombey*, or were read to from it. In a pre-television age, reading aloud was a favourite domestic pastime in what were often large Victorian families, with a parent or, perhaps, an older child reading a serial part to a group which might even include servants. And it was clearly easier in every way to lend, borrow or otherwise circulate a pamphlet of 32 pages than a heavier, bulkier and more expensive book. Altick gets to the figure of half a million just referred to by relying on a rule of thumb that as many as fifteen people had access to each number, a fact of social life which enormously increased the reach of the sales of between thirty-two and thirty-four thousand achieved for each number after the second.[4]

What are perhaps just as interesting, and useful, in such a controversial area are subjective impressions, those of Dickens himself and of the public. Whatever the reality, which is now probably irrecoverable in strictly numerical terms, Dickens and his readers *felt* that his influence was immense, not merely in respect to a numerically large audience but across a wide range of social classes. Anecdotes can again be brought into play to illustrate the perceived depth and range of Dickens's fame. It is impossible not to quote in this context the much referred-to comments of the writer Mary Russell Mitford in a letter to a friend in Ireland:

> So you have never heard of the *Pickwick Papers!* Well, they publish a number once a month and print 25,000. The bookseller has made £10,000 by the speculation. It is fun – London life – but without anything unpleasant: a lady might read it all *aloud*; and it is so graphic, so individual, and so true, that you could courtsey to all the people as you met them in the streets. I did not think there had been a place where English is spoken to which 'Boz' had not penetrated. All the boys and girls talk his fun – the boys in the streets; and yet those who are of the highest taste like it the most. Sir Benjamin Brodie [a leading surgeon] takes it to read in his carriage, between patient and patient, and Lord Denman [the Lord Chief Justice] studies *Pickwick* on the bench while the jury are deliberating. Do take some means to borrow the *Pickwick Papers*. It seems like not having heard of Hogarth, whom he resembles greatly, except that he takes a far more cheerful view, a Shakespearian view, of humanity. It is rather fragmentary, except the trial which is as complete and perfect as any bit of comic writing in the English language. You must read the *Pickwick Papers*.[5]

The enthusiasm of this outburst is infectious although it is distinguished as much by intelligent criticism as warmth of feeling. But the contradiction it embodies is a familiar one from daily life, asserting as it does the 'universal' appeal of something to someone who has in fact never heard of it. It seems to this highly intelligent observer that everyone has read or, at the very least, heard of Boz to a degree that renders ignorance of him amazing. A similar point is made by responses to Dickens's death, one of which implies the universal esteem in which he was held by the poor. Dickens's son Henry recalled the report of a friend who was in a tobacconist's shop on the day of Dickens's death:

> Whilst there a working man came in for a screw of tobacco, and, as he threw his twopence on the counter, he said: 'Charles Dickens is dead. We have lost our best friend.'[6]

What we are involved in here is myth, personal as well as social, although myth rooted in a solid basis of fact. Dickens's sales and readership *were* very large throughout his career, and we have clear evidence that he was read across class barriers. The submerged and illiterate lumpen-proletariat, the class represented by Jo in *Bleak House*, could not have read Dickens, by definition, or have heard of him either. But from the respectable, literate working class up – those who could afford to buy a monthly number or an issue of *Household Words* and later *All the Year Round* or who had access to a public library – Dickens was read by and known to a large percentage of his fellow Victorians:

> He was to be seen, by those who knew him, everywhere – and who did not know him? Who had not heard him read, and who had not seen his photograph in the shop-windows? The omnibus-conductors knew him, the street boys knew him; and perhaps the locality where his recognition would have been less frequent ...was Pall Mall.[7]

This comment has its own biases, of course, in being both London-orientated and class conscious (Dickens did not frequent the haunts of the upper classes), but can still take its place in the mosaic which testifies to the mythic perception that Dickens was universally known and loved. That said, it remains the case that his core audience was middle-class-defined, given the Byzantine complexity of the British class system, as lower, middle and upper (excluding the aristocracy), a fact verified by the authority of Altick.[8] There were many reasons for this, some obvious and some less so. Clearly, the biggest segment of the reading public, if not of the population at large, was middle class. And it was from the lower reaches of the middle class that Dickens himself had emerged, deeply familiar with that world of shabby gentility which he reproduced apparently effortlessly in his writing from *Sketches by Boz* onwards. Relevant also is that note of hostility to Dickens sounded early on and which ebbed and flowed throughout his career as a counter-weight to the loving admiration he was generally accorded. This frequently centred, as we have seen, on the 'lowness' of serial publication which was often related to Dickens's social manner in ways that marked him as not a gentleman. Edward Eigner has interesting things to say on this as well as the personal need in Dickens which accounts for the importance to him of the myth of his huge and wide readership: 'No writer needed a relationship with his readers more desperately than Dickens did, and few people have ever valued friendship more highly. Nevertheless for him, novel writing was not a membership card to a gentleman's club', a suggestive comment which relates to what Eigner sees as the 'unthreatening writer of the realistic novel' and the fact that 'we are not in polite society when we read Dickens'.[9] If Dickens is, in some senses, a threatening writer of non-realistic fiction, then his need for the cushioning belief in his huge and adoring public becomes all the more understandable.

On the other hand, this myth seems to have been almost as important to the public itself, as though Dickens were necessary to its personal and social well-being. From this perspective, Dickens can be read as constructed out of a mass of needs, desires and aspirations, although it is easier to describe this construction than to account for it. A useful starting point is to grasp the sense in which Dickens can be seen as a media personality, one of the most famous, and one of the first, examples of a phenomenon with which we have become deeply familiar. In the nineteenth century, great singers were treated with a degree of public adulation afforded to film stars in the 1920s, 1930s and 1940s, the kind of widespread public hysteria most memorably generated in recent times perhaps by the Beatles, but before Dickens, 'no novelist, no writer, had ever achieved such national acclaim' (Ackroyd 835). This fame took a whole series of forms. One was recorded by his son Henry, towards the end of Dickens's life: 'To walk with him in the streets of London was in itself a revelation; a royal progress; people of all degrees and classes taking off their hats and greeting him as he passed.' This celebrity ranged from recognition by teenage girls ('Oh, mummy! mummy! it is Charles Dickens!')[10] through 'Forgery of my name is becoming popular' (Nonesuch III, 685) to responses to 'that earnest, animated, mobile, delightful face, that we all knew by heart through his ubiquitous photographs'.[11] Although many of Dickens's letters exult in his success in public speaking and at other glamorous occasions, the more human side of what public recognition meant to him is registered in a touching little encounter: 'I was brought very near what I sometimes dream may be my Fame, when a lady whose face I had never seen stopped me yesterday in the street, and said to me, *Mr Dickens, will you let me touch the hand that has filled my house with many friends*' (Nonesuch III, 52).

The roots of this public response can be traced in a number of ways. The excitement generated by the identity of 'Boz' was one factor, harking back to the stimulating mystery as to the authorship of the initially anonymous 'Waverley' novels (by Sir Walter Scott), an excitement increased when the extreme youth of the brilliant new author was revealed. Again, contemporary technological advances in engraving techniques and photographic reproduction allowed Dickens to be associated with his work in a peculiarly intimate way: 'The fact that Dickens was no longer advertised as Boz but actually had his portrait as the frontispiece to the volume publication of *Nickleby* gives some idea of how the cult of a Dickensian personality or sensibility had gone'.[12] The painting of Dickens by his friend Daniel Maclise in 1839 known as the Nickleby portrait was a potent, if minor, factor in generating this personality cult. It shows a beautiful young man, eyes beaming with ardent intensity and hair arranged in artistic locks, gazing at the world while his left hand holds down the paper on his desk to which he is obviously about to return to record his observations. Its combination of Romantic ardour and Victorian earnestness projects a perfect image of the Dickens many readers must have imagined on the basis of the early work and which Dickens himself might well have subscribed to. Dickens was also the recipient of a very modern form of communication between celebrities and their public, the fan mail made possible by the improvements introduced through the reform of the postal system: 'Dickens probably received more fan letters than did any other nineteenth-century writer, including Scott, Byron, and Tennyson, but he destroyed virtually all of them, and the only record we have is a second-hand one, in such few of his replies as have been preserved'.[13] And this manifestation of public interest received added impetus from its attempted intervention in his works' serial progress: 'I am inundated with imploring letters recommending poor little Nell to mercy. – Six yesterday, and four today (it's not yet 12 o'Clock) already!' (Pilgrim II, 153.)

It is probably reasonable to mark Dickens's major entry on to the public stage with the dinner held for him in Edinburgh in 1841. This signal honour for a man not yet thirty was promoted by most of the city's literary, professional and social establishment, and some measure of the occasion's importance can be taken if we remember that Edinburgh was still basking in the glow of its reputation as the 'Athens of the North', one of the leading capitals of European cultural life in other words. For Dickens 'It was the most brilliant affair you can conceive; the completest success possible, from first to last' (Forster I, 149). His pleasure must have been great even on the score of numbers alone since the event was attended by over 450 people, including 200 women who obeyed the current convention of not dining but entering the gallery to listen to the speeches. This public recognition was soon followed by Dickens's first trip to America in 1842 which was more or less what a contemporary said of the second expedition years later, a visit which 'could in no respect be considered a private event, but, from first to last, was regarded, and reasonably regarded, as a public and almost international occurrence'.[14] America carried Dickens's exposure to his audience several degrees beyond anything he had previously experienced, aided no doubt by the more democratic flavour of American social behaviour and the role of the popular press which was roughly equivalent to that of contemporary British tabloids. This attention reached a climax at the Boz Ball in New York in February 1842, the sheer scale of which still takes one's breath away. Three thousand were present and the handshaking with hundreds of guests was a particularly tiring aspect of the whole affair. The experience generated some of Dickens's most hilarious letters as well as the fantastic comedy of the American scenes of *Martin Chuzzlewit*, the former well represented in a letter to Maclise:

> Imagine Kate and I – a kind of Queen and Albert – holding a Levee every day (proclaimed and placarded in newspapers) and receiving all who choose to come. Imagine...how now and then a republican boy, of surpassing and indescribable free and easiness comes in among the company, and keeping cap on his head, inspects me at his leisure. We had one the other day who remained two hours, and took no other refreshment during the whole time than an occasional pick of his nose, or survey of the street from the open window, whence he invited other boys to come up, and do the like.
>
> (Pilgrim III, 154)

All this was great raw material for a comic novelist and the 'clutching eye' of one of English literature's sharpest social observers, but some of its more wearing effects are indicated in a letter to his oldest friend, Thomas Beard, apologizing for not having written sooner: '[I] have been...so beset, waylaid, hustled, set upon, beaten about, trampled down, mashed, bruised, and pounded by crowds, that I never...had less time for those confidential interviews with myself whereby I earn my bread, than in the United States of America'.[15] As so often in Dickens, in even the funniest or apparently most light-hearted outbursts, there is matter for speculation. He clearly senses here the danger that the very activity which has provoked the furore by which he is surrounded may be destroyed by the trivializing effects of public attention. Given the level of media attention to which contemporary celebrities are subjected it is hardly surprising that promising talents in many fields sometimes disappear in a welter of interviews, chat shows and Sunday supplement exposure. American interest in Dickens was unabated on his second visit only two years before his death: 'I have now read in New York city to 40,000 people, and am quite as well known in the streets there as I am in London. People will turn back, turn again and face me, and have a look at me, or will say to one another, "Look here! Dickens coming!"' (Forster II, 335). And the prying eyes of the press had lost none of their interest in irrelevant and contradictory detail:

> Every night I read I am described...from the sole of my boot to where the topmost hair of my head ought to be but is not. Sometimes I am described as 'evidently nervous'; sometimes it is really rather taken ill that 'Mr Dickens is so extraordinarily composed'. My eyes are blue, red, grey, white, green, brown, black, hazel, violet, and rainbow-coloured. I am like a 'well-to-do-American gentleman', and the Emperor of the French, with an occasional touch of the Emperor of China, and a deterioration from the attributes of our famous townsman, Rufus W.B.D. Dodge Gumsher Pickville.
>
> (Nonesuch III, 631)

How can we account for this extraordinary link between the individual and his public? At one level it can be seen as a fusion of needs between Dickens and his audience, although it is not easy to disentangle the threads which make up this complex pattern of emotional, social and technological elements. Contemporaries were themselves aware of something new in this rage for lectures, readings and large-scale public occasions which were such a feature of Victorian life. Philip Collins has pointed out 'a new cult of literary personality which made the public eager to see as well as to read their favourite authors. Thus, a newspaper noticing Dickens's first reading-tour, and alluding to his recent marital difficulties, saw the publicity about such episodes as a sign of the times.'[16] But seeing the chosen spirit was not enough, for 'nowadays the public must know all about your domestic relations, your personal appearance, your age, the number of your children, the colour of your eyes and hair – must peep into the arcana of your social existence'.[17] Such a hunger was fed, but also stimulated, by the increasing spread of visual representations of contemporary celebrities through engravings and especially the development of photography. One sign of the times in this area is the popularity of the *Illustrated London News* from 1842 on and the practice of using personal photographs as visiting cards. The spread of literacy, however slow, and reductions in the price of journals also made an increasingly large number of newspapers and periodicals available to a gradually widening public. We can see here the beginnings of that insatiable appetite for material which has climaxed, if only temporarily, in television's ruthless consumption of facts and opinions which have instantly to be replaced by others. Any medium of communication which appears on a regular basis is forced to fill itself with something. Newspapers cannot choose not to appear if there is no news; rather, it must somehow be discovered or manufactured in order to fill the vacuum. Something in the Victorian psyche seems to have demanded that at least part of this material should be concerned with the doings of the famous, and no single individual seems to have fulfilled this role more satisfyingly than Charles Dickens, for the American almost as much as the British public.

This study is not the place for a full-scale exploration of the depths of the Victorian unconscious, but we can catch a glimpse of it in a contemporary's account of the public dinner held in November 1867 to take farewell of Dickens before his second visit to America. The very holding of such events is itself of interest. Why did the Victorians feel the need to express emotion in such a publicly organized manner? The description of it may provide a clue:

> Most of the men who were carrying on the literary, dramatic, and artistic work of London were present...When Dickens arose he had to stand long while the shouts stormed upon him. Men leaped on chairs, tossed up napkins, waved glasses and decanters over their heads – and there was a pressing up from the lower tables until Dickens was girt about by a solid wall of friends. As he stood there silent I watched his face; it was flushed with excitement, and those wonderful eyes flamed around like a searchlight...Dickens tried to speak, but could not; the tears streamed down his face.[18]

It is hard not to feel an edge of hysteria in all this despite the positive aspects of its willingness to channel emotion through the explicit celebration of an individual by way of food, drink, speeches and a public avowal of feeling. The stresses of Victorian life need to be evoked here. Extremes of huge wealth and abject poverty, which for us belong to the Third World, were a constant affront to the sensitive and responsible. The struggle to maintain a position in a world of fierce competition with no safety net of welfare support for those who failed also needs to be remembered. And the conflict between the ideal of domestic married bliss and the realities of prostitution, pornography and child abuse, to name only a few aspects of the darker side of Victorian life, may well have been a source of strain for many. As so often we can see a link between Dickens and his public in taking his full share of all of these tensions, especially from the period when his marriage began to disintegrate.

Dickens and his audience were locked in a mutual embrace which stemmed initially from the fun and pathos created by a wonderful young man in a series of works which brought laughter and moral speculation into people's homes in an easily accessible form. The resolution of the social indignation of *A Christmas Carol* in the spirit of Christmas tightened the embrace and identified Dickens with the joy of an annual celebration, centred in the home, of which his own contribution of special Christmas books and numbers was an eagerly anticipated part. The impact of all these activities, plus the success of *Household Words* and *All the Year Round*, caused Dickens to take on the status of a national institution, but one in which laughter, tears, and anger at social abuses were personalized in a single individual. It needed only the public readings to bring about the final consummation of this extraordinary love affair.

The first hint of public readings as a possible extension of Dickens's professional activities is probably the mention of them in a letter to Forster as early as 1846, prompted no doubt by the successful reading of the second number of his current Christmas Book, *The Battle of Life*, to a group of friends. But it was not until 1853 that the idea bore fruit, even if in only a modified form. Dickens's passionate interest in education for the working and lower classes prompted an interest in the Birmingham and Midland Institute which culminated in his giving unpaid readings for its benefit on 27, 29 and 30 December in the Birmingham Town Hall. Inspired by his success, Dickens gave a number of charity readings between 1853 and 1858, most of which took place around Christmas and involved, with a single exception, a performance of *A Christmas Carol*, what the expert in the field, Philip Collins, calls 'the quintessential Dickens Reading' of what is 'one of the great popular classics of world literature'.[19] Having once embarked on this activity, Dickens found it hard to control: 'I cannot do what the Chester Institution want me to do, simply because I am asked to do the like some fifty times a week. Five such letters I have answered this morning, and many more in the course of this last week' (Pilgrim VII, 702). And the range, as well the scale of these demands, is suggested by the fact that in September 1855 he had 'answered in the last fortnight thirty applications to do the like all over England, Ireland, and Scotland. Fancy my having to come from Paris in December to do this, at Peterborough, Birmingham, and Sheffield – old promises' (Pilgrim VII, 701). It is, then, hardly surprising that the idea of reading for a fee germinated between 1853 and 1858. And this is reinforced by Dickens's negative response, in a letter of May 1854, to Forster's views on 'paid lecturing', which for him represented a loss of dignity both for Dickens as an individual and for the status of the profession which they both held so dear. Dickens believed that the lecturing would, in fact, 'tend the other way' (Nonesuch II, 557) and clearly returned to the attack in the months leading up to the first paid readings, asking Forster 'to think of this reading project...solely with a view to its effect on that particular relation (personally affectionate and like no other man's) which subsists between me and the public' (Nonesuch III, 15). The disagreement centred on the desirability of Dickens reading for money and it is hard not to see it as rooted in a class difference between Dickens and his friend which grew more acute as Forster hardened into a narrowing conception of respectability under the pressures of age, literary success and a financially advantageous marriage. It goes without saying that, Dickens having made up his mind, the project went ahead. In all, he gave some 400 paid readings, beginning with eighty-three on his first provincial tour which lasted from August to November 1853, the administrative arrangements being in the capable hands of his manager, Arthur Smith. The American tour lasted from December to April 1868 and Dickens gave a London farewell in January and March 1870 during which he read the *Carol* and the Trial from *Pickwick*. His total earnings from this hugely popular activity were in the region of £45 000, thus amounting to nearly half of the enormous sum he left in 1870, £93 000, which in contemporary terms means that Dickens died a millionaire.[20] Dickens's professionalism is everywhere evident in his approach to the readings. The materials were carefully selected and just as carefully prepared for their appearance in the new medium. Philip Collins interestingly points out how few of the readings actually came from the novels themselves:

> Of the twenty-one items that were prepared, only nine...came from the novels (and two of these were never performed); of the rest, four came from the Christmas Books and eight from the Christmas stories...Thus, of the six most frequently-performed items...two were from *Pickwick Papers* (*The Trial* and *Bob Sawyer*), one was the *Carol*, two were from the Christmas Stories (*Boots* and *Marigold*), and the other was *David Copperfield*.[21]

The clue to this selectivity is provided by another interesting fact, that one major deletion from the readings' sources were 'passages of social criticism', even to the extent of omitting the children named as Ignorance and Want from the *Carol*.[22] Dickens clearly had a conception of the readings as celebratory entertainments and so not the place for his darkly savage criticisms of social abuses. Equally professional was Dickens's determination to learn his readings by heart 'so as to have no mechanical drawback in looking after the words' (Nonesuch III, 527) and his willingness to rehearse some items over 200 times in the interests of the most perfect reading he could achieve.

As with any kind of development, Dickens's readings emerged from a context, a tradition even, but one modified by technology, social developments and his own specific input. Philip Collins has described a tradition of monologuists, of actors and elocutionists giving readings from Shakespeare and other writers, of authors as varied as Hazlitt and Coleridge beginning a tradition of public lectures in the Romantic period which was then carried on by Thackeray, Trollope and others (interestingly, Dickens always refused to lecture). The 1840s and 50s saw a big increase in this kind of activity, partly in response to the demands of new bodies such as Mechanics' Institutes and large venues such as town halls. Tours of the kind undertaken by Dickens were essentially a product of the railway age; such a punishing schedule organized around specific dates and times would not have been possible by stage-coach. But if we turn again from fact to perception, it is clear that for many contemporaries there was something essentially new in Dickens's enterprise: 'Mr Dickens has invented a new medium for amusing an English audience....This is a novelty in literature and in the annals of "entertainment"'.[23] In another summing-up of the readings, Philip Collins places his emphasis on the uniqueness of Dickens's achievement: 'It is part of his originality and quiddity to have invented this form of "publication", as, years earlier, he had virtually invented the serialisation of fiction'.[24] The suggestion that the readings were a form of publication is borne out by an excited letter to Forster towards the end of the first tour:

> The men with the reading books were sold out, for about the twentieth time, at Manchester. Eleven dozen of the Poor Traveller, Boots, and Gamp being sold in about ten minutes...and Manchester became green with the little tracts, in every bookshop, outside every omnibus, and passing along every street. The sale of them, apart from us must be very great....Did I tell you that the agents for our tickets who are also booksellers, say very generally that the readings decidedly increase the sale of the books that they are taken from?
>
> (Nonesuch III, 70)

The idea of public readings as a form of publication was reinforced by Dickens's address to the audience before his first professional reading: 'Thus it is that I come, quite naturally, to be among you at this time; and thus it is that I proceed to read this little book, quite as composedly as I might proceed to write it, or to publish it in any other way' (Ackroyd, 805). We know, in fact, that the reading books did not turn out to be as profitable as Dickens supposed as their price hardly covered their costs, but it is impossible to doubt that the readings did have the effect, as Dickens believed, of opening up 'a new public who were outside before' (Nonesuch III, 92). In other words, we can see here yet another precursor of our own time, the increase in sales and library borrowings that follows from the showing of a 'classic serial' on television. It is also worth noting that railway travel enabled this reaching out to a new audience to occur far outside the major urban centres: 'Little Darlington...covered itself with glory. All sorts of people came in from outlying places, and the town was drunk with the Carol far into the night' (Nonesuch III, 57-58).

Again, we need to ask what all this meant for Dickens and his audience. For the reader himself some of the answers seem clear enough:

> But I must say that the intelligence and warmth of the audiences are an immense sustainment, and one that always sets me up...the people lift me out of this [what Dickens called 'the downs'] directly; and I find that I have quite forgotten everything but them and the book, in a quarter of an hour.
>
> (Nonesuch III, 52)

The sources of this need to forget are various. The previous letter was written shortly after Dickens's separation from his wife, and his state of mind of only a few months before is recorded in a letter to Wilkie Collins:

> The domestic unhappiness remains so strong upon me that I can't write, and (waking) can't rest, one minute. I have never known a moment's peace or content, since the last night of The Frozen Deep. I do suppose there never was a man so seized and rended by one spirit. In this condition though nothing can alter or soften it, I have a turning notion that the mere physical effort and charge of the Readings would be good, and another means of bearing it.[25]

Almost as deep-seated is his savage dissatisfaction with the Condition-of-England as it has been called, only part of which was vented in the dark satirical comedy of *Little Dorrit*, whose serial

publication ceased in June 1857, an anger expressed in a brilliant series
of letters in 1855, one of the most scathing of which was addressed to
the politically radical actor, Macready:

> As to the suffrage, I have lost hope even in the Ballot. We appear
> to me to have proved the failure of Representative Institutions, with-
> out an educated and advanced people to support them. What with
> teaching people to 'keep in their stations' – what with bringing up
> the Soul and Body of the land to be a good child, or to go to the
> Beershop to go a-poaching and go to the Devil – what with having
> no such thing as a Middle Class (for, though we are perpetually
> bragging of it as our safety, it is nothing but a poor fringe on the
> mantle of the Upper) – what with flunkeyism, toadyism, letting the
> most contemptible Lords come in for all manner of places – mak-
> ing asses of ourselves for Prince Albert [Queen Victoria's husband]
> to saddle – reading the Court Circular for the New Testament – and
> bearing such positively awful slaver in the papers, as I saw the other
> day about a visit of Lord Palmerston's [the prime minister] to
> Woolwich arsenal – I do reluctantly believe that the English peo-
> ple are, habitually, consenting parties to the miserable imbecility
> into which we have fallen, *and never will help themselves out of it.* Who
> is to do it, if anybody is, God knows. But at present we are on the
> down-hill road to being conquered, and the people *will* be content
> to hear incapable and insolent Premiers sing Rule Britannia, and
> *will not* be saved.

> (Pilgrim VII, 715-6)

And under the private pain and the social rage lurked the psychic
wound of the blacking factory, for there is good reason to believe that
Dickens's childhood suffering, overlaid by the earlier years of fame
and success, resurfaced under the pressure of later troubles, thus following a well-recognised pattern in the reappearance of seemingly
buried traumas.

We can see from this why Dickens felt himself to be in the downs
and how the readings helped to lift him out of them, but what of his
audiences and their responses? Despite the foregoing emphasis on
the readings bringing him to a new public, it is also clear that many
came because they already knew and loved his work. Rather like fanatical audiences for Gilbert and Sullivan, Dickens's contemporaries often
knew in advance what he was about to read so that their smiles at the
imminent arrival of a comic passage 'simultaneously anticipated the
laughter which an instant afterwards greeted the words themselves

when they were articulated'.[26] For example, a much anticipated moment from the favourite reading, *A Christmas Carol*, was the reformed Scrooge's instructions to the boy in the street from his bedroom window concerning the purchase of the turkey for Bob Cratchit. In the words of one contemporary periodical, it was a 'famous moment: every word of it was watched for and listened to by audiences like celebrated passages from a great standard play'.[27] But beyond the sheer pleasure of what for most was an evening of magical entertainment, the experience often seemed to involve an ethical dimension for people who to some extent found themselves lost in the morally confusing world of mid-Victorian capitalism, the sense that 'audiences left the hall, after hearing the *Carol*, better moral beings; unlike the other Readings, there was about this one an element of a rite, a religious affirmation'.[28] That this moral effect was not accidental for Dickens is implied by his concern to reach the widest possible audience from a class point of view; hence his dislike of morning readings 'both as distasteful to me, and as not addressing my large miscellaneous following, which is limited to no class'; his point being of course that working people were necessarily prevented from attending morning sessions (Nonesuch III, 458). Dickens cared about this enough to be willing to make trouble about it, as he did in the case of his reading in 1855 at Folkestone, one of his favourite holiday spots and so a place where he was particularly well known:

> I am going to read here, next Friday week. There are (as there are everywhere) a Literary Institution and a Working Men's Institution, which have not the slightest sympathy or connexion. The stalls are five shillings, but I have made them fix the working men's admissions at threepence, and I hope it may bring them together.
>
> (Pilgrim VII, 707)

In passing, it is worth noting that Dickens was just as concerned to reach the poorer sections of the public through cheaper prices once he had become a professional reader.

One sign of the seriousness with which Dickens took this whole enterprise is his willing co-operation with Charles Kent in compiling the material which was published two years after his death as *Charles Dickens as a Reader*:

> Everything that I can let you have in aid of the proposed record (which, *of course*, would be far more agreeable to me if done by you than by any other hand) shall be at your service. Dolby [his manager after Arthur Smith's death] has all the figures relating to

America, and you shall have for reference the books from which I read.

(Nonesuch III, 768)

But as with so many of his activities Dickens's practical good sense and business acumen were brought to bear on a project motivated by some of the deepest strands of his personality. A glance at the biographies and his letters reveals the profound importance of friendship in Dickens's life and there is a sense in which this need for friendship extended to his feelings about the public which thronged to these events: '...everywhere I have found that peculiar personal relation between my audience and myself on which I counted most when I entered on this enterprise' (Nonesuch III, 253). But something more disturbing than friendship is indicated by an early comment on reading for charity: 'Ah! It is a brave thing, by Heaven it is, to walk out of the room where one is shut up for so many hours of such a short life, into a sea of agitated faces, and think they are always looking on' (Pilgrim IV, 61). His pleasure here is perfectly understandable at the common sense level as the escape from the loneliness of the writer's life into companionship on a large scale. But triumphalism is also signalled by the excited emphasis of the sentence's opening, and a sense of power being exerted through the ability to evoke agitation in a mass of humanity which can then be roused to laughter or calmed by pathos. This is similar to the power, acknowledged by a kind of guilty glee, which Dickens experienced in taking over the lives of Leigh Hunt and Walter Savage Landor for artistic transformation, into the characters of Harold Skimpole and Boythorn in *Bleak House*. And under this again is an almost primitive delight in striding from solitude into the glare of lights, faces and eyes, a being looked at with delight, admiration, love and laughter which can be related directly to perhaps the deepest trauma of Dickens's life. Readers of *Oliver Twist* are bound to notice how often eyes and being looked at figure in that novel. After his murder of Nancy, Bill Sikes is haunted by the image of her eyes in the moment of death and this motif is picked up by the eyes that for him stare accusingly on his mad wanderings through London, a nightmare which reaches its climax as he is remorselessly scrutinized by the crowds at his accidentally self-induced 'execution'. Fagin is subjected to the same horrific gaze during his trial when we are again persuaded by the power of Dickens's language that he is the sole object of interest to a thousand eyes.

One is bound to speculate on a possible source for this almost obsessive preoccupation with the look which permeates *Oliver Twist* and one might be found in the often-told but still fascinating episode of the young Charles in the shoe polish factory, Warren's Blacking. It was clearly important for Dickens to believe, what was probably true, that despite the misery of his position he was determined to do his work as well as possible. As the skill and speed with which he applied labels to the bottles of polish increased, he found himself an object of interest to passers-by in the street outside the window where he worked who lingered to look at his dexterity for a passing moment. It has been suggested that such public exposure was instrumental in his escape from Warren's, his father quarrelling with the manager over his son's being seen in this way. True or not, this facet of the story is suggestive enough with its implication that John Dickens did not mind the son of a 'gentleman' doing the work as long as he was kept from the vulgar gaze. But it is hard not to believe that the experience was a deeply painful one for a boy brought up in lower middle class comfort whose childish talents had been appreciated and who seemed destined to be educated for some modestly respectable profession. The humiliation of being gazed at in such a context is obvious and we have the evidence of David Copperfield that his boyish mind was troubled by thinking of the reactions which would have been provoked in his new schoolfellows if they had known of David's earlier life in London, one remarkably similar to that of Dickens himself, of course. There is no evidence that Dickens harped on what he saw as his degradation every moment of the day, certainly in the early years of his first success, but there is ample reason to believe that he never forgot it either. The fierce indignation evoked by the plight of abandoned and abused children in the novels shows clearly enough how frequently Dickens translated his own experience into fiction. The self-transformation of this lonely and rejected boy into the triumphantly successful man of the world could not, however, fully heal such a painful early wound and so it does not seem far-fetched to see the public readings, even more than the theatricals, as the expression of a burning desire to be gazed at in a way at the furthest possible remove from the curiosity of idlers outside Warren's. In the theatricals Dickens was acting a role, but in the readings he could be seen and adored for himself, the almost overpoweringly charismatic embodiment of one of the greatest success stories of the nineteenth century. That there was something insatiable in this desire is demonstrated, comically, by the letters Dickens writes on his tours in which however earth-shatteringly responsive one audience is, it is bound to be outdone by the next and so on. At least part of the complexity of what the whole reading experience meant for Dickens – fun, companionship, money, professional skill, an escape from home, power over crowds of people, the satisfaction of a deep psychic need – is hinted at in a letter describing his reception in Paris in 1863:

> It is really the general Parisian impression that such a hit was never made here. The curiosity and interest and general buzz about it are quite indescribable. They are so extraordinarily quick to understand a face and gesture, going together, that one of the remarkable points is, that people who don't understand English, positively understand the Readings! I suppose that such an audience for a piece of Art is not to be found in the world....You have no idea what they made of me. I got things out of the old Carol – effects I mean – so entirely new and so very strong, that I quite amazed myself and wondered where I was going next. I really listened to Mr Peggoty's narrative in Copperfield, with admiration.
>
> (Nonesuch III, 340)

The public readings do, then, provide yet another example of the symbiotic relationship between Dickens and his audience, a fulfilment of needs which lay deep in his psyche as an individual and in his audience as a group. Adulation is evident enough in all this, but how far did this loving admiration act as a constraint on Dickens as a man and a writer? How far was Dickens's work, journalistic as well as fictional, affected by his sense of the size and importance of his public? As we would expect, the answers to such complex questions are bound to be mixed. A long letter to Forster of 1856 shows the extent to which Dickens had thought seriously about problems of art, morality and public opinion:

> I have always a fine feeling for the honest state into which we have got, when some smooth gentleman says to me or to some one else when I am by, how odd it is that the hero of an English book is always uninteresting – too good – not natural, etc. I am continually hearing this of Scott from English people here [on holiday in Boulogne] who pass their lives with Balzac and Sand. But O my smooth friend, what a shining imposter you must think yourself and what an ass you must think me, when you suppose that by putting a brazen face upon it you can blot out of knowledge the fact that this same unnatural young gentleman (if to be decent is to be necessarily unnatural), whom you meet in those other books and in mine, *must be* presented to you in that unnatural aspect by

reason of your morality, and is not to have, I will not say any of the indecencies you like, but not even any of the experiences, trials, perplexities, and confusions inseparable from the making and unmaking of all men!

(Nonesuch II, 797)

This is remarkably similar to a passage in which Thackeray complains that public opinion will not allow writers to present the fictional development of a young man in the way open to eighteenth century novelists such as Fielding. However, it is often suggested that although this limitation was damaging to Thackeray it was not to Dickens because he was so much in tune with his public that he felt no strain in avoiding difficult or dangerous areas of human experience. But the letter just quoted suggests that Dickens too felt hampered by the prohibitions of a public opinion which in some crucial ways was hypocritical. A full-scale treatment of the topic in Dickens's life and art lies outside the scope of this study, but his attitude to sexuality was clearly marked by the opposing tendencies which are such a strongly marked feature of his personality. The 'attraction of repulsion' came into play in his reforming interest in prostitution and enjoyment of the more raffish forms of entertainment in the company of the younger and sexually highly active Wilkie Collins. But apart from his relationship with Ellen Ternan, which whatever its precise nature was clearly stable and enduring, there is absolutely no evidence that Dickens indulged in casual sexual encounters despite the evident susceptibility shown in his intense friendships with a number of interesting and lively women throughout his life. In this sense, the sexually restrained lives of his young men are in keeping with his own experience rather than forced upon him by an externally imposed morality, although it is quite clear that Steerforth in *David Copperfield* has seduced Rosa Dartle as well as Emily and generally leads the life of a dissolute young man about town. A major thread in the last completed novel, *Our Mutual Friend,* is the determined attempt at seduction of the lower-class Lizzie Hexam by the gentleman Eugene Wrayburn, too complex a character to be described as either the hero or the villain of the piece.

We have seen that for Dickens his periodicals were, amongst other things, valuable commercial properties and he was therefore keenly alive to anything in their contents that might be damaging to sales. He worried, for example, about an article by Collins on schools and asked Wills 'not to leave anything in it that may be sweeping and unnecessarily offensive to the middle class. He has always a tendency to overdo that...Don't be afraid of the Truth, in the least; but don't be unjust' (Nonesuch III, 58). Dickens clearly always desired to take his audience with him in any medium in which he worked. To drive it away through excess was not merely bad business; it also meant that his influence for social and moral change was nullified. But the truth was a guiding principle and in its service Dickens was prepared to challenge his audience in ways that he clearly hoped would expand its limitations and modify its prejudices. Nowhere was this clearer than in his rejection of its chauvinist tendencies. Dickens adored Italy and France, lived abroad for significant periods of his life, and attained proficiency in Italian and French. He never wearied of rejecting Victorian misconceptions, of France especially, in life, in the journalism and in novels such as *Little Dorrit*. He writes to Wills, for example, of a projected article for *All the Year Round* centring on a Londoner 'having – say seven – quiet visitors from the country (Rule Britannic Britons every one of them, regarding other Empires and States as in mere outer darkness); and giving the particulars of their all being knocked down, garotted, choked, robbed, and half-murdered in one day'; that is, by their fellow countrymen and not the villainous foreigner (Nonesuch I, 321–2).

In trying to reach some conclusions on the adulation and constraint involved in Dickens's relationship with his audience it is helpful to return to Kathleen Tillotson's description of it as a love affair. The phrase is a particularly happy one in a number of ways. A love affair is not, of course, a marriage and settled domesticity is hardly a satisfactory way of indicating the ferment in which Dickens remained throughout his career *vis-à-vis* his public. On the other hand, it is hard to see what consummation could have meant in such a situation. Dickens went to his grave in some ways an unhappy and unfulfilled man, although it is a mistake to paint his later years in completely gloomy colours. His wonderful letters alone are enough to suggest how vivid his life remained, to himself as well as to others, until the very end. No one could have enjoyed life more or entered more fully into its pleasures, simple and complex. He seems never fully to have lost a sense of fun and an extraordinary vivacity, and he always retained his joy in the creative process itself and his deep sense of responsibility towards it. One aspect of this positive side of his nature is an almost lover-like anticipation of and delight in his audience, whether through the fiction and journalism, the theatricals and public readings, the speeches and the recognition by strangers in the street.

A lesser man might have been hopelessly spoilt by all this, but Dickens had the knack of swimming in public adulation rather than drowning in it. Graham Greene has pointed out that the huge success of *Pickwick* might have impelled another writer to endless repetitions of this initial triumph.[29] Indeed, there were calls throughout his career for a return to the apparently uncomplicated fun of Sam and Mr Pickwick, especially in the face of the social and moral indignation of the so-called 'dark' novels. Making Greene's point, Dickens followed *Pickwick* with *Oliver Twist*, almost as different a novel from its predecessor as could be imagined. In addition, his personal life was marked by a kind of modesty. He was noted as a good listener, interested in drawing others out, and he hardly ever played the great man or traded on his reputation out of vanity. Once again we are confronted by dualities: exuberance and reserve, wild enjoyment and a commitment to earnestness as a guiding principle, full awareness of his greatness and pleasure in the talents of others. He may eagerly have adopted the title conferred on him by his schoolmaster, the Inimitable, and signed himself in a variety of extravagant ways (as the Sparkler of Albion, for example), but without negative role-playing he seems both to have been 'our illustrious countryman' (Pilgrim VII, 452) and the quietly amused observer of this grandiose figure, a duality related to his delight in assuming a role in acting: 'Assumption has charms for me – I hardly know for how many wild reasons – so delightful, that I feel a loss of O I can't say what exquisite foolery, when I lose a chance of being some one, in voice etc not at all like myself' (Pilgrim VI, 257).

Perhaps a last word can be drawn from this complex and contradictory subject. A contemporary has described the extraordinary sight of the Strand in London on the publication day of a monthly serial. It is hard to believe that any other writer in English literature has been loved in quite this way and the effects of Dickens knowing that his work was so eagerly anticipated and so voraciously seized on are worth pondering. In all the welter of possible responses, one clue is provided by a highly authoritative source, Richard D. Altick, when he remarks that 'Dickens's true complexity, to say nothing of his subtleties, seems to have gone largely unnoticed in his own time.'[30] In other words, Dickens's originality and the precise forms in which it was embodied were hardly recognized by his contemporaries, a neglect all the more striking given Dickens's stress on 'making it new' (in Ezra Pound's phrase) from almost the earliest novels. He thought, for example, that 'Mrs Nickleby's love scene will come out rather unique'

(Pilgrim I, 527) and remarked, famously, of the relationship between his own life and David Copperfield: 'I really think I have done it ingeniously, and with a very complicated interweaving of truth and fiction' (Pilgrim V, 569). Dickens hoped that 'the general idea of *Dombey* is interesting and new' (Pilgrim IV, 586). And, like Yeats, he was stirred by 'the fascination of what's difficult' as Butt and Tillotson suggest:

> The conclusion of *Great Expectations* was straightforward by comparison [with the resolution of *Little Dorrit*] though 'the general turn and tone of the working out and winding up, will be away from all such things as they conventionally go,' and 'the planning out from week to week ' was declared to be unimaginably difficult.'[31]

Conclusive proof that Dickens thought seriously about his original approach to fiction is contained in a letter to Forster on the presentation of Miss Wade in *Little Dorrit*:

> I don't see the practicability of making the History of a Self-Tormenter, with which I took great pains, a written narrative. I do see the possibility...of making it a chapter by itself, which might enable me to dispense with the necessity of the turned commas. Do you think that would be better? I have no doubt that a great part of Fielding's reason for the introduced story, and Smollett's also, was, that it is sometimes really impossible to present, in a full book, the idea it contains (which yet it may be on all accounts desirable to present), without supposing the reader to be possessed of almost as much romantic allowance as would put him on a level with the writer. In Miss Wade I had an idea, which I thought a new one, of making the introduced story so fit into surroundings impossible of separation from the main story, as to make the blood of the book circulate through both. But I can only suppose from what you say that I have not exactly succeeded in this.

(Forster II, 184–5)

Despite the support provided by unflagging sales figures there is something heroic in Dickens's willingness to trust his own originality in the face of incomprehension and, on occasion, hostility. In referring to the 'indifferent reception' accorded *A Tale of Two Cities*, Philip Collins points out that its 'predecessor, *Little Dorrit*, was widely regarded as a failure...and *Hard Times*, just before that, had excited little enthusiasm'. His conclusion is that by 1859 'many critics had written Dickens off, as having entered a gloomy dotage'.[32] What forces drove and enabled Dickens in this pursuit of the highest levels of an

artistic excellence which he was aware would not be fully appreciated? One motive was sheer delight in the task in and for itself, as a letter on *A Tale of Two Cities* makes clear:

> Nothing but the interest of the subject, and the pleasure of striving
> with the difficulty of the form of treatment – nothing in the mere
> way of money, I mean – could else repay the time and trouble of
> the incessant condensation. [Of weekly serialization.]
>
>   (Forster II 281)

But this personal dedication was reinforced by the confidence inseparable from the knowledge that a huge audience looked forward to,
and read, his work in undiminished numbers and with endlessly recur-
ring delight. Mention has already been made of the dissatisfaction felt
at what many now consider Dickens's most mature work because of
its differences from *Pickwick* and *Nickleby*. Critics and reviewers were
not slow to make invidious comparisons between Dickens and rivals
such as Thackeray and George Eliot when they began to share a stage
that had been occupied almost exclusively by Dickens in the early
stages of his career. But the fact remains that the hold on the public
mind described in this chapter hardly faltered throughout Dickens's
career and the sales of his fiction continued unabated so that he could
say of the first serial number of his eleventh novel, '*Little Dorrit* has
beaten even *Bleak House* out of the field. It is a most tremendous start,
and I am overjoyed at it' (Pilgrim VII, 759). We can only speculate as
to what it must have meant for a writer embarking on the creation of
one of the greatest, and most experimental, works in European and
American fiction to know that his efforts were supported by a public
eager to give him financial and moral support by purchasing his work
in such numbers. What the evidence of the novel itself suggests is that
Dickens was inspired by this almost unconditional approval to the creation of daring formal effects, but that his originality was tempered
by a concern that the adulation bestowed on him should be returned
in the shape of a work which could accommodate its originality to the
demands of entertainment.

If, then, Dickens's lifelong love affair with his public was uncon-
summated in one sense, in another it bore fruit through the trust which
enabled him to satisfy his own complex artistic ambitions and the
needs of his audience in a single work.

7

Dickens and Social Institutions

The subject of this book is the description and analysis of those aspects of Dickens's working life which have a direct bearing on his professional career. It is not intended to be either a conventional biography or literary criticism; it is difficult, however, to make a rigid separation between these genres and the work in hand, and in this case perhaps not even desirable. Dickens's personal involvement with the social world of his own time is one of the most fascinating aspects of his life and the transformation of this material into the social panoramas of the novels is a touchstone of his artistic process. The point is well made by one of his young male collaborators on *All the Year Round*, Percy Fitzgerald, when he remarks that attacks on social abuses:

> supplied him with a certain dramatic stimulus or motive-power. Once started, and furnished with something *real* or living to work on, his imagination kindled; fancies rushed upon him, and he put the topic in all sorts of forms. It supplied him with characters and situations.[1]

Dickens's powers of observation were extraordinary, but so also was his willingness to be stimulated by sensory impressions as an exclamation from the *Sketches* shows: 'What inexhaustible food for speculation do the streets of London afford!'[2] That Dickens was fully aware of this aspect of his personality is shown by a letter from as early as 1838 and another from 1843. Replying to a correspondent who asked for some biographical details, he replied:

> As to my means of observation, they have been pretty extensive. I have been abroad in the world from a mere child, and have lived in London and travelled by fits and starts through a great part of England, and a little of Scotland, and less of France, my eyes open.
> (Pilgrim I, 424)

He clearly saw foreign travel as something more than an opportunity for a holiday: 'If I had made money, I should unquestionably fade away from the public eye for a year, and enlarge my stock of description and observation by seeing countries new to me.' (Pilgrim III, 587.) What did being 'abroad in the world' mean for Dickens? It meant, for a start, being a semi-abandoned child in the streets of London, a little wanderer between his lonely lodgings and his workplace with visits to the Marshalsea Prison on Sundays to be with his family. Dickens met with real kindness on this odyssey, both at work and in the streets, but he could just as easily have met the worst kinds of abuse and he undoubtedly saw the horrific poverty and vice of the streets of London in addition to all their fun, bustle and wealth. An incident from *David Copperfield*, David's meeting with a tinker and his woman on the way to Betsey Trotwood's, comes unforgettably to mind with all the force of a remembered reality; the tinker accuses David of 'wearing my brother's silk handkercher' and seizing it from him throws it to the woman:

> The woman burst into a fit of laughter, as if she thought this a joke, and tossed it back to me, nodded once, as slightly as before, and made the word 'Go!' with her lips. Before I could obey, however, the tinker seized the handkerchief out of my hand with a roughness that threw me away like a feather, and putting it loosely round his own neck, turned upon the woman with an oath, and knocked her down. I never shall forget seeing her fall backward on the hard road, and lie there with her bonnet tumbled off, and her hair all whitened in the dust; nor, when I looked back from a distance, seeing her sitting on the pathway, which was a bank by the roadside, wiping the blood from her face with the corner of her shawl, while he went on ahead.

(Chapter 13)

There was nothing in the least sheltered about this phase of Dickens's development, although it was followed by less threatening opportunities for social experience.

After his fairly brief period as a solicitor's clerk, Dickens became a freelance shorthand reporter in 1828, aged sixteen. His work for the bizarre legal institution known as Doctors' Commons brought him into close contact with some of the eccentric vagaries of the English legal system, an exposure to what he regarded as expensive nonsense which became a permanent fixture in his personal and novelistic vision of the world. More broadly based experience was the fruit of Dickens's time as a reporter on a number of newspapers, which involved travelling to many different parts of the country, mainly reporting parliamentary elections and related political activity. Dickens is so often, and rightly, seen as the chronicler of urban life, that it is salutary to be reminded of his vivid observation of small town and rural existence. This can be enjoyed in a number of ways, but one of the most interesting, and hilarious, is the speech he made to the dinner of the Commercial Travellers' Schools in December 1854. This is too long to quote in any detail, but some idea of the flavour of this wonderful evocation of the contrast between travelling in the past and present may be gained from the following:

> I dare say most of us remember certain modest post-chaises dragging us down interminable roads through slush and mud, to little country towns with no visible populations except half a dozen men in smock frocks smoking pipes under the lee of the Town Hall; half a dozen women with umbrellas and pattens, and a washed-out dog or so shivering under the gables to complete the desolate picture. We can all discourse, I dare say, if so minded upon our recollections of the 'Talbot', the 'King's Head', or the 'Lion' of those days. We have all been in that room on the ground floor on one side of the old inn yard, not quite free from a certain fragrant smell of tobacco, where the cruets on the sideboard were usually absorbed by the skirts of the box coats that hung from the wall...With the travelling characteristics of later times we are all, no doubt, equally familiar. We know all about that station of which we have a clear idea although we were never there; we know that if we arrive after dark we are certain to find it half a mile from the town, where the old road is sure to have been abolished, and the new road is going to be made, where the old neighbourhood has been tumbled down, and the new one not half built up.

> (Speeches 172–3)

If Dickens never forgot the impression made on him by his early acquaintance with the legal profession, the impact made by his period as a parliamentary reporter was just as strong, coinciding as it did 'with the years of the most intense political excitement for the nineteenth century'.[3] Although Dickens reported such major pieces of legislation as the First Reform Bill, he never weakened in his estimate of the House of Commons as a collection of windbags, reducing his son Henry to helpless laughter late in life by dictating mock parliamentary speeches to help him practise his shorthand. Dickens was approached on several occasions to stand as a Member of Parliament but always declined, partly on grounds of expense since members were not then paid, but also because he had no confidence in his ability to play a useful role in what he regarded as a totally useless body. On the other hand, Dickens did not so easily surrender the desire to occupy an official position of the kind expressed in a letter of 1846:

> I have an ambition for some public employment – some Commissionership or Inspectorship, or the like, connected with those subjects in which I take a deep interest...the Education of the People...the treatment of Criminals...I have hoped, for years, that I may become at least a Police Magistrate.
>
> (Pilgrim IV, 566–7)

Dickens gradually abandoned the idea as his ever-increasing fame began to put him on a secure financial footing, an end he was unswervingly determined to achieve. From the middle years of his career onwards, however, Dickens saw his social role and influence as stemming from his position as a professional writer, although he still found time for a huge range of contacts and activities.

Dickens might well be regarded as one of the first exponents of 'networking', an idea justified by his claim to Miss Coutts: 'I know everybody at Manchester, and in most of those places' (Pilgrim VI, 645.) His ability to move freely in society was helped by the fact that by the standards of his time Dickens lived an unconventional social life, ignoring the formal rules governing the etiquette of Victorian invitations:

> We are very homely and unceremonious people, and Mrs Dickens labours under some apprehension that there should have been previous callings and interchanges of formality. I have undertaken, however, to dispense with any such preliminaries, trust that as we (i.e. you and I) understand each other moderately well, Mrs Blanchard and Mrs Dickens may arrive at a similar interchange of friendliness without first playing at company.
>
> (Pilgrim I, 478)

Ignoring the to and fro of visiting cards hinted at here probably left him all the more time for a social activity he loved, dining with interesting and influential people, contacts which bore fruit in the fiction, the journalism and in his practical work as a philanthropist, above all in acting as unofficial agent for the immensely wealthy Angela Burdett Coutts. Dickens's letters are studded with innumerable asides such as 'I am engaged to dine with Brunel' (Pilgrim VI, 411), the great builder of railways, steamships and bridges. It is impossible to follow the ramifications of all these contacts, but a single example may do something to suggest how deeply Dickens's life was interwoven with some of the dominant intellectual and practical forces of his time. In 1851 he informed a close friend, Mark Lemon the editor of *Punch*, that he had 'to meet Chadwick at the Labourers Model cottages by the Exposition at 11' (Pilgrim VI, 402). The editors of the great Pilgrim Edition of Dickens's letters explain that these cottages were '"Model Houses for Families" erected, at his own expense, for the Great Exhibition, by Prince Albert...instigated by the Society for Improving the Condition of the Labouring Classes' (Pilgrim VI, n. 3 402). Chadwick was Sir Edwin Chadwick, one of the greatest of Victorian social reformers and author, in 1842, of *The Sanitary Conditions of the Labouring Population* which, despite its off-putting title, is a riveting account of the living conditions endured by masses of the poor. Chadwick was for many years an assistant to Jeremy Bentham, the founder of Utilitarianism, perhaps the most important philosophical system of the period and a key foundation of nineteenth-century reforms of the criminal law, judicial organization and the parliamentary electorate, much of which was implemented by Bentham's disciples. Chadwick was largely responsible for the passage of the Public Health Act of 1848 which established the General Board of Health of which Dickens's brother-in-law, Henry Austen, became secretary in 1850. Giving in to vested interests, Parliament omitted London from the firm control of abuses exerted by the General Board and, an act which only reinforced Dickens's contempt, left the capital city to the mercies of the ineffectual Metropolitan Board. As Philip Collins points out, in his capacity as secretary Henry Austen was 'able to keep Dickens in touch with official developments, send him the latest reports, and advise him about the numerous articles on the sanitary question written for *Household Words*'.[4] He was bitterly opposed to another of Chadwick's contributions, the New Poor Law, but Dickens's political acumen ensured that they did not fall out: '[He] is the head and front of this matter in England [the New Poor Law]...with whom my differences of opinion are no cause of division between us, as he has done, unquestionably, much good for the people' (Pilgrim VII, 849). Dickens co-operated with Chadwick, and a wide range of like-minded people, in an unceasing and sometimes savage campaign to improve the sanitary condition of London and the country as a whole, using his periodicals as a major channel of communication to a large public. The nature of this help is indicated by his offer to the radical member of Parliament, A. H. Layard: 'If you ever see any new loophole, cranny, needle's-eye, through which I can present your case in Household Words, I do most earnestly entreat you...to count upon my being Damascus Steel to the core.' (Pilgrim VII, 582) In addition to his own aid, Dickens 'recruited Mark Lemon (of *Punch*), Shirley Brooks (*Illustrated London News* and the *Weekly Chronicle*), Douglas Jerrold (*Lloyd's Weekly News*), and undertook to speak "carefully" to Forster (of the *Examiner*)' (Speeches, 191). These passionate convictions also found expression in brilliant public speeches and in the novels, from the hideous graveyard in *Bleak House* in which Nemo is buried and beside which Lady Dedlock dies, to the dust heaps of *Our Mutual Friend*.

Dickens's life and interests make up such a complex pattern that it is difficult to disentangle a single thread and separate it out from the others with which it is interwoven. It is clear, for example, that his hatred of legal mumbo-jumbo and parliamentary do-nothingism is permeated by a strong vein of class-consciousness. A few of his best friends may have been upper class, but Dickens had a deep suspicion bordering on contempt for what he persistently referred to, in his 'vulgar' way, as the nobs, an attitude that persisted throughout his life and which he expressed ironically in the 'high principle' of Montague Tigg in *Martin Chuzzlewit*, that 'Nature's Nobs felt with Nature's Nobs...all the world over'(Chapter 7). Given the true principles of the appalling Tigg it is clear that Society's Nobs are every bit as suspect as Nature's in Dickens's eyes. In 1836, aged twenty-four, we find him delighting in a modest financial 'scam' at their expense occasioned by his having been asked to write 'a series of small sketches' for the upper-class *Carlton Chronicle*: 'The circulation I believe is a small one. So much the better – Fewer people will see the Sketches before they are collected. It is all among the nobs too – Better still. They'll buy the book.' (Pilgrim I, 160) This dislike found expression in numerous ways. For example, he loathed the annuals which appeared every Christmas because of the snob-appeal generated by their reliance on material from titled contributors and always declined to write for them, even for the superior example edited by his friend, the notorious Countess of Blessington. His rage against items such as *Portraits of the Nobility* which appeared between 1838 and 1841, and consisted of a series of engravings accompanied by verses, is barely containable:

> These books are the gall and bitterness of my life. I vow to God they make me wretched, and taint the freshness of every new year...What

do you think of a book in serious earnest – a true, sledgehammer book – about the children of the people; as much beaten out of Nature by iron necessity as the children of the nobility, by luxury and pride? It would be a good thing to have the two extremes – Fairlie and Fielding – Hogarth and Chalon – the Princess Royal whom the nurse daren't kiss – and the baby on the step whose mother tried to strangle it...[In] different towns in England, and...in London whenever I walk alone into its byeways at night...such miseries and horrors among these little creatures – such an impossibility of their ever growing up to be good or happy – that these aristocratic dolls do turn me sick. I know only one good these books are likely to achieve. If I were a poor labouring man and saw them in the shop windows as I went slouching home, I should think of my own children and the no-regard they had from anybody, and be a greater Radical than ever. I hope they may be productive of some advantage that way.

(Pilgrim II, 201)

This outburst may have been playing up to some extent to the radicalism of its recipient, Mrs Gore, but that these feelings related to matters of general principle is demonstrated by his reluctance to own land, the traditional source of aristocratic wealth:

I could purchase the piece of ground without interference, and have the money in the funds. But I don't care to have land, because I don't understand it, and because that sort of proprietorship is not in my way, and seems to me to put a public man of my notoriety – with a good-natured reputation – at a disadvantage with tenants.

(Nonesuch III, 299)

There is a principled resistance to the dominant codes of his society at work here akin to his unwillingness to make his servants wear livery, rather than their own clothes: 'I hope you are not surprised; I do not consider that I own enough of any man to hang a badge upon.'[5] A similar spirit can be observed in the domestic arrangements of his various households as recorded by a guest:

A peculiarity of the household was the fact that, except at table, no servant was ever seen about. This was because the requirements of life were always ready to hand, especially in the bed-rooms [including tea-things]...so that [it] was always attainable without even the trouble of asking for it.[6]

Or, one might add, causing the servants to make and bring it.

Another passionately embraced resistance was to patronage of the working classes and any inclination to treat them with a disrespect which slighted their individual dignity. The roots of this attitude undoubtedly lie in what can only be called Dickens's love for the poor:

> what the working people have found me towards them in my books, I am throughout my life...whenever I have tried to hold up to admiration their fortitude, patience, gentleness, the reasonableness of their nature, so accessible to persuasion, and their extraordinary goodness one towards another, I have done so because I have first genuinely felt that admiration myself, and have been thoroughly imbued with the sentiment which I sought to communicate to others.
>
> (*Speeches*, 155)

This emotion crystallized into a principle at least as early as 1836 in the pamphlet *Sunday Under Three Heads*, a brilliant rejection of an attempt to legislate for Sunday closing whose major effect would have been to cause suffering and deprivation to the poor. However, a note of tiredness often creeps into Dickens's later writings on the issues that enraged him, a near despair stemming from the fact that most of the causes he championed remained essentially unaltered at his death. *The Uncommercial Traveller's* praise of a new dining establishment for working people, for example, is qualified by its refusal to sell beer which Dickens sees as an insult to the working man:

> [It] is to suppose that he is a baby, and is again to tell him in the old wearisome condescending patronising way that he must be goody-poody, and do as he is toldy-poldy, and not be a manny-panny or a voter-poter, but fold his handy-pandys, and be a childy-pildy.[7]

Dickens's consistency in this area is revealed by his untiring insistence that working people should, as far as possible, take responsibility for their own lives. He was perfectly willing to criticize them whenever he thought they were failing in this duty as he does in relation to the Mechanics Institutions that were springing up in the Victorian period:

> They have fallen into an accursed habit of looking round for external patronage – of abandoning the self reliance which should be a main part of their existence – and lashing themselves into frothy speech-makings under the presidency of Lords. One of the natural results of this perversion of their duty, is, that the Working Man has never had his proper share in their management – has been

required to give a great deal of confidence where he received very little – and so has been missed and lost.

(Pilgrim VII, 230–1)

He is, therefore, perfectly consistent in declining to accept the Presidency of a People's Concern Committee because 'I most earnestly desire to see a working man in that position.' (Nonesuch II, 798). Dickens responded in a similar way to the request of a number of working men for assistance in their attempts to prevent a ban on 'Sunday bands in the Parks':

> I think it essential that the working people should, of themselves and by themselves, assert that right. They have been informed, on the high authority of their first Minister (lately rather in want of House of Commons votes, I am told), that they are almost indifferent to it. The correction of that mistake...lies with themselves.
>
> (Nonesuch II, 774)

Dickens subscribed ten pounds to their cause but declined, for the above reasons, to attend a meeting in 'our Parish Vestry Hall'. Dickens's stance here needs to be seen in the context of a range of responses to working people in the period. The intrusiveness of do-gooders, on the one hand, and unfeeling contempt on the other were equally a source of what Thomas Carlyle memorably summarized as 'to be heart worn, weary, yet isolated, unrelated, girt-in with a cold universal laissez-faire'.[8] And Humphrey House's version of the summing-up of working men and women by Thomas Malthus, the founder of modern population studies, can only leave us amazed that it was seen as the basis for a theory of human social behaviour: '...the...unthrifty, careless, ignorant, but not evil person whom Malthus took to be the backbone of the working-class'.[9] Dickens was not unique in his recognition of the essential dignity of even the poorest members of society, but the depth of his passionate concern did not inhibit the rational development of emotion into a principle, as a late letter on contributions to *All the Year Round* makes clear:

> I want the Article on Working Men's Clubs to refer back to The Poor Man and his Beer in No.1, and to maintain the principle involved in that effort...to show that trustfulness is at the bottom of all social institutions, and that to trust a man, as one of a body of men, is to place him under a wholesome restraint of social opinion, and is very much better than to make a baby of him...to point out that the rejection of beer in this club, tobacco in that club, dancing or what

not in another club, are instances that such clubs are founded on mere whims, and therefore cannot successfully address human nature in general, and hope to last...to urge that patronage is the curse and blight of all such endeavours, and to impress upon the working men that they must originate and manage for themselves...and...encourage them to declare...that these clubs...do not need educational pretences or flourishes. Do not let them be afraid or ashamed of wanting to be amused and pleased.

(Nonesuch III, 381–2)

Given the complex interrelations of Dickens's social thought and feeling it is not easy to separate out one issue from another in the area. He clearly hated patronage in all its forms and regarded its indulgence as a central weakness of his society as we can see from a letter to an unknown correspondent: 'Make me a patron if you like though I very much dislike the word. In so doing I know you will make [me] the patron of a failure. If these things cannot be done without patronage, they will never, never, never, be done with it' (Pilgrim VI, 391). Dickens obviously had in mind the full range of patronage operating in the Victorian era, from the patronizing attitudes towards the poor we have just been looking at to the nepotism that secured profitable positions for people unqualified by training or abilities in the upper reaches of society. But a key stimulus of this complicated range of reactions was probably patronage in its sense of support for the artist, a phenomenon which particularly roused Dickens's ire, and which a speech of 1853 brought together with his feeling for working people:

To the great compact phalanx of the people, by whose industry, perseverance, and intelligence, and their result in money-wealth such places as Birmingham, and many others like it, have arisen – to that great centre of support, that comprehensive experience, and that breathing heart – Literature has turned happily from individual patrons, sometimes munificent, often sordid, always few, and has found there at once its highest purpose, its natural range of actions, and its best reward.

(Speeches 156)

We have seen earlier that Dickens had seriously considered undertaking some kind of public office, although he steadfastly resisted requests to become a Member of Parliament. It is not surprising that the story we have been following in this chapter should have led him actively into questions of political reform. Dickens pursued them in a series of thoughtful letters; in agitation of all kinds in his periodicals, from action against cholera to attacks on governmental red tape; and in his support of the Administrative Reform Association, founded in 1855. The Association had come into existence through anxieties aroused by the so-called Condition-of-England-Question, exacerbated by the specific inefficiencies revealed by the conduct of the Crimean War which had led to the wanton suffering and death of thousands of British soldiers, a scandal exposed in *The Times* by the investigative reporting of W. H. Russell. Russell's damning indictment of this callous disregard for human life was reinforced by the Parliamentary Committee on the Army before Sebastopol under the chairmanship of the radical John Roebuck. Despite its horrific revelations, the Establishment escaped unscathed, except with regard to its reputation, although a start was made in reform of the Civil Service and the administration of the Army. It was in this general climate that Dickens's friend and Member of Parliament, A. H. Layard:

> gave notice in the Commons...of his intention to move a series of resolutions expressing concern about the state of the nation; (i) that at all times the administration of public affairs should be entrusted to those best qualified and the more so at a time of national emergency; (ii) that the way merit and efficiency had been sacrificed to personal influence and adherence to routine in appointments was opposed to the interests of the State; and (iii) that the Commons would give its best support to a ministry prepared to aim for 'the efficiency of the public service and the vigorous prosecution of the war, as the only means of securing an honourable and lasting peace.'...The resolutions...were defeated (46 to 359).
>
> (Pilgrim VII, 586)

Layard's failure to influence Parliament was undoubtedly a factor in the formation of the Reform Association in June 1885.

Dickens's commitment to the Association can be deduced from his subscription of twenty pounds, 'as a kind of example to a large class', (Pilgrim VII, 620) when membership could cost as little as a guinea a year and life membership ten guineas. Dickens 'enrolled himself as a member...because I believe it to be impossible for England to hold her place in the world, or long be at rest within herself, unless the present system of mismanaging the public affairs, and mis-spending the public money, be altogether changed'. (Pilgrim VII, 646–7). Dickens lent his support mainly by example and through urging his friends to become involved, but he also made a major speech to the Association on 27 June 1855 in which he stated that 'this was the first political meeting I have ever attended' and that his 'trade and calling is not politics' (Speeches, 200). This long, funny and reflective speech needs to be read in full if its statement of Dickens's political position is to be fully grasped, but its general direction can be glimpsed from the comments of K. J. Fielding who points out that a month after the speech Dickens began writing *Little Dorrit*:

> It is wrong to look for the origin of any of the themes of the novels simply in the author's activities in real life, since life and fiction were both closely twisted round the core of the writer's personality. In this case, Dickens would never have spoken for the association, if it had not expressed convictions he already held. Yet as well as 'the common experience of an Englishman', and the evidence given before the Sebastopol Committee – both of which he mentioned in the Preface to *Little Dorrit* – the origin of the Circumlocution Office was no doubt closely associated with the campaign for Administrative Reform.
>
> (Speeches 208)

The strength of Dickens's feelings on public affairs is also memorably expressed in a letter to Macready of June 1855: 'The subject is surrounded by difficulties, the Association is sorely in want of able men, and the resistance on the part of all the Phalanx who have an interest in corruption and mismanagement, is the resistance of a struggle against Death' (Pilgrim VII, 664). The Association published a number of pamphlets on administrative reform, but gradually lost its sense of direction and a year later the new chairman, John Roebuck, 'announced that it was proposed to act through Parliament in future, rather than independently; and with that it certainly lost Dickens's interest, if not before' (Speeches 208). But that he never lost interest in the subject itself is proved by a long letter of 1867, the annual New Year correspondence he kept up with W. F. de Cerjat, a friend from his days in Lausanne:

> As to the Reform Question, it should have been, and could have been, perfectly known to any honest man in England that the more intelligent part of the great masses were deeply dissatisfied with the state of representation, but were in a very moderate and patient condition, awaiting the better intellectual cultivation of numbers of their fellows....The intolerable injustice of vituperating the bribed to an assembly of bribers, has goaded their sense of injustice beyond endurance....It is certain that every inventor of anything designed

for the public good, and offered to the English Government, becomes *ipso facto* a criminal, to have his heart broken on the circumlocutional wheel. It is as certain that the whole Crimean story will be retold, whenever this country again goes to war. And to tell the truth, I have such a very small opinion of what the great genteel have done for us, that I am very philosophical indeed concerning what the great vulgar may do, having a decided opinion it can't be worse.

(Nonesuch III, 500)

The inevitable tendency of this discussion is towards a confrontation with one of the most vexed questions in Dickens studies, the degree and extent of his radicalism as a political thinker, whether in the fiction, journalism or in his life. That Dickens was, in fact, a thinker it is part of this book's point to demonstrate, although not one who articulated a position with the extended abstractions of a political economist or a philosopher. For Dickens, ideas and emotions were inseparable, arising simultaneously out of some profound reaction to human experience. These reactions took many forms – laughter, pathos, satirical anger, moral indignation – and that they can reasonably be described as ideas seems indisputable. Many of Dickens's letters and speeches were of a length to permit the thoughtful exploration of a problem, and his demand that periodical articles should be entertaining in no way disbarred them from intelligent content. But this is an aspect of Dickens that was misunderstood or ignored by even distinguished writers on him. Until the radical revisionism of his *Dickens the Novelist*, the major British critic of the twentieth century, F. R. Leavis, saw Dickens as essentially an entertainer, with the sole exception of *Hard Times*. Dickens was not infrequently attacked in his own day for his lack of a university, meaning Oxford or Cambridge, education. And after claiming that Dickens is 'utterly deficient in the faculty of reasoning', even the distinguished Walter Bagehot gives perfect expression to the conventionalities of the Victorian mind in explaining Dickens's supposed lack of taste: 'Nor has Mr Dickens the gentlemanly instinct which in many minds supplies the place of purely critical discernment, and which, by a constant association with those who know what is best, acquires a second-hand perception of that which is best'.[10]

Any doubts as to Dickens's intellectual powers should, of course, be removed by a close examination of the novels themselves, although this position has been disputed, in Dickens's day as well as our own.

One of the most reductive of contemporary attacks was that of James Fitzjames Stephen, in an article in the *Edinburgh Review* of July 1857, 'The License of Modern Novelists'. Stephen set out to rebut the social criticism of *Little Dorrit*, and a novel by Charles Reade, arguing that they 'beget hasty generalisations and false conclusions' in addressing 'themselves almost entirely to the imagination upon subjects which properly belong to the intellect'. For Stephen this weakness 'applies even to those ordinary domestic relations, which are the legitimate province of novels' because the 'representations of novelists are... false' and 'often in the highest degree mischievous when they apply, not to the feelings, but to the facts and business transactions of the world'.[11] That Fitzjames Stephen was an intelligent and distinguished man makes his misunderstanding of the nature of fiction all the more revealing of the context within which Dickens, and indeed any truly creative mind, has to work. Stephen's separation of imagination and intellect is a fundamental error in relation to creative thought and he clearly sees the 'real world' of politics, business and administration as superior to the realm of feeling and human relationships. His inability to read a novel, in the fullest sense, caused his disastrous misreading of *Little Dorrit*, in claiming that Dickens's superficial reliance on topical events led him to take the collapse of the Clennan house from 'the recent fall of houses in Tottenham Court Road, which happens to have appeared in the newspapers at a convenient moment'.[12] In his brilliant reply in *Household Words*, 'Curious Misprint in the Edinburgh Review', Dickens demonstrated that this catastrophe had been part of his novel's plan and texture from the beginning. The fact is that Stephen showed himself unable to appreciate Dickens's thought in the sense in which it is being defined here. The house's physical downfall is a fictional idea, a combination of imagination and intellect, which is convincing on a purely realistic level and capable also of interpretation as symbolic of the state of society the novel so richly evokes.

This issue is of such central importance that it is worth pursuing a little further; two passages are particularly appropriate in testifying, first, to the seriousness with which Dickens took the form of the novel and, second, the insights he was capable of infusing into that form. Daniel Doyce, the inventor frustrated by the bureaucratic indifference of the Circumlocution Office in *Little Dorrit*, stands as a type of the creative mind, contrasted favourably with the dilettantism of the upper-class painter, Henry Gowan, and patronisingly misunderstood even by his friend Mr Meagles. Meeting a more sympathetic response in Arthur Clennam, Doyce describes the formal structure of the invention that has brought him nothing but neglect and distrust:

> He had the power, often to be found in union with such a character, of explaining what he himself perceived, and meant, with the direct force and distinctness with which it struck his own mind. His manner of demonstration was so orderly and neat and simple, that it was not easy to mistake him. There was something almost ludicrous in the complete irreconcilability of a vague conventional notion that he must be a visionary man, with the precise, sagacious travelling of his eye and thumb over the plans, their patient stoppages at particular points, their careful returns to other points whence little channels of explanation had to be traced up, and his steady manner of making everything good and everything sound, at each important stage, before taking his hearer on a line's-breadth further. His dismissal of himself from his description, was hardly less remarkable. He never said, I discovered this adaptation or invented that combination; but showed the whole thing as if the Divine artificer had made it, and he had happened to find it. So modest was he about it, such a pleasant touch of respect was mingled with his quiet admiration of it, and so calmly convinced he was that it was established on irrefragable laws.

(Book the Second, Chapter 8)

It is hard not to see this as a tribute to originality in all fields, including novel writing, and also as a description of the kind of book Dickens is writing in *Little Dorrit*. We have seen that Dickens was conscious of a need to do new things in a new way in his writing. But despite his continuing popularity there is evidence, one example of which will be discussed in the final chapter, that he failed to be awarded general critical understanding in his lifetime. Evidence also exists that Dickens took an objective pleasure in his own work and sometimes referred to it as if it were not his own creation, as in his remark on Fagin in *Oliver Twist* that he is 'such an out and outer that I don't know what to make of him' (Pilgrim 1, 441). Finally, the description of Doyce's invention as a complex unity in which all the parts come together for a common purpose is a way of characterizing the formal unity of the novel itself, in which an immense range and variety of material is woven together in an organic whole.

For insights in the realm of politics in the widest sense we could turn to a relatively little noticed passage in *David Copperfield* which occurs towards the end of the novel, on David's return home after a considerable absence. David dines at the Gray's Inn Coffee-house where he attempts to learn what progress his friend Traddles is making in his profession only to discover that the waiter regards Traddles's three years in the law as being beneath consideration:

> As I followed the chief waiter with my eyes, I could not help thinking that the garden in which he had gradually blown to be the flower he was, was an arduous place to rise in. It had such a prescriptive, stiff-necked, long-established, solemn, elderly air. I glanced about the room, which had had its sanded floor sanded, no doubt, in exactly the same manner when the chief waiter was a boy – if he ever was a boy, which appeared improbable; and at the shining tables, where I saw myself reflected, in unruffled depths of old mahogony; and at the lamps, without a flaw in their trimming or cleaning; and at the comfortable green curtains, with their pure brass rods, snugly enclosing the boxes; and at the two large coal fires, brightly burning; and at the rows of decanters, burly as if with the consciousness of pipes of expensive old port-wine below; and both England, and the law, appeared to me to be very difficult indeed to be taken by storm...and...all seemed to unite in sternly frowning on the fortunes of Traddles, or on any such daring youth.
>
> (Chapter 59)

The conservatism of a culture weighed down by its own history could hardly be caught more brilliantly. Not the least of the passage's virtues is its acknowledgement of the beauty and comfort afforded by the time-honoured practices of a long-established civilization. It reads almost like an anticipation of the heritage industry in its celebration of all that is most English in Englishness. But the sting in the tale is unmistakable. This is no country for young men, but a place where the servants of the Circumlocution Office would feel happily at their ease.

Where to begin, then, in charting the complex map of Dickens's radical and conservative impulses? It is tempting to start with the rather näive excitement of the 29-year-old: 'By Jove how radical I am getting! I wax stronger and stronger in the true principles every day' (Nonesuch II, 357). From the same period comes a rather more extended version of this slightly self-congratulatory tone. Dickens is replying to his brother Fred about the question of trying to use political influence to get him promoted in his job as a Treasury clerk:

> But I cannot possibly apply to the Tories for *anything*. I dare say they would be glad enough if I would; but I cannot with any regard

to honour, consistency or Truth, ask any favour of people whom, politically, I despise and abhor. It would tie my hands, seal my lips, rob my pen of its honesty, and bind me neck and heels in most discredited fetters.

(Pilgrim II, 379)

The high drama being played out here cannot fail to strike us as a shade exaggerated, with its image of the young writer as hero manfully holding at bay opponents who would be only too pleased to see him in their camp. We might be inclined to think that Dickens's radicalism was only skin deep at this stage, a participation in a politics which Kathryn Chittick has argued was fashionable in the early 1830s.[13] She cites Disraeli as an example, but points out that he slowly moved to the right as the Whig Reform Parliament began to falter, allowing the Tories to return to office in 1841. We have seen that Dickens quickly became disillusioned with both parties, indeed with Parliament itself as an institution. Furthermore, he would have found it impossible to give his support to a Whig administration responsible for one of his most hated pieces of legislation, the Poor Law Amendment Act (the New Poor Law as it was popularly known) of 1834. Whether or not his views at this time were superficial, Dickens's two years as a reporter on the *Morning Chronicle* must have embroiled him in some of the most interesting radical tendencies of the period. Dickens always warmly remembered the paper's editor, John Black, as his first hearty admirer and he was, according to John Stuart Mill, the first journalist to bring 'criticism and the spirit of reform into the details of English institutions' and to introduce 'Bentham's opinions on legal and judicial reform into newspaper discussion'.[14] Clearly, Dickens was being exposed to politics and political thinking at an exciting moment in British social life and this exposure played its part in forming that map of his political thought already referred to. The word map is chosen advisedly in preference to growth or development. It goes without saying that Dickens's thinking matured with age and experience, but it would clearly be a mistake to believe that he gradually evolved a systematic programme for social change. The positions Dickens started from were laid down early. Indeed, it might be said that the map of his political thinking remained essentially unaltered, modified only by the changes inseparable from the stresses of actual living.

For Dickens politics began in suffering, his own in the deprivation of the Warren's Blacking period, and then, by a process of sympathetic transference, that of the great mass of the Victorian poor. The result of this direct, and vicarious, experience of poverty was to make him, in Graham Greene's words from *The Confidential Agent*, one who had 'chosen certain people who've had the lean portion for some centuries now' (Part 1, Chapter 2). At one level, his concern was directly for creature comforts. Dickens loved the primitive pleasures of warmth, food and shelter, and – unlike many of those who attain wealth by their own efforts – never affected to despise their importance, an attitude expressed in the surprised tone of a letter from the first trip to America:

> There is no man in this town [Boston], or in this state of New England, who has not a blazing fire and a meat dinner every day of his life. A flaming sword in the air would not attract so much attention as a beggar in the streets. There are no charity uniforms, no wearisome repetition of the same dully ugly dress, in that blind school. All are attired after their own tastes, and every boy and girl has his or her individuality as distinct and unimpaired as you would find it in their own homes....A man with seven heads would be no sight, at all, compared with one who couldn't read and write.
>
> (Pilgrim III, 749–50)

Dickens was to express deep reservations about American society as his stay lengthened, but the contrasts at this level are clearly all in favour of Britain's youthful rival. And Dickens's approval does not end with warmth and food; it extends to dress as something more than just a protection against cold and immodesty, and to what can only be called respect for individual worth, regardless of wealth or rank. Dickens's views on dress are one of the most interesting examples of how radical attitudes permeated his vision of the world. For example, he loathed the uniforms that pupils at charity schools had to wear, seeing in them a badge of degradation which consigned their wearers to the ranks of the patronized. One of the most liberating examples of Dickens's concern for the individuality of dress relates to his involvement with the Home for Homeless Women, Urania Cottage, which he helped to set up and organize on behalf of the philanthropist, Angela Burdett Coutts. Urania Cottage was basically an attempt to offer prostitutes a new way of life with the ultimate possibility of emigration, usually to Australia, and marriage. Dickens and Miss Coutts were bound together by mutual respect and affection, but their extensive correspondence on Urania Cottage provides a fascinating example of differences in approaching this major Victorian problem. Miss Coutts was a remarkable woman, but her general outlook was essentially conservative and conventional. For example, despite being herself a lover of fine clothes, she believed that the Home's inhabitants should wear what was essentially a dull and unadorned uniform. Dickens combated such views in letters that are witty, forceful and which reveal a convincing insight into the nature of the problems that Urania Cottage is seeking to solve. He argues that life in the Home is bound to seem dull and routine to at least some of its inhabitants compared to their former experience, and that to rob them of the colour associated with the finery of their previous occupation is to create too large a divide between one life and the other, and to sink their individualities in the drabness of a uniform.

The prostitute is to be respected for her humanity regardless of the uses to which she has put, or been forced to put, her body, and this respect for the poor is one of Dickens's most frequently reiterated themes. He remarks, for instance, in relation to the excesses of bad government that 'there is a sense and humanity in the mass, in the long run, that will not bear them', and that despite the prevailing statistical, Utilitarian response to social problems not 'all the figures...would stand in the long run against the general heart' (Pilgrim IV, 609). The repetition of 'the long run' shows that he has no sentimental expectation of instant change or immediate insight into problems as far as the poor are concerned. It is too much to expect that uneducated people whose lives are dominated by the struggle for existence will be able to find short-term solutions to their social problems. This explains, of course, his hatred of a ruling class who have the education and the leisure to examine problems and who postpone action for the sake of short-term political gains and personal advancement. In the end, however, as a well-known formulation from a speech late in his life makes clear, his 'faith in the people governing, is, on the whole, infinitesimal; my faith in the People governed, is, on the whole illimitable' (Speeches 407). Respect, love and sympathy were the bedrock of his attitude to the poor, but this solid foundation allowed for great variety in its specific expression, from tenderness to savagery. Dickens adored babies and his delicacy of response to them emerges clearly in an *Uncommercial Traveller* piece, 'Wapping Workhouse', which refers to babies 'who had not appropriated to themselves any bad expressions yet, and might have been...Princes Imperial, and Princesses Royal. I had the pleasure of giving a poetical commission to the baker's man to make a cake with all despatch and toss it into the oven for one red-headed young pauper and myself, and felt much the better for it.'[15] The consistency of Dickens's responses in this area is clear when we remember that this passage echoes something from as early as *Oliver Twist*:

> What an excellent example of the power of dress, young Oliver Twist was! Wrapped in the blanket which had hitherto formed his only covering, he might have been the child of a nobleman or a beggar; it would have been hard for the haughtiest stranger to have assigned him his proper station in society. But now that he was enveloped in the old calico robes which had grown yellow in the same service, he was badged and ticketed, and fell into his place at once – a parish child – the orphan of a workhouse – the humble half-starved drudge – to be cuffed and buffeted through the world – despised by all, and pitied by none.
>
> (Chapter 1)

The degradation of the uniform that places Oliver in his 'proper' station and the passage's cutting irony makes a useful contrast with the image of Dickens playing 'Pat-a-cake' with a pauper infant in 'Wapping Workhouse', and leads into the ironically controlled savagery of 'The Paradise at Tooting' which appeared in *The Examiner* in 1849. The 'Paradise' was a so-called baby farm at Tooting in London run by a man called Drouet where many babies had died as a result of the careless running of this home for orphaned, abandoned and unwanted children. For Dickens, cholera 'broke out in Mr Drouet's farm for children, because it was brutally conducted, vilely kept, preposterously inspected, dishonestly defended, a disgrace to a Christian community, and a stain upon a civilised land'.[16] We might not be surprised to discover that the punishment meted out to Drouet for these outrages was, to put it mildly, light. As a conclusion to this side of Dickens's life and career, the summary of Anthony Trollope seems essentially fair and accurate: 'he was a radical at heart, – believing entirely in the people, writing for them, speaking for them, and always desirous to take their part'.[17]

It is perhaps worth remembering some of the negative results of adopting radical positions in the aftermath of the upheavals generated by the French Revolution. A recent biography of Charles Darwin has charted the conflict between his scientific daring and a timidity fearful of the results of publishing what would have been regarded as unChristian. These fears were intensified in Darwin's case by a conservative hunger for respectability and fear of losing his status as a gentleman. It is easy to dismiss such anxieties as cowardly, but they have to be seen in the context of the case of a surgeon, William

Lawrence, a republican who 'had been forced to resign his post at the College of Surgeons after a vicious attack in the Tory Quarterly Review....The Court of Chancery ruled his *Lectures on Man* blasphemous, which destroyed his copyright.'[18] These actions were obviously designed to remove Lawrence's livelihood and occurred as late as 1838 when Dickens was already twenty-six. Incidents of this kind help us to understand the force of Walter Bagehot's influential summing-up of Dickens's political position in his important essay of 1858. Bagehot's views are particularly worth heeding given his activities as economist, political thinker and journalist, his joint editorship of the *National Review* from 1855 and his editorship of the *Economist* from 1861. His summary is as interesting for its analysis of the period as of Dickens himself:

> The most instructive political characteristic of the years from 1825 to 1845 is the growth and influence of the scheme of opinion which we call radicalism. There are several species of creeds which are comprehended under this generic name, but they all evince a marked reaction against the worship of the English constitution and the affection for the English *status quo*, which were then the established creed and sentiment....Benthamite or philosophical radicalism of the early period...[and] Manchester or 'definite-grievance' radicalism....Mr Dickens represents a species different from either. His is what we may call 'sentimental radicalism;' and if we recur to the history of the time, we shall find that there would not originally have been any approprium attaching to such a name. The whole course of the legislation, and still more of the administration of the first twenty years of the nineteenth century were marked by a harsh unfeelingness...[Dickens] began by describing really removable evils in a style which would induce all persons, however insensible, to remove them if they could...he has ended...[with] a tone of objection to the necessary constitution of human society.[19]

Bagehot does believe that Dickens's political stance shifted during the course of his career, although not for the better, and it remains a question whether he would have recognized this as a process of development, as opposed to mere change, a question the remainder of this chapter will try to confront.

It is important to reinforce Bagehot's point that he implies nothing pejorative in defining Dickens as a *sentimental* radical. By sentimental in this context he clearly implies strong feeling and, we might add, an imaginative sympathy with the sufferings of the poor. It is at this level of response that we can try to grasp the radicalism of Dickens's personal style in relation to the minutiae of social mores, habits, ways of thinking and feeling that are seemingly instinctive. This instinctiveness is, of course, constructed and it is part of Dickens's distinction to have been aware of, and resistant to, these constructions in his personal, daily life as well as in the fiction and journalism. The conflict in Charles Darwin is again relevant here. As with Lydgate in George Eliot's *Middlemarch*, Darwin's prejudices 'were half of them such as are found in ordinary men of the world: that distinction of mind which belonged to his intellectual ardour, did not penetrate...the desirability of its being known (without his telling) that he was better born than other country surgeons' (Book 2, Chapter 15). In other words, as Darwin's biographers bring out, the fascinating conflict of his life is between the revolutionary radicalism of his scientific theories and his hatred of radicalism in any other sphere. Another instructive contrast is provided by Dickens's distinguished fellow-novelist, Anthony Trollope, whose most recent biographer, Victoria Glendinning, provides a good general description of what it meant to be a gentleman in the Victorian period:

> Servants and the lower classes, Anthony always said, were good judges of who was and was not a gentleman; deference was accorded to a gentleman, whatever one's private opinion of him. It was extremely difficult to challenge a gentleman's authority, in the deference society.
>
> Gentlemen recognised one another by complex codes of dress, gesture, taste, use of language and shared references. Gentlemen not only acknowledged and accepted one another, they selected one another – as friends, as suitable husbands for their sisters and daughters, as the holders of commissions, posts, church livings, official positions, parliamentary seats, high office.
>
> To be a gentleman was to have access to power, influence and 'society'...Radicals, artists and mavericks who contested or wholeheartedly rejected class demarcations were true rebels.[20]

This was the code that Trollope, and the great majority of middle- and upper-class Victorians lived by, and we have already examined a number of ways in which Dickens rejected it, in his attitude to the 'nobs' and his treatment of servants. His rise to wealth and fame were, of course, bound to introduce contradictions into Dickens's life, but the extent to which he kept himself free of establishment pressures is remarkable. He was, for example, consistent in his attitude to the 'society' referred to above as we can see from letters as far apart as 1844 and 1866. The only difference between them, perhaps, is in the strength of feeling which increases over the years. The earlier letter is strong enough:

> I declare I never go into what is called 'society' that I am not a weary of it, despise it, hate it, and reject it. The more I see of its extraordinary conceit, and its stupendous ignorance of what is passing out of doors, the more certain I am that it is approaching the period when, being incapable of reforming itself, it will have to submit to be reformed by others off the face of the earth.
>
> (Pilgrim IV, 74)

This is a firm statement of principled beliefs, but it seems to be held in check by the conviction that such a charade cannot long sustain itself and that its inanities will sooner or later bring it to an end. More than twenty years later, at a Lord Mayor's Banquet, his feelings are almost uncontrollably bitter:

> I sat pining under the imbecility of constitutional and corporational idiots...O! no man will ever know under what provocation to contradiction and savage yell of repudiation I suffered at the hands of —, feebly complacent in the uniform of Madame Tussaud's own military waxers, and almost the worst speaker I ever heard in my life.
>
> (Nonesuch III, 456)

This is Bagehot's 'tone of objection to the necessary constitution of society' with a vengeance. Can we account for the ferocity of such a truly amazing outburst? We know, of course, that Dickens's health was no longer good. In June 1865 he played a heroic role in a serious railway accident in which ten people were killed and roughly fifty injured, a trauma exacerbated by the fact that he was travelling with Ellen Ternan and deeply anxious to keep this fact secret in the face of the publicity generated by the disaster. He never fully recovered from the accident and its combination of physical and social danger must have been a particularly potent reminder of the perils of mortality in the context of his complex private life. Dickens's personal radicalism did not extend to living openly with Ellen Ternan, supposing she had been willing to do so which is highly unlikely. Ternan would have been cast as a mistress at best and at worst a prostitute, while it would have been impossible for his daughters to be accepted in respectable society, thus irretrievably damaging their marriage prospects. Such constraints must have seemed almost intolerable to a powerfully emotional man with a passionate loathing of the hypocrisies of organized society. In addition, his earlier dreams of social amelioration and change were beginning to fade. Historians and other scholars have testified to the slow progess of reform in all fields in Dickens's lifetime, from the First Reform Bill of 1832 (when he was twenty) until his death in 1870. And so there is an almost frenzied disgust at things going on in the same old way, the endless cycle of Lord Mayor's Banquets, the idiots and wax dummies, the uniforms as fatuous as the minds, and in the midst of it all the famous and loved author who proposed the Lady Mayoress's health at the Mansion House banquet while secretly longing to repudiate it all with a savage yell of rejection. We have seen that there were conservative strains in Dickens's thinking which strengthened as he grew older. 'The Ruffian' (from *The Uncommercial Traveller*) demonstrates that clearly enough, although it must be pointed out that it is surrounded by essays which have lost nothing of Dickens's old tenderness for the dispossessed and hatred of the forces that abuse them. Those for whom 'The Ruffian' is a milestone on Dickens's road to an almost brutal conservatism, need also to consider 'Lying Awake' with its totally laudable response to some 'late brutal assaults':

> I strongly question the expediency of the revival of whipping for these crimes...going down into the dark to grope for the whip among the rusty fragments of the rack, and the branding iron, and the chains and gibbet from the public road, and the weights that pressed men to death in the cells of Newgate.[21]

On the negative side, there are undoubted elements of racism in his dismissal of the 'Noble Savage'[22] and adoption of a reactionary position in the arguments which raged periodically over Britain's treatment of the 'natives' in its Colonial Empire. These are qualifying elements in a complex picture, but the dominant tendency is towards a stance that can reasonably be called radical in both the life and the work that lasted for the whole of Dickens's career.

The general tenor of Dickens's response to his social world does not really alter throughout his life, especially with regard to such touchstones of incompetence as the law, parliament, education and so on. For example, he echoes *Bleak House* in writing to Angela Burdett Coutts concerning the seeming impossibility of the legal system protecting her from the persecution of a certain Richard Dunn: 'A more striking illustration of what I deliberately believe to be the only intelligible and consistent principle of the English law – the principle of making business for itself – could scarcely be conceived' (Pilgrim VII, 21). Dickens's 'I deliberately believe' is clearly meant to be a claim for seriousness in the face of the reactions likely to be provoked by such condemnation, in our own time as much as his. You don't really mean that, do you? or Of course, you're a comic writer and entertainer so this must be a joke. Or you simply don't have the ability or education to understand such complicated matters and if there are any problems their solution should be left to your betters. Dickens's stance, in the face of this dismissiveness, is a kind of sublime common sense. This book is being written at a moment in British history when corruptions of every kind abound in society and where the sums paid in golden handshakes to company directors and public servants who have actually *failed* in their responsibilities are recognized by ordinary people as wrong, although objections are smoothed over with an unction similar to that which infuriated Dickens. The British Establishment has a self-renewing capacity to muffle criticism by adopting malcontents into its ranks and this technique was adopted by countless special interest groups, lawyers above all. There are many examples of their formalized tributes to and celebration of Dickens which fall essentially into the let's-have-a-good-laugh-and-be-moved-and-then-get-back-to-making-money category. Dickens did, naturally enough, use laughter as one of his weapons as in the hilarious 'Thousand and One Humbugs', an attack on government and administration based on the *Arabian Nights* which includes 'The Story of Scarli Tapa and the Forty Thieves'. But as *Little Dorrit* makes clear, Dickens went beyond the simple class-based attacks on the 'nobs' that he was frequently accused of in his own time. Part of that novel's subtlety is to reveal the basically good Mr Meagles as caught in a complex web of snobbery and deference in which he has to be seen as complicitous. The novel's poor and humble characters are also revealed as blameworthy in their willingness to turn to the crooked Mr Merdle as their financial saviour.

Mr Meagles must share some responsibility for the state of society and Dickens's unwillingness to see any group as blameless is reflected in a *Household Words* piece of 1855, 'A Slight Depreciation of the Currency', which contains one of his more far-reaching statements on the social ills which spread wider than any one class: 'The few words that I wish to note down here, bear reference to one particular misuse of Money, and exaggeration of its power, which presents itself to my mind as a curious rottenness appertaining to the age'.[23] Such a strong condemnation reinforces the view that in the mid-1850s *Household*

Words pursued a consistent line of radical criticism of Victorian society however tempered this may have been by its editor's desire to ensure that it remained lively and entertaining. His speech to the Newsvendors' Benevolent Institution of May 1855 was made in the midst of the revelations of 'the disaster in the Crimea', at the detail of which, 'the suffering of the troops, and the mismanagement that caused them, he had grown more angry and embittered...Dickens relieved his exasperation...by a stream of articles in *Household Words*' from February to June (Speeches, n 1 190). Further evidence is provided by 'Ground in the Mill' which was written by one of Dickens's young men, Henry Morley, who was particularly trusted in such areas as abuses in the workplace, in this case the hideous injuries resulting from the lack of safeguards surrounding factory machinery. Morley's piece provoked a rancorous and ongoing dispute with the reformer Harriet Martineau, previously a contributor to the periodical who had turned into a defender of the mill-owners. In commissioning the article, Dickens wrote to Wills, 'He will be perfectly fair and just, of course; but I hope he will not turn the equitable balance, one hair's weight in favour of the Mill Owners...I have the strongest feeling of indignation and horror on the subject' (Pilgrim VII, 297–8). The end result, in the words of the editors of the Pilgrim Edition of the letters, was a piece 'savagely critical of the mill-owners' attempts to evade the provisions of the Factory Act' (Pilgrim VII, n 1 298). Despite the emphasis in this study on Dickens's commitment to a wide-ranging popularity, these essays cannot always have made for comfortable reading for all sections of his audience and this willingness to go against the grain is evident in his response to the political events of 1848. Of the revolution in France he remarked, 'The aristocratic feeling of England is against it, of course. All the intelligence and liberality, I should say, are with it, tooth and nail.' Dickens clearly felt the support of like-minded people in such a response, but his isolation is more apparent in his dislike of the preparations made for the presentation to Parliament of the Chartist Petition in April 1848, fear of which led to 150 000 special constables being sworn in as defenders of the status quo against violence and destruction, which failed to occur: 'I have not been special constableing, myself, today. Thinking there was rather an epidemic in that wise abroad, I walked out and looked at the preparations without any baggage of staff, warrant or affidavit' (Pilgrim V, 274).

The foregoing evidence amply confirms Bagehot's judgement that Dickens was a sentimental, or what we might call a non-ideological, radical. He was motivated by a warm-hearted concern for the underdog, but this did not preclude an extensive concern for the health of society above the level of material comfort and sanitary conditions. His essentially reformist tendencies emerge clearly from a letter on *Household Words* business of 1851:

> I want a great paper done, on the distribution of Titles in England. It would be a very remarkable thing to take the list of the House of Peers, the list of Baronets and Knights, and (without personality) divide the more recent titles into classes and ascertain what they were given *for*. How many chemists, how many men of science, how many writers, how many aldermen...How much...of improvements in Machinery, of any sort of contribution to the happiness of mankind...How much soldiering. How much Law...if you can get a powerful array of the facts together, plainly stated for my use, *I* will do the paper...with great advantage to us, and to the question!
>
> (Pilgrim VI, 467–8)

Although we have seen that Dickens was not simply the slave of public opinion, it is clear from this that he sees the wellbeing of his periodical and of the country as being linked in significant ways. In other words, Dickens's constant ambition to amuse and entertain his large audience is suffused with an educational purpose, in the widest sense, and his respect for the public is such that he was convinced that the second could do no lasting damage to the first.

If Dickens was radical in his life and thought, and in the journalism, this was also true of his art. For his contemporaries, serial publication was a radical, almost revolutionary, form of publication, a judgement reinforced by a widely held view of his choice and use of language: 'Boz is regius professor of slang, that expression of the mother-wit, the low humour of the lower classes, their Sanscrit, their hitherto unknown tongue'.[24] This is one facet of a dominant sense of Dickens as an explorer of contemporary urban life, reporting back to an amazed and amused public on the unknown worlds that exist round the corner from them but of which they are unaware. Another constant refrain, however, is the delicacy with which this *reportage* is handled in terms of descriptive detail as well as language. The consensus is that 'a coarse transcript would not be tolerated'[25] and for most of his readers Dickens kept within the bounds of what was shocking but acceptable. Dickens himself was explicitly conscious of his radical purpose in creating works such as *Little Dorrit*, which he must have known would not be well received critically if the experience of *Bleak House* and *Hard Times* was anything to go by:

Your friend and servant is as calm as Pecksniff, saving for his knit-
ted brows now turning into cordage over Little Dorrit. The theatre
has disappeared, the house is restored to its usual condition of order,
the family are tranquil and domestic, dove-eyed peace is enthroned
in this study, fire-eyed radicalism in its master's breast.

(Nonesuch II, 831)

This letter to Macready is fascinating for its revelation of how deeply
Dickens lived in his own created world, seeing himself as the appalling
Pecksniff and issuing a profound challenge to Victorian society from
the apparent calm of a settled domesticity. There is no mistaking the
deadly seriousness of this enterprise for Dickens in another letter concerning *Dorrit*, this time to Forster: ' I have a grim pleasure upon me to-
night in thinking that the Circumlocution Office sees the light and in
wondering what effect it will make. But my head really stings with the
visions of the book.' (Nonesuch II, 738.) Such fierce political commitment helps to reinforce a perhaps surprising remark by Jerome Meckier:

Although nineteenth-century novelists were never a confederacy,
many stood together against Dickens, striving to prevent his spir-
ited delineation of an impersonal, irresponsible society in the throes
of decomposition from becoming the popular conception and, as
such, passing into history.[26]

This is a bold claim, but it remains true that Dickens's major contemporaries – George Eliot, Thackeray, the Brontës, and Trollope –
held radically dissimilar views on both the nature of the novel and of
the society of which they were all a part. Dickens cast a shadow from
which it was hard to emerge and they all expressed their admiration
for him, in varying degrees, but it is hard not to agree with Meckier
that there was something disturbing for them in a writer who managed to combine huge popularity with a discomfiting vision of their
social world. Richard D. Altick offers a possible explanation for this:

The predominant conclusion we are forced to reach through a review
of our data is that from the beginning of the nineteenth century
down to the dawn of the Welfare State, the readers of Great Britain
were supplied by authors the great majority of whom had sprung
from the 'solid' middle class. They had, for the most part, whatever intellectual advantages the formal education of their time offered
them; and socially and politically they were, with conspicuous
exceptions that come immediately to mind, in sympathy with the
attitudes of their class and era.[27]

Dickens stood outside the boundaries of this solid middle class and its ideology through birth, background, experience and education, a position which helped to form his distinctive view of the Victorian world and which was reinforced by profound feelings and intellectual commitment. This complex of forces motivated him, at one level, to tackle very specific abuses, as we can see from a letter on *Household Words* in the context of the Crimean War: 'I set my heart on doing the real good of not allowing the remembrance of the cholera to die away, even in the louder miseries and appeals of War – under which...the Do Nothings will endeavour to shelter themselves for the next ten years' (Pilgrim VII, 436). But that Dickens had set his sights on something more than a series of one-off attacks on individual abuses is revealed by the fact that, from its inception, *Household Words* had a section entitled 'Social, Sanitary, and Municipal Progress' (Pilgrim VI, n 1 19). His capacity to think more broadly is also clear, however lightheartedly, in a letter of 1867: 'The extinct prize-fighters, as a body, I take to be a good subject [for *All the Year Round*]...Their patrons were a class of men now extinct also, and the whole ring of those days...is a piece of social history' (Nonesuch III, 521). Dickens's use of a phrase such as social history is highly revealing of his grasp of society as a large, interrelated mass of events and individuals, but we need to remember that even as late as 1867 sociology as a discipline was in its infancy and so Dickens was unable to profit from fully worked-out analyses of social structures. It can be shown that, via Carlyle, Dickens anticipated Marx in his understanding of phenomena such as alienation and the economic bases of social organization, but it is futile to claim him as a quasi-Marxist since he was quite unaware that Marx was working in the British Museum at the very moment as his contemporary, and Marx was not translated into English until long after his death. As with so much else in his life, Dickens worked out his social and political position essentially for himself, but he did so from a perspective the very reverse of that stated by one of his most persistent critics, Sir James Fitzjames Stephen:

> It is not a little curious to consider what qualifications a man ought to possess before he could, with any kind of propriety, hold the language Mr Dickens sometimes holds about the various departments of social life. Scott, we all know, was a lawyer and antiquarian. Sir Edward Lytton had distinguished himself in political life, and his books contain unquestionable evidence of a considerable amount of classical and historical reading. Mr Thackeray hardly ever steps beyond those regions of society and literature which he has carefully explored. But in Mr Dickens's voluminous works, we do not

remember to have found many traces of these solid acquirements; and we must be permitted to say...that his notions of law, which occupy so large a space in his books, are precisely those of an attorney's clerk....The greatness of our statesmen, lawyers, and philosophers would shrink from delivering any trenchant and unqualified opinion upon so complicated and obscure a subject as the merits of the whole administrative Government of the empire. To Mr Dickens the question presents no such difficulty. He stumbles upon the happy phrase of 'the Circumlocution Office'...and proceeds to describe, in a light and playful tone, the government of his country.[28]

This is precisely the position of those who find it impossible to believe that the lower-middle-class, grammar school-educated Shakespeare could have written the plays, and are desperate to assign them to the Cambridge-educated Marlowe or some apparently suitable candidate from the aristocracy. The whole argument of this chapter has been to justify that Dickens *was* qualified to undertake a profound examination of Victorian society through a unique blend of abilities and experience. Dickens was in a position to know a very great deal of what went on in his own time, and he had the observational and analytical powers to profit from this experience. The last word on this complex matter may be safely left to a contemporary better fitted than Stephen to judge it, Dickens's most successful son, Henry:

His political views were, of course, strongly radical; he was very intolerant of much that he found in the body politic. Nor did he see much to admire in Parliament or its methods; but he was absolutely loyal, and was never in any sense of the word a revolutionary...He had a very strong love of his country, though he himself used to say, laughingly, that his sympathies were so much with the French that he ought to have been a Frenchman.[29]

8

*Great Expectations:*Literary Career and Literary Text

The preceding chapters of this book have described and analysed Dickens's career as a professional writer. In doing so they have tried to ignore the twin pulls of conventional biography and literary criticism. The failure to achieve complete success in this ambition is, of course, inevitable. No treatment of Dickens, whatever its perspective, can avoid discussion of, say, his period in Warren's Blacking Factory or fail to perceive some connections between his life and the novels. This book is committed to the view that Dickens's professional career is interesting in its own right. On the other hand, we are surely only interested in this career because we begin with a fascination with the fiction. It would be perfectly feasible to write a literary life of a completely minor writer, but this would seem to many to be a somewhat futile enterprise. Dickens's complexity can be felt in many different ways, but its primary source has to be those books which constitute one of the outstanding achievements in the European and American, as well as the British, novel.

However interesting in itself, a professional career only exists, in the last analysis, in relation to the creative work it brings into being. This final chapter will, therefore, involve some change of emphasis from what has gone before. Dickens the literary producer will not be jettisoned, but an attempt will be made to see how he fused with Dickens the literary creator. The distinction offered here is, of course, an artificial one and used only for clarity of argument. The Dickenses that have been separated out from one another in this study are, in the last analysis, a single Dickens. In other words, it would be false to the spirit of my undertaking to suggest that Dickens the literary producer and Dickens the creator exist in different worlds, and that the second follows after and is in some sense superior to the first. At the moment of writing, the material discussed in earlier chapters was available for the whole range of Dickens's concerns as a writer because it was continuously being mediated by his own special vision of the world.

How can this process best be described? Given the limitations of space, and the reader's patience, perhaps the best method would be the detailed examination of a single novel, in this case *Great Expectations* which has been chosen for a number of reasons. Without descending to a desert island choice of 'favourite' books, it has seemed to many readers and critics that this novel is one of Dickens's masterpieces. It is the shortest of the so-called dark novels (*Bleak House, Little Dorrit* and *Our Mutual Friend*), those panoramas of social evil, which means that it lacks the extravagant richness of detail which some consider a blemish, although for others it is one of the joys of reading Dickens. In Pip it has a protagonist who is generally considered Dickens's outstanding achievement in psychological realism, a field in which he is often seen to be inferior to, say, George Eliot. In its turn this relates to the depiction of a love relationship, between Pip and Estella, which is regarded as having an adult maturity compared with what are thought to be weaknesses in his treatment of love and sex in earlier novels. In short, *Great Expectations* is perhaps the work which fits most easily into the paradigm of creativity discussed in Chapter 1. The novel is near perfect formally and makes a mature examination of human and social corruption that puts it at odds with the wildness of books produced in apparently slapdash circumstances. This makes *Great Expectations* a candidate for the kind of work whose appearance is governed solely by artistic considerations, far removed from the turmoil of literary production. What follows will show that such a view is unsustainable, but also that the creation of *Great Expectations* in the circumstances of literary production is mediated by the intervention of Dickens as the literary artist.

The first rebuff to the notion that it should be seen as a novel in the Jamesian mode – that is, as a work of formal perfection crafted into existence as a unified whole far from the pressures of vulgar commercialism – comes from its genesis. The context in which it came into existence was as far removed as possible from the myths of Romantic creativity supposedly embodied in the creative processes of novelists such as Flaubert, Conrad and Henry James. *Great Expectations* (1860–61) came out soon after Dickens's novel of the French Revolution, *A Tale of Two Cities*, which appeared in weekly instalments in his periodical *All the Year Round* in 1859. *A Tale of Two Cities* is one of the shorter novels, of a length similar to *Great Expectations* in fact, and followed two massive books, *Bleak House* (1852–53) and *Little Dorrit* (1855–57). After the relative brevity of *A Tale of Two Cities* Dickens had been thinking of returning to the larger format of monthly serialization, but circumstances intervened to cause a change of mind, one that reveals a great deal about Dickens's status as a professional writer and the commercial consider- ations that came into play even in the creation of a novel as deeply med- itated as *Great Expectations*. We know that the distinguishing feature of *All the Year Round* was its weekly serialization of high quality fiction, including of course his historical novel. Dickens's book was followed by Charles Lever's *A Day's Ride*, which proved unsuccessful; it result- ed, in fact, in the first and only fall in the magazine's weekly sales. As a result, Dickens abandoned his plan to produce his new novel in the nineteen monthly parts format which he had done so much to make his own. We can follow this change of direction in fascinating detail in the letters of the period. The imagery in which Dickens's intervention is embodied strikingly reinforces his sense of himself as an active pro- fessional far removed from the anguished contemplation of artistic con- science of the ivory-towered writer:

> I called a council of war at the office on Tuesday. It was perfectly clear that the one thing to be done was, for me to strike in. I have therefore decided to begin a story, the length of the Tale of Two Cities, on the First of December – begin publishing, that is. I must make the most I can out of the book.
>
> (Nonesuch lll, 182)

The germ of the idea for *Great Expectations* had come to Dickens as a sketch for *The Uncommercial Traveller* series, but it was put aside because, as he told Forster, ' it so opens out before me that I can see the whole of a serial revolving on it, in a most singular and comic manner' (Nonesuch III, 182). But its potential as a large-scale serial could not be allowed to take priority over the financial health of *All the Year Round* and so, 'by dashing in now, I come in when most want- ed...A thousand pounds are to be paid for early proofs of the story to America' (Nonesuch III, 183). That quality in Dickens I have called triumphalism is well to the fore here with its accompanying military language and pugnacity. On the other hand, 'I must make the most I can out of the book' does not, I think, refer to its monetary success. Rather, Dickens is referring to his need not to spoil the aesthetic pos- sibilities of such an idea, with its 'pivot on which the story will turn...the grotesque tragi-comic conception that first encouraged me' (Nonesuch III, 186), by turning the two-year, monthly serial into the much short- er weekly format.

The achievement of *Great Expectations*, arising out of such circum- stances, adds another dimension to the professionalism that has been a major focus of this study. It has mainly been taken to relate to that side of Dickens that was preoccupied with sales figures, advertising, contracts with publishers, financial returns, and so on. But it can also be read as the ability to use external pressures as an opportunity to express what I have called a deeply meditated fictional idea into a new, even experimental, form. Dickens achieved this with *Hard Times* where the pressures of weekly serialization enabled him to refine his stylistic exuberance into a spareness of form and directness of impact unique in his fiction. Similarly, rather than bemoaning the losses to be suffered in surrendering the larger format, Dickens seized the chance to embody his by now profound understanding of the human and social in a purity of form that abandoned the digressive richness of *Bleak House* and *Little Dorrit*. On the other hand, he was clearly not interested in repeating the somewhat skeletal effect of *Hard Times*. As a result, we have a book which almost perfectly combines what is most truly Dickensian with psychological realism, balanced by a formal structure that is complex without being complicated. One explanation of this surprising fusion may be found in a technical matter which throws light on Dickens's craftsmanship. Even though *Great Expectations* was to be a weekly serial Dickens planned it, in his working notes, as if it were to be a monthly one. Organizing for monthly appearances and writing for weekly ones may help to account for a spareness in the writing and formal structure of *Great Expectations* which never seems rushed and which implies the amplitude of the longer fiction, for the attentive reader, even if it lacks the space to fill it in.

Dickens was thus able to create, in commercial circumstances, a work of art with wide popular appeal and financial necessities were not ignored after its first publication. The novel appeared in *All the Year Round* between 1 December 1860 and 3 August 1861, but it was also appearing in the American *Harper's Weekly* from 24 November 1860 to 3 August 1861. It was published in three volumes in 1861, and this was followed by four more impressions in the same year. There were a number of American editions in 1861 and a one-volume edition came out in 1862. Beautiful work of art as it is, *Great Expectations* was clearly not a delicate flower but a product, as well as a creation, which was expected to fight its way in the market-place through Dickens's by now time-honoured practice of working his copyrights.

We can perhaps begin to see at this point ways in which the previous chapters of this book are more than merely informational. They may, in fact, suggest an explanation for a key aspect of Dickens's achievement, his combination of popular success with artistry of the highest order. If, at the moment of writing, his mind was filled with the materials I have described some explanation is required for us to understand how these were transformed into fiction. This is not to say that Dickens's mind was simply a chaos of random information and impressions. He was fascinated by the full range of what came to him from the social world and this was no doubt sifted even as impressions were being made on him, as well as in further thought on what he so richly observed. But something more seems needed to account for the ways in which these experiences became part of the novels. Dickens's personal intervention, at this point, might be described as the mediating effect of imagination which created a fictional order out of the ordering process which was presumably always going on as part of the drama of his inner life. A way of describing this order would be to see it embodied in the work in a series of levels, fused rather than separated from one another. Readers are thus offered a range of experiences, from simple entertainment to involvement with the depths of Dickens's human and social insight. An 'ideal' reading might combine all these elements, but there is no authorial pressure to do so. Indeed, there is a case for seeing Dickens as a truly democratic writer, in keeping with his lifelong hatred of patronage, who empowers readers by leaving them free to make their own choices from the wealth of material on offer. If we turn to the world of theatre and popular entertainment, for example, we find that the whole of Chapter 12 in Volume 2 (Chapter 31 in editions that are not divided into volumes) is given over to an hilarious evocation of Victorian popular theatre. Mr Wopsle, the clerk of Pip's village church in his childhood, was the possessor, in addition to 'a Roman nose and a large shining bald forehead', of 'a deep voice which he was uncommonly proud of' (Volume 1, Chapter 4). Having failed to find scope for his talents in his rural backwater, Mr Wopsle takes himself off to London to be an actor where, before he declines into bit parts in melodramas and pantomimes, he is seen by Pip and Herbert as Hamlet. The production is of the most threadbare kind with 'a noble boy in ancestral boots' playing a range of 'inconsistent' roles, and poor Mr Wopsle being subjected to audience participation on a devastating scale:

> Upon my unfortunate townsman all these incidents accumulated with playful effect. Whenever that undecided Prince had to ask a question or state a doubt, the public helped him out with it. As for example; on the question whether 'twas nobler in the mind to suffer', some roared yes, and some no, and some inclining to both

opinions said 'toss up for it'; and quite a Debating Society arose. When he asked what should such fellows as he do crawling between earth and heaven, he was encouraged with loud cries of 'Hear, hear!' When he appeared with his stocking disordered (its disorder expressed, according to usage, by one very neat fold in the top, which I suppose always got up with a flat iron), a conversation took place in the gallery respecting the paleness of his leg, and whether it was occasioned by the turn the ghost had given him. On his taking the recorders – very like a little black flute that had just been played in the orchestra and handed out at the door – he was called upon unanimously for Rule Britannia. When he recommended the player not to saw the air thus, the sulky man said, 'And don't *you* do it, neither; you're a deal worse than *him!*' And I grieve to add that peals of laughter greeted Mr Wopsle on every one of these occasions.

The tone of the whole episode is quite unpatronizing. Shakespeare is clearly a robust enough part of the national heritage to be undamaged by this treatment while the audience is perfectly within its rights to find its enjoyment in derision of the production's inadequacies rather than in the play itself. At one level, this chapter could be seen as a self-contained piece of writing, a sketch by a more mature Boz or an offering from *The Uncommercial Traveller*. From this perspective, it is an amusing and entertaining interlude which contributes to a sense of the novel as a miscellany similar to the mixed ingredients that make up, say, *The Vicar of Wakefield*. On this reading, intense pleasure could be derived from a whole number of episodes: Pip's thrilling early encounter with Magwitch; the eerie fairy-tale atmosphere of Satis House with a Miss Havisham who is both a witch and a, false, fairy godmother; Pip's visit to Wemmick's eccentric little home in Walworth where he meets the Aged P and the bizarre Miss Skiffins. However unlikely this way of reading the novel may seem from a contemporary perspective, there is evidence to suggest that this was how it was seen on its first appearance. It was praised by *The Times*, for example, as a return to 'the old Pickwick style',[1] and *Pickwick Papers* is the most episodic of all Dickens's novels.

If we continue with these comments from *The Times* we can understand something of what Dickens was up against in terms of critical response, if not audience approval as measured by sales figures:

> *Great Expectations* is not, indeed, his best work, but it is to be ranked among his happiest. There is that flowing humour in it which disarms criticism, and which is all the more enjoyable because it defies

criticism. Faults there are in abundance, but who is going to find fault when the very essence of the fun is to commit faults?

This was an unsigned review, but it is interesting to know that it was written by E. S. Dallas, one of the liveliest literary critics of his time, and a man able to apply for the Chair of Rhetoric and Belles-lettres at the University of Edinburgh. In other words, it was an intelligence of real quality that committed itself to this fundamentally limited view of the novel. We can only speculate as to how deeply disappointed Dickens was by such mind-numbing absurdities, supposing he caught sight of them. It is, of course, possible to respond to the book in general, and the episode of Pip's visit to the theatre in particular, at quite another level without, and this is crucial, annihilating the pleasure and fun involved in the first reading. It is surely significant that Mr Wopsle is playing Hamlet rather than, say, King Lear or Macbeth. Although the point is nowhere stated explicitly, we are clearly empowered by the text to see Pip himself as an unheroic and comic Hamlet. Laurence Olivier's film of the play has been heavily criticized for describing itself as the tragedy of a man who could not make up his mind, but this is a facet of Hamlet which is obviously applicable to Pip, who can hardly make up his mind about anything. Like Hamlet, Pip is engaged in a 'singular kind of quarrel with myself which I was always carrying on' (Volume 1, Chapter 17) and the novel evokes the appalling absence of peace of mind that stems from an overriding obsession, whether it be avenging a murdered father or worries that the criminal Magwitch will be arrested:

It was an unhappy life that I lived, and its one dominant anxiety, towering over all its other anxieties like a high mountain above a range of mountains, never disappeared from my view. Still, no new cause for fear arose. Let me start from my bed as I would, with the terror fresh upon me that he was discovered; let me sit listening as I would, with dread, for Herbert's returning step at night, lest it should be fleeter than ordinary, and winged with evil news; for all that, and much more to like purpose, the round of things went on. Condemned to inaction and a state of constant restlessness and suspense, I rowed about in my boat, and waited, waited, waited, as I best could. (Volume 3, Chapter 8 and Chapter 47)

Thus, as we meditate on our reading of *Great Expectations* we begin to experience how amusing and exciting episodes are unified and interrelated. We laugh at Mr Wopsle as Hamlet and through that laughter begin to see that the episode may be understood as a comic metaphor for the absurdities involved in Pip's hankering after gentility. John Sutherland has suggested that Dickens's 'dense thematic compositions, striking use of imagery, rhetoric and dramatic device advanced fiction technically to the threshold of modernism'.[2] If we accept Sutherland's judgement, it may suggest an explanation for the dichotomy between the banal critical response of Dallas and the continuing high sales enjoyed by the later novels. Dickens shifted the novel out of its dominant mode of social and psychological realism, but this left critics in the quandary of lacking the tools to analyse what was essentially a new form in literature. On the other hand, is there any reason to believe that Victorian readers did not understand the essential drift of Dickens's later work, although they may not have had a language in which to express it? It is hard to believe that readers went on buying one dark novel after another in the vain hope that it would be another *Pickwick* or, even more improbably, that they actually thought that they were reading a kind of *Pickwick* as they experienced the darker episodes of *Bleak House, Little Dorrit, Our Mutual Friend* and *Great Expectations*.

If the novel has been counted as rather special in the Dickens canon by modern critics and readers for its relative austerity of form and content, seen in the context of earlier chapters of this study it is in fact suffused in the popular and in those other elements that made up Dickens's public and private worlds. Indeed, its richness at the popular level takes such varied forms that they can only be suggested here. Dickens delights in proverbial language, but in a playfully manipulative manner rather than simply recording it. 'An Englishman's home is his castle', which dates from the late sixteenth century, is rendered literal by Wemmick's absurd little Gothic pile at Walworth, but in ways that make us think deeply about the nature of his divided life, between work and home, and the insecurity of his escapist fortress when the nightly setting off of the cannon, the Stinger, 'shook the crazy little box of a cottage as if it must fall to pieces' (Volume 2, Chapter 6 and Chapter 25). Nursery rhymes make their appearance, as in the action of one of Jaggers's clients in 'pulling a lock of hair in the middle of his forehead, like the Bull in Cock Robin' (Volume 2, Chapter 1 and Chapter 20). And in a remarkable passage in the same chapter, Dickens creates a fragment of urban popular culture in the making, in the response of a Jewish client to Jaggers's apparent omnipotence:

> I remarked this Jew, who was of a highly excitable temperament, performing a jig of anxiety under a lamp-post, and accompanying

himself, in a kind of frenzy with the words, 'Oh Jaggerth, Jaggerth, Jaggerth, Jaggerth! all otherth ith Cag-Maggerth, give me Jaggerth!'

Cag-Maggerth is a reference to shady dealers in 'scraps of bad meat and refuse'.[3]

We have seen that Satis House is suffused in a fairy-tale atmosphere and the motif is continued in relation to Herbert's fiancée, Clara, and her relations with her father: 'She really was a most charming girl, and might have passed for a captive fairy, whom that truculent Ogre, Old Barley, had pressed into his service' (Volume 3, Chapter 8 and Chapter 47). This nudges us in the direction of Dickens's reading and an interesting reference to Mary Shelley's *Frankenstein* as a reverse analogy of Pip's relations with Magwitch:

'The imaginary student pursued by the misshapen creature he had impiously made, was not more wretched than I, pursued by the creature who had made me, and recoiling from him with a stronger repulsion, the more he admired me and the fonder he was of me.'

(Volume 3, Chapter 1 and Chapter 40)

Also, it is significant that Dickens has recourse to his childhood immersion in stories of the East (in this case *Tales of the Genii*) as preparation for one of his novel's most important moments, the return of Magwitch into Pip's life and its consequent revelation of the true source of his expectations, the 'pivot on which the story will turn...the grotesque tragi-comic conception that first encouraged me' (Nonesuch, III,):

In the Eastern story, the heavy slab that was to fall on the bed of state in the flush of conquest was slowly wrought out of the quarry, the tunnel for the rope to hold it in its place was slowly carried through the leagues of rock, the slab was slowly raised and fitted in the roof, the rope was rove to it and slowly taken through the miles of hollow to the great iron ring. All being made ready with much labour, and the hour come, the sultan was aroused in the dead of the night, and the sharpened axe that was to sever the rope from the great iron ring was put into his hand, and he struck with it, and the rope parted and rushed away, and the ceiling fell. So, in my case; all the work, near and afar, that tended to the end, had been accomplished; and in an instant the blow was struck, and the roof of my stronghold dropped upon me.

(Volume 2, Chapter 19 and Chapter 38)

The move from the popular elements in Dickens's cultural context to his reading is, of course, a false dichotomy since some of the most important aspects of this reading were part of the general inheritance of his own time. This is clearly the case with Shakespeare and is even more evident in the Biblical echoes which sound throughout the novel. One of the most important occurs towards the end as a prelude to the stripping away of Pip's last remaining fantasy, that he can simply return to the forge and expect to find Biddy ready and waiting to marry him: 'my heart was softened by my return, and such a change had come to pass, that I felt like one who was toiling home barefoot from distant travel, and whose wanderings had lasted many years' (Volume 3, Chapter 19 and Chapter 58). The richness and beauty of this passage reveals a great deal about the roots of Dickens's imagination. It brings together echoes of Bunyan's *The Pilgrim's Progress* (a favourite book) and the story of the Prodigal Son, as well as imagery of life as a difficult journey through a vale of tears. Life as a pilgrimage is, in fact, one of the dominant metaphors in Dickens's late work; it figures prominently in *Little Dorrit*, and here it becomes integral to the whole formal structure of the novel both on the literal and metaphorical levels. Pip does travel from the country forge to London, thanks to his expectations, and ultimately back again, albeit temporarily. This spiritual journey from a flawed innocence via corruption to a hard-won goodness can only fully be accomplished by the passage of time which includes a spell of eleven years in the Colonies.

Dickens belonged to a world, one which his own work helped to create, in which what we would now call popular and high culture seemed able to coexist without too much strain. Shakespeare still formed part of popular entertainment, however robustly the audience may have responded on occasions. Dickens's world was essentially urban, but had not quite severed links with its ancient past through that amalgam of fairy and folk tales, city ballads, Christianity, proverbs and the lore of the streets, Shakespeare and melodrama, pantomime and the circus, that made up so much of the urban consciousness. (A novel such as Michael Moorhouse's *Mother London* suggests that this world can still be recreated at least for fictional purposes.) Dickens's immersion in all this gave him access to an elemental as well as a sophisticated inheritance. He plays games with Hamlet, Mr Wopsle and Pip on the one hand, but also deepens our experience of his protagonist's moral and spiritual regeneration through its embodiment in the elements of fire and water which are powerful symbols of cleansing and, paradoxically, forces of destruction. In his attempt to rescue Miss Havisham, Pip has to be burned in the fire that kills her and so finds himself on the ground with her 'struggling like desperate enemies' (Volume 3, Chapter 11 and Chapter 50), a metaphorical revelation of one level of his feeling towards her. And although it is Magwitch who nearly drowns in the water of the Thames during his attempted escape, this is also a crucial stage in the rigorous process of purification which is a key aspect of Pip's journey through *Great Expectations*:

> For now, my repugnance to him had all melted away, and in the hunted wounded shackled creature who held my hand in his, I only saw a man who had meant to be my benefactor, and who had felt affectionately, gratefully, and generously, towards me with great constancy through a series of years. I only saw in him a much better man than I had been to Joe.
>
> (Volume 3, Chapter 15, and Chapter 54)

The point to which this chapter is moving is that *Great Expectations* may help us to accept that the material presented in the earlier chapters of this book is not merely factual in some limited sense that is divorced from Dickens's major concerns as a creative writer. My intention is to demonstrate that the creative work is informed by this material in ways that enable Dickens to combine, in a manner that is apparently effortless, the popular and the serious in a seamless web. Again, the need for clarity tempts one towards a dichotomy that is familiar to us, but which would have been false to Dickens. For him the popular *was* serious, the serious popular. Since the point is central to my argument, it needs to be demonstrated at some length and the best way to do this seems to be through the detailed examination of a single chapter, Chapter 14 of Volume 3 (Chapter 53 in editions without volumes).

The chapter is a single weekly part from the original serialization of the novel in *All the Year Round* and so, as with Mr Wopsle, we are dealing with what can seem like a self-contained episode. If we begin by placing it in the context of the novel's plot we can see some of the functions it performs at the level of craftsmanship, as opposed to artistry. It is the seventh chapter from the end of the book and so has a major part to play in that winding up towards the conclusion that was such an important part of the process of serial composition for Dickens. We are approaching the finale, the attempt to get Magwitch to the Continent and freedom from the hanging he faces as a returned transportee to Australia. The failure of this rescue bid leads to Pip's total identification with his initially repulsive benefactor and so nearly completes the process of moral and spiritual regeneration towards which the later stages of the novel have been moving. Seen in this context 'our' chapter serves a time-honoured function in narrative, the interposing of a minor climax before the concluding one so as to avoid rushing towards the story's end too precipitately. Our chapter clearly fulfils this function very satisfactorily. Pip disappears from London without telling a soul as a result of the mysterious letter challenging him to come down to the marshes if he wants 'information regarding *your uncle Provis*' (Volume 3, Chapter 13 and Chapter 52), that is, Magwitch. Once there he is caught up in a hair-raising confrontation with his old enemy Orlick and is rescued in the nick of time on the very point of death. This is Dickens the entertainer at work with a vengeance, although in a mode very different from Pip's visit to the theatre. The episode is gripping in its sinister detail and provides a satisfying interruption in the onward flow of the narrative which leaves us eager to find out what happens next, responses which must have been especially strong for those reading the book for the first time in its weekly serialization. But once again we are empowered by the text to consider interpretation, if we choose to do so, with results that are bound to be interesting given Dickens's personal stake in the novel at the level of creativity as well as production.

If we return to the point that the novel is moving towards, Pip's personal regeneration, then we may be moved to consider whether Dickens is not killing at least two birds with one stone here by making our chapter play its part in this process as well as the other functions I have just outlined. The clue to this approach lies in the concluding paragraphs of the previous chapter which provide their contextualization for what is to follow. Some chance words of the landlord of the inn where Pip stops off before going on the marshes brings home to him the corruptions involved in his expectations with new force:

> I had never been struck at so keenly, for my thanklessness to Joe, as through the brazen imposter Pumblechook. The falser he, the truer Joe; the meaner he, the nobler Joe.
>
> My heart was deeply and most deservedly humbled as I mused over the fire for an hour or more. The striking of the clock aroused me, but not from my dejection or remorse, and I got up and had my coat fastened round my neck, and went out.

The events that follow, however exciting at the narrative level, invite us to remember that they are occurring in the context of Pip's very special state of mind. It is obvious, of course, that the novel's plot is completing a circle at this point with its return to the marshes and their prison hulks, to the place where the child had his first encounter with the criminality which led him into the lies and evasions recounted with charming comedy but complete moral seriousness in the book's opening chapter. Since the aid he offered, however unwillingly, to Magwitch was the source of Pip's expectations, it may well be that their value is about to be tested yet again. What Pip comes face to face with here is the seeming inevitability of sudden death at the hands of an individual who has played a special role in his own life and also in the artistic structure of the novel. It is significant that in his first outburst of menacing dialogue Orlick does not say something like 'I am going to kill you. You will soon be dead.' Instead of the predictable we get the far more frightening, and surprising: 'You was always in Old Orlick's way since ever you was a child. You goes out of his way, this present night. He'll have no more on you. *You're dead.*' (My emphasis.) The sense of immediate extinction produces all kinds of reactions in Pip, some quite unexpected, others less so, although none the less interesting for that. It is hardly surprising, for example, that his mind 'with inconceivable rapidity, followed out all the sequences of such a death', the most appalling of which is 'the dread of being misremembered after death' and its related agony that he would never be able to say he was sorry to those he had hurt. Quite unpredictable, however, is the following:

> I resolved that I would not entreat him, and that I would die making some last poor resistance to him. Softened as my thoughts of all the rest of men were at that dire extremity, humbly beseeching pardon, as I did, of Heaven; melted at heart, as I was, by the thought that I had taken no farewell, and never never now could take farewell, of those who were dear to me, or could explain myself to them, or ask their compassion on my miserable errors; still, if I could have killed him, even in dying, I would have done it.

What are we to make of this? Whatever the faults engendered by his rise in the world, Pip never loses the gentleness and sensitivity that marked him out as a special child. The common-sense rejoinder might well be that we would all try to kill our killers if we could, but something more than common sense is indicated by the contrast between Pip's Christian humility and his desire to murder at this crucial moment in his experience. A deeper answer may lie in 'Old Orlick's a going to tell you somethink. It was you as did for your shrew sister.' Pip is naturally outraged by this accusation, but Orlick goes on to make his meaning clearer:

'I tell you it was your doing – I tell you it was done through you...I come upon her from behind, as I come upon you to-night. *I* giv' it her! I left her for dead, and if there had been a limekiln as nigh her as there is now nigh you, she shouldn't have come to life again. But it warn't Old Orlick as did it; it was you. You was favoured, and he was bullied and beat. Old Orlick bullied and beat, eh? Now you pays for it. You done it; now you pays for it.'

It is true that Orlick struck down Mrs Joe with the leg irons that Pip had assisted Magwitch to remove by stealing a file from the forge, but such passages leave us to our own devices, and to the novel as a whole, in making sense of them. One answer may lie in the moral and physical brutality with which Pip is treated by his sister. Although these episodes are presented in a comic mode, this does nothing to lighten our sense that Pip is an abused child caught up in the power of those who 'were grown up and had their own way, and...made the most of it' (Volume 1, Chapter 13) with the single exception of Joe. Pip is too timid to rebel against this treatment, even in his thoughts, so far as we have access to them, but Orlick's claim that he is morally responsible for his sister's death opens the way to the possibility that the relationship between Pip and Orlick is yet another example of one of Dickens's favourite fictional devices, his use of the double to explore the darker sides of human nature below the level of conscious thought. If Orlick does represent Pip's double in acting out desires that lie too deep for Pip himself to acknowledge, then his need to kill Orlick, at the moment when he is softened to all of the rest of humanity, embodies yet another stage on his journey towards moral salvation, the destruction of the darkest side of himself as part of his movement towards light.

What seems to be Pip's final moment of life provokes yet another highly unexpected response as Orlick makes his last preparations before killing him:

He flared the candle at me again, smoking my face and hair, and for an instant blinding me, and turned his powerful back as he replaced the light on the table. I had thought a prayer, and had been with Joe and Biddy and Herbert, before he turned towards me again.

There is an amazing omission at this point of those whom Pip 'had been with' in the flash of heightened consciousness provoked by his seemingly unavoidable and inevitable death. In the earlier passage when his mind moved 'with inconceivable rapidity' there was mention of 'Estella's father' (Magwitch) and Estella's as yet unborn children, but she has no place at this moment. Given the intensity of Pip's love for her throughout the novel, the hopeless intensity of his passion, this is hard to understand. It might be argued that she is too important to need mentioning, but this is hardly sustainable given the moral anguish engendered at this moment. I think we must be forced to the view that a radical deepening of Pip's private world has occurred as a result of these terrifying events, one in which his priorities are sorted out at the most important level. Estella may enter his inner life again later, but in this split-second of time she has no place amongst those for whom Pip feels most deeply. It may be worth noting, in passing, that this reading seems in tune with the novel's original ending in which Pip encounters a much changed Estella on his return to London after years abroad. They 'looked sadly enough on one another' and Pip 'was very glad to have had the interview; for, in her face and in her voice, and in her touch, she gave me the assurance, that suffering had been stronger than Miss Havisham's teaching, and had given her a heart to understand what my heart used to be'. The pain in this lovely passage is for the memory of a love that is past, a process that may have begun for Pip at the moment when he faced death at the hands of Orlick.

Pip is rescued at the very last moment, by the same Trabb's boy whose pursuit of him through the streets of their home town as he paraded for the first time in his new clothes is one of the most hilarious episodes of social comedy ever created by Dickens. Pip's inner turmoil is objectified in the physical pain he endures from the rough treatment meted out by Orlick to the burns he received in attempting to rescue Miss Havisham. But after a night of sound sleep, the spiritual meaning of the experiences endured in this chapter are embodied in what is almost its final paragraph:

Wednesday morning was dawning when I looked out of window. The winking lights upon the bridges were already pale, the coming sun was like a marsh of fire on the horizon. The river, still dark and mysterious, was spanned by bridges that were turning coldly grey, with here and there at top a warm touch from the burning in the sky. As I looked along the clustered roofs, with Church towers and spires shooting into the unusually clear air, the sun rose up, and a veil seemed to be drawn from the river, and millions of sparkles burst out upon its waters. From me too, a veil seemed to be drawn, and I felt strong and well.

This passage clearly draws on those elemental aspects of Dickens's imagination that were discussed earlier. The life-giving power of sleep is followed by the start of a new day and sunrise, and in them is embodied the movement from moral, as well as literal, darkness into the light of spiritual and physical health. And if the novel is not explicitly Christian, the spiritual dimensions of Pip's movement towards a new life are reinforced by the fact that it is 'Church towers and spires' which are 'shooting into the unusually clear air'.

There may be an element of transcendence at work here, but Dickens's imaginative intervention into the materials discussed earlier in this book also operates at the level of social institutions, although a link can be established to these different areas of experience through his profound understanding of the depths of the human psyche. We can begin an exploration of the novel's social dimensions at the scene which initiates the revelation of what Dickens called the novel's 'pivot', the 'grotesque tragi-comic conception that first encouraged me'; in other words, the source of Pip's great expectations. This begins in the middle of a tremendous storm when Pip hears 'a footstep on the stair' leading up to the rooms he shares with Herbert:

> I stood with my lamp held out over the stair-rail, and he came slowly within its light. It was a shaded lamp, to shine upon a book, and its circle of light was very contracted; so that he was in it for a mere instant, and then out of it. In the instant, I had seen a face that was strange to me looking up with an incomprehensible air of being touched and pleased by the sight of me.
>
> (Volume 2, Chapter 20 and Chapter 39)

The mysterious power of the passage is bound to make us ask where this strange figure is coming from. We soon discover where he is coming from literally, but his metaphorical sources are more complex. The fact that Pip connects this footstep with 'the footstep of my dead sister' suggests, what is in fact the case, that he is coming from Pip's past as a deeply submerged memory. But the apparent stranger can also be seen as coming from the depth of his deepest and darkest fears, and Magwitch's appalling behaviour when he has made himself known takes Pip back to his first discovery that he was 'a common labouring-boy; that my hands were coarse; that my boots were thick...that I was much more ignorant than I had considered myself last night, and generally that I was in a low-lived bad way' (Volume 1, Chapter 8). In other words, that the world he thought his expectations had taken him away from forever, but which he secretly feared he could never finally shake off, has come back with a vengeance. But there is yet another dimension to this suggestive occurrence, that Magwitch is coming up into the light from the lower depths of the socially deprived, from what we would now call the underclass.

The grimly comic aspects of this wonderful conception are developed in the next chapter in, for example, Magwitch's response to Pip's question, 'What were you brought up to be?':

'A warmint, dear boy.'
He answered quite seriously, and used the word as if it denoted some profession.

Again, we remember his horrible eating habits, like those of a 'hungry old dog' and his apology for being 'a heavy grubber, dear boy'. And it is impossible not to smile at his driving Pip almost mad with irritation with his apologies for being 'low':

'Look'ee here, Pip. I was low; that's what I was; low. Look over it, dear boy.'
Some sense of the grimly-ludicrous moved me to a fretful laugh, as I replied, 'I *have* looked over it. In Heaven's name, don't harp upon it.'

But the tragic social dimensions of this pivot of the novel are worth further exploration since they take us into the heart of the book and illuminate Dickens's transformation of his lifelong interest in social institutions into fiction. Immediately after his reappearance in Pip's life, in the previous chapter, Magwitch begins to assert a terrible ownership over him:

'Yes, Pip, dear boy, I've made a gentleman on you! It's me wot has done it! I swore that time, sure as ever I earned a guinea, that guinea should go to you. I swore arterwards, sure as ever I spec'lated and got rich, you should get rich. I lived rough, that you should live smooth; I worked hard, that you should be above work. What odds, dear boy? Do I tell it, fur you to feel a obligation? Not a bit. I tell it, fur you to know as that there hunted dunghill dog wot you kep life in, got his head so high that he could make a gentleman – and, Pip, you're him!'

If Magwitch has made Pip in this literal sense, he goes on to assert ownership metaphorically and with a dreadful intimacy: 'I'm your second father. You're my son.' The claim takes us back to the comedy of Wopsle as Hamlet and its absurd embodiment of Pip's plight. But the laughter drains away at the reminder of Hamlet's anguish in contemplating the death of his real father and the substitute father and king foisted on him by Claudius's murder of Hamlet senior. Pip's moral corruption is brought to a focus at this moment by our realization that he had abandoned his loving 'father' Joe, only to find himself the 'son' of a criminal outcast. The relationship is worked through with terrible power, taking in the notion that Estella's 'bright eyes' shall be 'yourn, dear boy, if money can buy 'em', and climaxing with Magwitch's triumphant response to the Australian colonists who treated him with contempt: 'All on you owns stock and land; which on you owns a brought-up London gentleman?'

Without realizing it, Magwitch's assertion of possession is the most appropriate punishment that poor Pip could possibly receive. It joins a circle that began with the sudden realization of class consciousness that arose out of his treatment by Miss Havisham and Estella which, in its turn, leads directly to the ambition Pip confesses to Biddy as a boy, his desire to be a gentleman in order to win Estella. However, it is one thing to be made a gentleman through the unearned wealth he believes comes to him from a lady, Miss Havisham, quite another to discover that his benefactor is a violent criminal from the lowest depths of society. The novel's theme of class thus takes on an even stronger economic dimension than it possessed earlier and, once again, the sheer richness of the novel acts as an invitation to interpretation, if we wish to take this route. What kind of judgement is implied here on Pip's desire for wealth and social position? Pip's expectations may have a veneer of glamour that makes them acceptable, but the revelation that their source lies in the efforts of a criminal outcast puts them on a par with Wemmick's comic but sordid pursuit of 'portable property' (Volume 2, Chapter 5 and Chapter 24). On a larger scale, the ownership of Pip by Magwitch can be read as Dickens's own interpretation of some of the basic economic facts of his own society. If we ask what were some of the sources of the wealth that created the luxurious leisure of much of the Victorian world, we are bound to find the answer in the degrading labour of men, women and children: those who laboured in the depths of coal-mines; those who faced the hideous dangers involved in dealing with molten metals in steel-making; the night-marish conditions of factory life with its unfenced machinery and unimaginably long hours of toil. From this perspective it could be argued that Victorian men about town and ladies of leisure were, in a sense, made and owned by those groups in society for whom Magwitch is a representative, although heightened and exaggerated for artistic purposes. Whatever the complexities and contradictions of Dickens's views about riches in his society, it is clear that in the novel wealth is rooted in criminal exploitation. This is a vision, embodied in the novel's form and content, which all readers must judge for themselves. However, if we wished to apply it to our own circumstances, the point might be extended to the ways in which our own wealth and leisure are created by and dependent on the sweat-shops of the Third World, on those earning a pittance on tea and coffee plantations, and the rest.

Gentility as a theme is developed throughout the novel with great subtlety. Joe Gargery is clearly one of nature's gentlemen, and the text endorses Herbert Pocket and his father, although not uncritically, as a fine expression of gentlemanliness in its conventional sense. Wonderful play is made of the contrast in the fates of Magwitch and his criminal accomplice Compeyson who, despite being the initiator of their schemes, gets off more lightly because he possesses the superficial signs of gentility. Complex links are established between this theme and those of crime, imprisonment and the law, and if we consider the last of these in its institutional aspect, the novel's judgement of it is damning indeed. Magwitch is fatally injured in the failed rescue attempt in which he is finally able to destroy the hated Compeyson, but despite this he is brought into court to be sentenced to death:

> The whole scene starts out again in the vivid colours of the moment, down to the drops of April rain on the windows of the court, glittering in the rays of April sun. Penned in the dock, as I again stood outside it at the corner with his hand in mine, were the two-and-thirty men and women; some defiant, some stricken with terror, some sobbing and weeping, some covering their faces, some staring gloomily about. There had been shrieks from among the women convicts, but they had been stilled, and a hush had succeeded. The sheriffs with their great chains and nosegays, other civic gewgaws and monsters, criers, ushers, a great gallery full of people – a large theatrical audience – looked on, as the two-and-thirty and the Judge were solemnly confronted....The sun was striking in at the great windows of the court, through the glittering drops of rain upon the glass, and it made a broad shaft of light between the two-and-thirty and the Judge, linking both together, and perhaps reminding some among the audience, how both were passing on, with absolute equality, to the greater Judgement that knoweth all things and cannot err.
>
> (Volume 3, Chapter 17 and Chapter 56)

Such a passage clearly has a bearing on the issue of Dickens's politics in the widest sense of the term. We have noted that this is a vexed issue in Dickens studies and seen that some of his later utterances have a strongly reactionary tone. But if it is Dickens the novelist we are considering at this point, the radicalism of the passage is unmistakable, and is consistent with the other late fiction. Dickenses abound, as the first chapter of this study was at pains to point out, which raises the issue of whether it is legitimate to prioritize this Dickens over the writer of such conservative pieces from *The Uncommercial Traveller* as 'The Ruffian'. Some might feel uneasy with the view that the Dickens whom we should trust most is the Dickens who thought and felt at his highest pitch of intensity; that is, the novelist. On the other hand, one theme of this chapter is that creative writing gives meaning to a literary life rather than the other way round, although their mutual dependence is crucial. If this is so, then the views embodied, rather than merely stated, in the novels might be accorded the last word on such a complicated issue.

This might be an appropriate note on which to close a description and analysis of Dickens's literary life. The story of his involvement with all the elements that make up a writer's professional career is a gripping narrative in itself and has been presented here as an essential context for understanding his achievement. But the concluding thrust of the argument has been the attempt to show that the forces of professionalism – the conflicting demands made on the writer by the pressures of serial writing, publishers, public expectations, financial success, and so on – are not merely a background to the novels, but may actually shape them artistically through the mediating influence of Dickens's imagination. In doing so they provided an opportunity which Dickens seized with the eagerness of his deepest convictions, to create a literature that could speak to an extraordinarily wide cross-section of the Victorian public. In this context it would be appropriate to leave the last word with the illiterate old charwoman we have already encounted from Forster's biography: 'Lawk, ma'am! I thought that three or four men must have put together *Dombey*!' (l, 454) Compliments from such a source are rare in the history of literature. They were earned by an unshakable commitment to novel writing, in all its ramifications, and to its capacity to reach those with eyes to read and ears to hear.

Notes

1 Authorship and Literary Production

1. Walter Dexter, *The Love Romance of Charles Dickens Told in his Letters to Maria Beadnell (Mrs Winter)* (London: The Argonaut Press, 1936), pp. 99–100.
2. S.J. Adair Fitz-Gerald, *Dickens and the Drama* (London: Chapman and Hall, 1910), p. 54.
3. See 'A Background for *A Christmas Carol*,' *The Dickensian* 89, 1993, pp. 165–9.
4. Ruth Glancy (ed.), *Christmas Books* (Oxford: World's Classics, 1988), p. xii.
5. Ibid., p. xiii.
6. (London: Methuen, 1988), p. 191.
7. Philip Collins, *Interviews and Recollections*, 2 vols (London: Macmillan, 1981), vol. 2, p. 330.
8. Royal A. Gettman, *A Victorian Publisher: A Study of the Bentley Papers* (Cambridge University Press, 1960), p. 5.
9. B.W. Matz (ed.), *Miscellaneous Papers* (London: Chapman and Hall, 1914), pp. 47–8.
10. *Interviews and Recollections*, vol. 2, pp. 319, 297, 303.
11. Philip Collins, *Dickens: The Critical Heritage*, (London: Routledge, 1971), pp. 566–7.

2 Publishers and Serialization

1. Gettman, *A Victorian Publisher: A Study of the Bentley Papers*, pp. 3–4.
2. Op. cit., p. 22.
3. Elliot Engel and Margaret F. King, *The Victorian Novel Before Victoria: British Fiction during the Reign of William IV, 1830–37* (London: Macmillan, 1984), p. 18.
4. *Charles Dickens and his Publishers* (Oxford University Press, 1978), p. 59.
5. Op. cit., pp. 343–4.
6. Gettman, p. 231.
7. Op. cit., p. 260.
8. *Victorian Novelists and Publishers* (London, 1976), pp. 66–7.

9. Ella Ann Oppenlander, *Dickens's All the Year Round: Descriptive Index and Contributor List* (Troy: The Whitston Publishing Company, 1984), p. 10.
10. Kathryn Chittick, *Dickens and the 1830s* (Cambridge University Press, 1990), pp. 66 and 68.
11. *Bozland Dickens' Places and People* (Ann Arbor, Michigan: Gryphon Books, 1971), pp. 194–5).
12. Ibid., p. 65.
13. Collins, *Dickens: The Critical Heritage*, p. 264.
14. *Novels of the Eighteen-Forties* (Oxford University Press, 1954), p. 28.
15. *Dickens and Popular Entertainment* (London: Allen and Unwin, 1985), p. 104.
16. *Dickens at Work* (London: Methuen, 1968), n. 1, p. 154.
17. In *Victorian Novelists and Publishers* (London, 1976), p. 35.
18. Ibid., p. 37.
19. Chittick, *Dickens and the 1830s*, p. 144.
20. Harry Stone, *Charles Dickens' Uncollected Writings from Household Words 1850–1859*, 2 vols (Bloomington: Indiana University Press, 1968), p. 10.
21. Op. cit., p. 37.
22. In her edition of *Oliver Twist* (Oxford: Clarendon Press, 1966), p. xxxv.
23. Flora V Livingston (ed.), *Charles Dickens's Letters to Charles Lever* (Harvard University Press, 1933), p. 12.
24. In his *Charles Dickens as a Reader* (London: Chapman and Hall, 1872), pp. 45–6.
25. Collins, *Dickens: The Critical Heritage*, p. 228.

3 Dickens's Reading

1. Lawrence Hutton (ed.), *Letters of Charles Dickens to Wilkie Collins* (New York: Harper and Brothers, 1892), pp. 16–17.
2. Matz, *Miscellaneous Papers*, p. 126.
3. Collins, *Interviews and Recollections*, p. 348.
4. See Robert Fleissner, *Dickens and Shakespeare: A Study in Histrionic Contrasts* (New York: Haskell House, 1965).
5. Annie Adams Fields, *James T. Fields' Biographical Notes and Personal Sketches* (Boston: Houghton, Mifflin and Company, 1881), p. 156.
6. *The Uncommercial Traveller and Reprinted Pieces, etc.* (Oxford University Press, 1958), p. 153.
7. Glancy (ed.), *Christmas Books*, p. ix.

8. Stone (ed.), *Charles Dickens' Uncollected Writings from Household Words 1850–1859*, p. 397.

9. *Tales from the Thousand and One Nights*, trans. N. J. Dawood (Harmondsworth: Penguin Books, 1973), p. 9.

10. Ibid., p. 11.

11. *The Complete Works and Letters of Charles Lamb* (New York: The Modern Library, 1935), pp. 90–3.

12. Collins, *Interviews and Recollections*, pp. 312–14.

13. Ibid., p. 115.

14. See Grahame Smith, *The Novel and Society: from Defoe to George Eliot* (London: Batsford, 1984), pp. 147–8.

15. John Butt and Kathleen Tillotson, *Dickens at Work* (London: Methuen, 1968), p. 78.

16. Michael Slater, *The Composition and Monthly Publication of Nicholas Nickleby* (Menston: The Scholar Press, 1973), pp. 41–2.

17. Norman Page, *A Dickens Chronology* (London: Macmillan, 1988), p. 11.

18. *Encyclopaedia Britannica* (New York: The Encyclopaedia Britannica Company, 1910), vol. 12, p. 215.

19. Ibid., p. 218.

4 Periodicals, Journalism and the Literary Essay

1. J. H. Lobban (ed.), *Selections from The Spectator* (Cambridge University Press, 1929), p. xvi.

2. G. Gregory Smith (ed.), *The Spectator*, 4 vols (London: Dent, Everyman's Library No. 164, 1945), p. vii.

3. Lobban, p. xiii.

4. Smith, n. 10, p. 522.

5. *Charles Dickens as I Knew Him* (London: T. Fisher Unwin, 1887).

6. George S. Marr, *The Periodical Essayists of the Eighteenth Century* (London: James Clarke & Co. Ltd., 1923), p. 34.

7. Smith, *The Spectator*, pp. 43 and 46.

8. Ibid., p. 40.

9. Ibid., p. 50.

10. Ibid., p. 73.

11. Ibid., p. 65.

12. Ibid., p. 69.

13. Ibid., p. 21.

14. Oliver Goldsmith, *The Bee and Other Essays* (Oxford University Press, 1914), pp. 210–13.

15. Ibid., p. 195.

16. Ibid., p.195.
17. Ibid., p. 180.
18. Ibid., pp. 41–3.
19. *Encyclopaedia Britannica*, vol. 13, p. 566.
20. Martin Meisel, *Realizations: Narrative, Pictorial, and Theatrical Arts in Nineteenth Century England* (Princeton University Press, 1983), p. 98.
21. Peter and Linda Murray, *The Penguin Dictionary of Art and Artists* (Harmondsworth: Penguin Books, 1983), p. 195.
22. Meisel, p. 98.
23. E. V. Lucas (ed.), *The Works of Charles and Mary Lamb* (London: Methuen, 1903), vol. 1, p. 71.
24. Ibid., pp. 73, 74.
25. Ibid., p. 85.
26. Ibid., p. 86.
27. Ibid., p. 82.
28. 'Charles Lamb', *Table Talk* (London: Smith, Elder, & Co., 1882), p. 52.
29. Op. cit., pp. 114–15.
30. Ibid., p. 118.
31. Ibid., pp. 97, 99.
32. Stone (ed.), *Uncollected Writings from Household Words, 1850–59*, vol. 2, pp. 416–17.
33. Op. cit., p. 158.
34. Ibid., p. 210.
35. Ibid., pp. 193, 195.
36. *Bentley's Miscellany* (London: Richard Bentley, 1837), vol. 1, p. iii.
37. Chittick, *Dickens and the 1830s*, p. 107.
38. *Bentley's Miscellany*, p. 5.
39. Stone, *Uncollected Writings from Household Words*, vol. 1, p.13.
40. Ibid., vol. 1, p. 21.
41. Ibid., vol. 1, p. 19.
42. *The Uncommercial Traveller and Reprinted Pieces*, p. 409.
43. Stone, *Uncollected Writings*, vol. 1, p. 168.
44. Ibid., vol. 1, p. 176.
45. Ibid., vol. 1, p. 23.
46. Ibid., vol. 1, p. 27.
47. Oppenlander, *Dickens's All the Year Round: Descriptive Index and Contributor List*, p. 49.
48. Op. cit., vol. 1, p. 27.
49. Quoted in John Sutherland, *Victorian Novelists and Publishers* (London, 1976), p. 168.

50. Oppenlander, p. 23.
51. Ibid., p. 28.
52. Quoted in Ian Ousby (ed.), *The Cambridge Guide to Literature in English* (Cambridge University Press, 1992), p. 939.
53. Charles Dickens, *Uncommercial Traveller*, p. 2.
54. Ibid., pp. 116–17.
55. Ibid., p. 119.
56. Stone, *A Dickens Chronology*, p. 106.
57. *Uncommercial Traveller*, p. 126.
58. Ibid., p. 124.
59. Ibid., p. 326.
60. Ibid., p. 303.
61. Ibid., p. 346.

5 Theatre and Popular Entertainment

1. See Grahame Smith, 'Comic Subversion and *Hard Times*', *Dickens Studies Annual* 18, 1990, pp. 145–60.
2. Edgar Johnson, *Charles Dickens: His Tragedy and Triumph*, 2 vols (New York, 1952), p. 19.
3. Stone, op. cit., vol. 2, p. 416.
4. Charles Dickens, *Memoirs of Joseph Grimaldi*, 2 vols (London: Richard Bentley, 1838), vol. 1, p. xii.
5. Ibid., p. xii.
6. Dickens, op. cit., p. 291.
7. Stone, op. cit., vol. 1 p. 343.
8. *The Uncommercial Traveller and Reprinted Pieces*, pp. 30–6.
9. Ibid., pp. 243–4.
10. Henry D. Thoreau, *Walden; or, Life in the Woods* (1854), in the section on 'Economy'.
11. James Redmond, *Dramatic Dickens*, pp. 130–1.
12. Ibid., p. 137.
13. Regina Barneca, *Dramatic Dickens*, p. 87.
14. Fitzgerald, *Bozland Dickens' Places and People*, p. 231.
15. H. Philip Bolton, *Dickens Dramatized* (London: Mansell Publishing Limited, 1987), p. 3.
16. Ibid., p. 25.
17. Ibid., p. 46.
18. Fitz-Gerald, *Dickens and the Drama*, p. 85.
19. Bolton, op. cit., p. 26.
20. Ibid., p. 56.
21. See Fitzgerald, *Dickens and the Drama*, p. 129.

22. *Reprinted Pieces*, p. 342.
23. Fitzgerald, op. cit., p. 87.
24. Bolton, op. cit., p. 63.
25. See Harriette R. Shattuck, *Our Mutual Friend: A Comedy in Four Acts* (Boston: W. H. Baker and Company, 1879).
26. Op. cit., p. 108.
27. See Grahame Smith, 'Dickens and Adaptation: Imagery in Words and Pictures,' in Peter Reynolds (ed.), *Novel Images* (London: Routledge, 1993), pp. 49–63.
28. See Andrew Halliday, *Little Em'ly ('David Copperfield'), A Drama, in Four Acts* (New York: The De Witt Publishing House, n.d.).
29. Fitzgerald, op. cit., p. 253.
30. See Grahame Smith, 'Novel into Film: The Case of *Little Dorrit'*, *The Yearbook of English Studies*, vol. 20, 1990, pp. 33–47.
31. Leon Rubin, *The Nicholas Nickleby Story: The Making of the Historic Royal Shakespeare Company Production* (London: Heinemann, 1981), p. 11.
32. Robert Louis Brannan, *Under the Management of Mr Charles Dickens: His Production of 'The Frozen Deep'* (Ithaca: Cornell University Press, 1966), p. 50.
33. Ibid., p. 1.
34. Ibid., p. 69.
35. Ibid., pp. 74–5.
36. Ibid., p. 80.
37. Ibid., pp. 4–5.
38. Ibid., p. 88.
39. Fitzgerald, op. cit., p. xviii–xix.

6 Dickens's Public: Adulation and Constraint

1. Butt and Tillotson, *Dickens and Work*, p. 75.
2. David Trotter, *Circulation: Defoe, Dickens and the Economics of the Novel* (New York: St. Martin's Press, 1988), p. 76.
3. Richard D. Altick, *Writers, Readers and Occasions. Selected Essays on Victorian Literature and Life* (Columbus: Ohio State University Press, 1989), p. 152.
4. Ibid., p. 114.
5. Collins, *Dickens: The Critical Heritage*, p. 36.
6. Sir Henry F. Dickens, *Memories of My Father* (London: Victor Gollancz Ltd., 1928), p. 29.
7. Collins, *Interviews and Recollections*, p. 198.
8. Op. cit., p. 118.

9. *The Dickens Pantomime* (London: University of California Press, 1989), pp. 58–60.
10. Op. cit., p. 17.
11. Kent, *Charles Dickens as a Reader*, p. 32.
12. Chittick, *Dickens and the 1830s*, p. 137.
13. Altick, op. cit., p. 121.
14. Collins, *Dickens: The Critical Heritage*, p. 281.
15. Walter Dexter (ed.), *Dickens to his Oldest Friend: The Letters of a Lifetime from Charles Dickens to Thomas Beard* (London and New York: Putnam, 1932), p. 67.
16. Philip Collins, *Charles Dickens The Public Readings* (Oxford: Clarendon Press, 1975), p. lii.
17. Ibid., p. liii.
18. Collins, *Interviews and Recollections*, p. 341.
19. *The Public Readings*, p. 1.
20. See, *The Public Readings*, p. xxv.
21. Ibid., p. lxiv.
22. Ibid., p. xxxvi.
23. Ibid., p. xlvi.
24. Philip Collins, 'How Many Men was Dickens the Novelist?' in Jean-Claude Amalric (ed.), *Studies in the Later Dickens* (Montpellier, 1973), p. 155.
25. Page, *A Dickens Chronology*, pp. 97–8.
26. Kent, *Charles Dickens as a Reader*, p. 20.
27. Collins, *The Public Readings*, n. 1, p. 31.
28. Ibid., p. 4.
29. See 'The Young Dickens', in *Collected Essays* (London: The Bodley Head, 1969).
30. *Writers, Readers and Occasions*, p. 139.
31. *Dickens at Work*, p. 31.
32. *Dickens The Critical Heritage*, p. 421.

7 Dickens and Social Institutions

1. *Bozland Dickens' Places and People*, p. 237.
2. Thea Holme (ed.), *Sketches by Boz Illustrative of Every-Day Life and Every-Day People* (Oxford: Oxford University Press, 1957), p. 59.
3. Chittick, *Dickens and the 1830s*, p. 9.
4. Collins, *Dickens: The Critical Heritage*, p. 105.
5. Collins, *Interviews and Recollections*, p. 236.
6. Ibid., pp. 282–3.

7. *Reprinted Pieces*, The New Oxford Illustrated Dickens (London: Oxford University Press, 1958), p. 259.
8. Thomas Carlyle, *Past and Present*, (ed.), A. M. D. Hughes (Oxford: Clarendon Press, 1918), p. 190.
9. *The Dickens World* (Oxford: Oxford University Press, 1942), p. 86.
10. Collins, *Dickens: The Critical Heritage*, p. 400.
11. Ibid., p. 367.
12. Ibid., p. 368.
13. *Dickens in the 1830s*, p. 20.
14. Collins, *Interviews and Recollections*, p. 14.
15. *Reprinted Pieces*, p. 23.
16. Matz (ed.), *Miscellaneous Papers*, p. 146.
17. Collins, *Dickens: The Critical Heritage*, p. 325.
18. Adrian Desmond and James Moore, *Darwin* (London: Michael Joseph, 1991), p. 253.
19. Collins, op. cit., pp. 397–9.
20. *Trollope* (London: Hutchinson, 1992), pp. 52–4.
21. *Reprinted Pieces*, p. 437.
22. Ibid., p. 467.
23. *Miscellaneous Papers*, p. 561.
24. Collins, *Dickens: The Critical Heritage*, p. 83.
25. Ibid., p. 83.
26. *Hidden Rivalries in Victorian Fiction: Dickens, Realism, and Revaluation* (Lexington: The University of Kentucky Press, 1987), p. 43.
27. *Writers, Readers and Occasions*, p. 107.
28. Collins, *Dickens: The Critical Heritage*, p. 369.
29. *Memories of my Father*, p. 28.

8 *Great Expectations:* Literary Career and Literary Text

1. Collins, *Dickens: The Critical Heritage*, p. 431.
2. *The Longman Companion to Victorian Fiction* (London: Longman, 1988), p. 186.
3. Angus Calder (ed.), *Great Expectations* (Harmondsworth: Penguin Books, 1965), n. 4, p. 504.

Index